MARC Manual

MARC Manual

Understanding and Using MARC Records

DEBORAH J. BYRNE

LIBRARIES UNLIMITED, INC.
Englewood, Colorado
1991

LIBRARIES UNLIMITED, INC.
P.O. Box 6633
Englewood, CO 80155-6633

Library of Congress Cataloging-in-Publication Data

Byrne, Deborah J.
  MARC manual : understanding and using MARC records / Deborah J.
Byrne.
    xxi, 260 p. 22x28 cm.
    Includes bibliographical references and index.
    ISBN 0-87287-813-9 (soft)
    1. MARC System--United States--Handbooks, manuals, etc.
2. Cataloging--United States--Data processing--Handbooks, manuals,
etc. 3. Libraries--United States--Automation--Handbooks, manuals,
etc. I. Title.
Z699.4.M2B94   1990
025.3'16--dc20   90-13413
                                                           CIP

Dedicated to
Tim, Amanda, and Melanie
for making it possible
and to
Deb and Lois
for making it probable

Contents

PREFACE xvii

ACKNOWLEDGMENTS xxi

1 – MARC THEORY AND DEVELOPMENT 1
   Introduction 1
   Pre-MARC Formats 2
   Pre-MARC Library Records and Systems 4
   MARC Research and Development: MARC I and MARC II 8
   MARC Format: Finesse and Culture 11
   MARC II Evolution: MARBI and the USMARC Advisory Group 12
   Variations of MARC Format 13
   MARC Format Integration 14
   MARC Realities: Twenty Years Later 15
   Notes 16
   Related Readings 17

2 – MARC FORMAT STRUCTURE AND CONTENT DESIGNATION 18
   Introduction 18
      MARC Record Structure 19
      MARC Content Designation 19
      MARC Record Content 19
   Structure and Content Designation 19
      Leader 20
      Directory 21
      Variable Fields 21
   MARC Variable Fields 23
      Variable Control Fields 23
      Variable Data Fields 24
   Other Aspects of Record Structure 27
      Field and Subfield Repeatability 27
      Display Constants 28
      National Level Requirements 28

2—MARC FORMAT STRUCTURE AND CONTENT DESIGNATION (*continued*)

MARC Format Integration..29
The USMARC Formats—Underlying Principles................31
Notes...40
Related Readings...40

3—PATTERNS IN THE MARC FORMAT..................................41

Introduction..41
Fixed Field Codes: Basics..41
Fixed Field Codes: Patterns......................................42
    Single Numeric Characters..42
    Single Alphabetic Characters.....................................42
    Combinations of Two or More Alphabetic Characters................44
    Combinations of Four to Eight Numeric Characters.................44
Variable Data Field Patterns: Generalities.......................45
    Tag Patterns: Tag Groups...45
    Tag Patterns: Numerical Order and Other Orders...................46
        0XX Tags (Control and Call Number Fields)....................46
        1XX Tags (Main Entries)......................................46
        2XX Tags (Body of Entry).....................................47
        3XX Tags (Physical Description)..............................47
        4XX Tags (Series Statement)..................................47
        5XX Tags (Notes)...47
        6XX Tags (Subject Headings)..................................48
        7XX Tags (Added Entries).....................................48
        8XX Tags (Series Added Entry—Traced Differently)............48
        9XX Tags (Local Fields)......................................48
    Tag Patterns: MARC "9" Tags......................................49
    Tag Patterns: Function and Form (Repetition).....................49
    Indicator Patterns: Repetition...................................50
    Subfield Code Patterns: Repetition...............................50
    Subfield Code Patterns: Alphabetical Order.......................51
    Subfield Code Patterns: Abbreviation.............................51

4—MAJOR MARC BIBLIOGRAPHIC CODES.................................52

Introduction..52
MARC Fixed Field..53
    MARC Leader Information...53
    Major Leader Codes...53
        Record Status (Offset Character 5)...........................53
        Type of Record (Offset Character 6)..........................55
        Encoding Level (Offset Character 17).........................58
        Descriptive Cataloging Form (Offset Character 18)...........60
    MARC 008 Fixed-length Data Elements..............................62

Major 008 Field Codes..62
   Type of Date/Publication Status (008/06)..........................62
   Date 1/Beginning Date of Publication (008/7-10)..................63
   Date 2/Ending Date of Publication (008/11-14)...................64
   Place of Publication Code (008/15-17)............................65
   Illustration Code (008/18-21)....................................66
   Target Audience (008/22)...67
   Form of Item Code (008/23).......................................68
   Nature of Contents Code (008/24-27)..............................68
   Government Publication Code (008/28).............................69
   Conference Publication (008/29)..................................70
   Festschrift (008/30)...71
   Index (008/31)...71
   Fiction (008/33)...72
   Biography (008/34)...73
   Language Code (008/35-37)..73
Variable Control Fields...74
   001 Control Number...74
   005 Date and Time of Latest Transaction..........................77
   007 Physical Description Fixed Field.............................78
   008 Field (Described in MARC 008 Field Codes Section Above).......79
   009 Local Use Field (Not Described Herein).......................79
Variable Data Fields...80
   01X-09X Numbers and Codes..80
   010 Library of Congress Control Number...........................80
   020 International Standard Book Number............................82
   041 Language Code..83
   050-099 Call Numbers (Introduction)..............................84
   050 Library of Congress Call Number..............................86
   082 Dewey Decimal Call Number....................................87
   086 Government Document Classification Number.....................87
   09X Local Call Numbers...88
   1XX Main Entries...88
   100 Main Entry — Personal Name...................................89
   110 Main Entry — Corporate Name..................................90
   111 Main Entry — Meeting Name....................................91
   130 Main Entry — Uniform Title...................................92
   245 Title Statement..94
   250 Edition Statement..96
   260 Publication, Distribution, Etc. (Imprint)....................97
   300 Physical Description...98
   4XX Series Statements..99
   440 Series Statement/Added Entry — Title.........................101
   490 Series Statement...103
   5XX Notes...104
   500 General Note..104
   504 Bibliography Note..105
   505 Formatted Contents Note......................................106
   520 Summary, Abstract, Annotation, Scope, Etc., Note.............106

4 — MAJOR MARC BIBLIOGRAPHIC CODES (*continued*)

Variable Data Fields (*continued*)

6XX Subject Access Fields.....................................107
600 Subject Added Entry — Personal Name.........................108
610 Subject Added Entry — Corporate Name.........................109
611 Subject Added Entry — Meeting Name..........................110
630 Subject Added Entry — Uniform Title..........................111
650 Subject Added Entry — Topical Term..........................112
651 Subject Added Entry — Geographic Name.......................113
700-740 Added Entries..114
700 Added Entry — Personal Name...............................114
710 Added Entry — Corporate Name..............................115
711 Added Entry — Meeting Name................................116
730 Added Entry — Uniform Title...............................117
740 Added Entry — Variant Title...............................118
830 Series Added Entry — Uniform Title.........................119

MARC Format Integration.....................................120
Notes..122
Related Readings..122

5 — MARC RECORDS ON MAGNETIC TAPE AND FLOPPY DISK..............123

Tape and Disk: Some Introductory Comparisons.................123
Tape and Disk: Some Commonalities...........................124
Bits and Bytes..124
ASCII, EBCDIC...125
MARC Records on Tape......................................126
Introduction...126
How Computer Tapes Work....................................127
MARC Tape Characteristics...................................127
Nine-track Tape...127
BPI (Bytes Per Inch).....................................127
Parity..127
Blocked, Unblocked Records................................128
Physical Records, Logical Records..........................129
Headers and Trailers.....................................129
Tape Labels...129
ANSI Z39.2-1985 (American National Standard for Bibliographic
Information Interchange)...............................130
Care and Storage of Tapes...................................130
Checking the Tapes.......................................130
Backup Copies of Tapes......................................134
Tape Storage..134
Temperature...134
Humidity..134
Position of Tapes..134
Other Considerations.....................................134

Tape Shipment...135
   Containers...135
   Internal Packing.....................................135
   Enclosures...135
Tape Format vs. Screen Display vs. Printed Cards.......135

Records on Floppy Disk...............................139
Introduction...139
How Floppy Disks Work..................................139
Floppy Disk Characteristics............................139
   Size...139
   Tracks and Sectors...................................139
Care and Storage of Floppy Disks.......................140
   Checking the Disks...................................140
   Backup and Recovery of Data on Floppy Disk...........140
   Disk Storage...141
   Shipping Disks.......................................141

Notes..141
Related Readings...................................141

6 – MARC DATABASE PROCESSING......................142

Introduction......................................142
Deduping..144
Computer Programs and Other Vendor Responsibilities....145
Library Specifications and Other Considerations........148
Holdings Consolidation............................149
Computer Programs and Other Vendor Responsibilities....149
Library Specifications and Other Considerations........150
Special Select....................................150
Computer Programs and Other Vendor Responsibilities....150
Library Specifications and Other Considerations........151
Filing Indicator Correction.......................152
Computer Programs and Other Vendor Responsibilities....153
Library Specifications and Other Considerations........154
Smart Barcode Processing..........................154
Computer Programs and Other Vendor Responsibilities....156
Library Specifications and Other Considerations........156
Authority Control Processing......................158
Computer Programs and Other Vendor Responsibilities....162
Library Specifications and Other Considerations........164
Pricing of MARC Database Processing Services.......166
Setup Fees...167
Processing Charges (Per Record or Unit Charges)........167
Customization (Custom Programming).....................168
Charges for Output.....................................168
Charges for Shipping, Insurance, and So Forth..........168
Product Support..168
Extras...169

6 – MARC DATABASE PROCESSING (*continued*)

   Notes 169
   Related Readings 170

7 – MARC DATABASE PRODUCTS 171

   Introduction 171
   Preliminary Considerations 172
      Database Characteristics 172
      Preprocessing of the Database 172
      Time Frames and Scheduling 172
      Computer Filing 173
   Catalogs 175
      Computer Output Microform Catalogs (Comcatalogs) 176
         Description and Background 176
         Input Considerations 176
         Output Specifications 177
      CD-ROM Catalogs 178
         Description and Background 178
         Input Considerations 178
         Output Considerations 178
      Printed Catalogs 179
         Description and Background 179
         Input Considerations 179
         Output Considerations 179
   Bibliographies 180
         Description and Background 180
         Input Considerations 181
         Output Considerations 181
   Collection Analysis 182
         Description and Background 182
         Input Considerations 183
         Output Considerations 184
   Contracting for MARC Database Products 184
      Researching Vendors 184
      RFIs, RFPs, RFQs 185
      Technical and Other Specifications 185
      Costs 186
      Product Evaluation 186
   Related Readings 186

8 – MARC-BASED ONLINE SYSTEMS 187

   Introduction 187
   Computer Capabilities 188
      Storage 188
      Routines 189
      Speed 190

System Specifications 191
   Initial Specifications 191
      Modules 191
      System Capacities 192
      Input and Output Capabilities 192
   Ongoing Specifications 193
Preprocessing the MARC Database 194
Loading and Maintaining MARC Records 195
   Loading Records to an Online System 195
   Database Maintenance 196
Troubleshooting and Problem Solving 197
   Diagnosing System Problems 197
      Hardware: Machinery 198
      Hardware: Operating Software 198
      Applications Software: Vendor Computer Programs 199
      Applications Software: Library Specifications and Changes 199
      Database: Medium by Which Records Are Entered 200
      Database: Profile and Computer Programs of Cataloging Vendor 201
      Database: Local Cataloging Practice and Procedure 201
      Database: MARC Coding 202
      Database: Text of the MARC Record 204
   Common Database Problems and Possible Resolutions 204
      Missing Records 204
      Missing or Incorrectly Displayed Data 205
      Misfiled Entries 206
Related Readings 207

9 — MARC AUTHORITY FORMAT 209

Introduction 209
MARC Authority Records: Names and Subjects 212
   Name Headings 212
      Personal Name 212
      Corporate Name or Jurisdiction Name 212
      Meeting Name 213
      Name/Title Combination 213
      Uniform Title 213
   Subject Headings 214
      Topical Subject Heading 214
      Geographic Name That Is Not a Jurisdiction 214
      Name Heading with Subject Subdivision Term 215
      Terms and Names Used as Subject Subdivision Terms 215
Structure and Codes of the MARC Authority Format 216
   Major Leader Codes 217
      Record Status (Offset Character 5) 217
      Type of Record (Offset Character 6) 218

9 – MARC AUTHORITY FORMAT (*continued*)

Structure and Codes of the MARC Authority Format (*continued*)

Major 008 Codes..219

Direct/Indirect Geographic Subdivision Code (008/06)................219

Kind of Record Code (008/09)...................................220

Heading Use Code – Main or Added Entry (008/14)....................220

Heading Use Code – Subject Added Entry (008/15)....................221

Heading Use Code – Series Added Entry (008/16)....................222

Variable Data Fields..222

1XX Headings...222

4XX and 5XX Tracing Fields................................223

260 and 360 Complex See References for Subjects Fields............225

663 Complex See Also Reference – Name........................226

664 Complex See Reference – Name...........................226

665 History Reference....................................226

667 Name Usage or Scope Note.............................227

Potential Uses for MARC Authority Records........................227

Online Authority File..227

Offline Batch Authority Control.................................228

Cross-referencing for Public Access Catalogs......................228

Editing and Exceptions List Production...........................229

Global Changes..229

LSP – The Linked Systems Project..............................230

Related Readings...232

10 – MARC FORMAT FOR HOLDINGS DATA..........................233

Introduction...233

Pre-MARC Holdings Formats and Uses...........................234

Uses of the MARC Holdings Format.............................234

Major MARC Holdings Codes..................................235

Leader..235

008 Field...235

Notes Fields (583, 841, 843, 845 Fields)........................235

852 Field (Location)...235

Captions and Pattern Fields (853, 854, 855 Fields)................236

Enumeration and Chronology Fields (863, 864, 865 Fields)..........236

Textual Holdings Fields (866, 867, 868 Fields)....................236

Notes...237

Related Readings...237

11 – MARC USE IN DIFFERENT TYPES OF LIBRARIES 238
   Introduction 238
   Academic and Research Libraries 238
      MARC Implementation 238
      Collections 239
         Serial Publications 239
         Serials Union Listing 240
         Microforms 240
         Technical Reports 241
         Government Documents 241
         Analytical Entries 242
         Archival and Manuscript Materials 242
         Special Collections 243
         Foreign Language Materials 243
      Classification and Call Numbers 244
      Patron Needs 244
   Public Libraries 245
      MARC Implementation 245
      Collections 246
         Paperback Materials 246
         Multimedia Collections 247
         Pseudonyms 247
      Classification and Call Numbers 248
         Non-unique Call Numbers 248
         High Duplication Rates 248
         Biographies 248
      Patron Needs 249
         Bibliographic Instruction 249
         Sears Subject Headings 249
   School Libraries 250
      MARC Implementation 250
      Collections 251
         Paperback Materials 251
         Multimedia Collections 251
         Pseudonyms 252
      Classification and Call Numbers 252
         Non-unique Call Numbers 252
         High Duplication Rates 253
         Biographies 253
      Patron Needs 253
   Notes 253
   Related Readings 254

GLOSSARY 255

INDEX 257

Preface

WHY MARC FORMAT?

We have always relied upon library catalog records to gain access to the library's collection. The earliest catalogs were in book format, and it was hard to interfile records in such catalogs. Access could be provided by only one or a few access points, such as author or title.

Card catalogs have accommodated interfiling of new entries and have more readily allowed access by multiple access points, including author, title, and subject entries. However, maintenance of the card catalog is a very time-consuming endeavor. Just the task of filing, in and of itself, is always a slow, burdensome process. Card sets must be filed for new items, pulled from the catalog and refiled for updating and correction purposes, and pulled again when items are removed from the library's collection.

The limitations of the card catalog are obvious. Card catalogs are primarily useful for "known item" requests, that is, when a library patron has a specific work in mind and knows either the author's name or the title of the work. The patron must know the "title proper" in the correct order, as well. If only the last few words are remembered (for example, "Ladies of the club" instead of the correct title "... and ladies of the club"), then the card catalog probably will not be of use to the patron.

Subject access through the card catalog is more flexible than author or title "known item" searching; however, the "rule of three" (no more than three subject headings are supplied for any item cataloged), which has been applied as a practice in most libraries, has limited the usefulness of library materials.

How many library patrons have requests that are not served by the card catalog? How many library materials are underutilized because their scope has been artificially limited by the constraints of the card catalog?

The computer was initially seen as a means for saving some of the time and money that was being invested in accomplishing library activities manually. Although this expectation has not necessarily proven true, the computer has the potential for satisfying library and patron needs far, far beyond the capabilities of manual systems. And, the computer can allow libraries to utilize their materials to a far greater extent than has previously been possible, which is a valuable benefit indeed in this era of shrinking budgets and rising costs.

We now have the capability of accessing library catalog records by any piece of information found in the catalog record, be it author, title, subject, publisher, place or date of publication, key word or phrase. And, we can access catalog records by information that formerly may have been only implicit within the catalog record. We can limit our searches to biographies; fiction or nonfiction; government publications at various levels; conference publications; reference works of specific types, such as dictionaries or handbooks; or braille materials. We can even search for specific types of illustrations, such as maps, coats of arms, and photographs, and we can limit our searches to juvenile or adult materials.

Computer hardware and software are essential for performing such sophisticated operations. But, it is the development of the MARC (*Ma*chine-*R*eadable *C*ataloging) format that has made such library services a practical reality for libraries. When a library's collection is represented by MARC catalog records, the library has the option of using any MARC-based service available for processing records, producing lists, generating statistics, providing access to materials, and participating in the sharing of resources. As the world of library automation grows and matures, more and more opportunities will open up to libraries and their patrons for taking advantage of the benefits of MARC format.

WHY THIS BOOK?

Having worked with instructional technology for 19 years and with MARC records and MARC-based systems for 16 years, I have been fortunate in being able to fully appreciate the value and potential of MARC. And, having worked with literally hundreds of libraries in their automation plans and projects, I have found a needy and ever-increasing contingency of librarians, administrators, systems specialists, vendors, and others who want to understand MARC and its uses. The world of MARC automation offers many daunting challenges. The purpose of this book is to turn those daunting challenges into exciting opportunities. My primary reasons for writing this book are discussed in the following paragraphs.

Librarians need to understand what MARC is and how it works. Only with that understanding will they be able to understand why and how it provides for a quantum leap in the provision of library services, the fulfillment of patron needs, and the effective use of library resources.

A library's MARC database is its most expensive investment in library automation. Although cataloging is considered as a given for libraries, the costs of building and maintaining a MARC database will, all told, involve a greater financial investment than either computer hardware or software. One rule of thumb that has maintained its validity over the years is that libraries migrate from one system to another every seven years, on the average. However, no library could afford to completely replace its database every seven years. Fortunately, a good MARC database will maintain its value regardless of the system that is used.

A library's MARC database is the most crucial factor in the success of the library's automation. Hardware, software, and even personnel are, to a great extent, interchangeable. And, it is much easier to upgrade hardware or software than to upgrade the quality of a MARC database. The maxim "garbage in, garbage out" is at least as true within the library automation environment as within other computerized functions. Even if a library acquires the most expensive, advanced, sophisticated hardware and software, unless the library also provides a complete and accurate MARC database, the automated system will not provide the services for which it was designed (and for which the library is paying).

As consumers, librarians have a right and a responsibility to know what they are getting for their money when they invest in MARC records, MARC database processing, MARC products, and MARC-based systems. In too many instances, librarians do not know what to ask for or how to evaluate whether a specific product or service will fulfill their library's or patrons' needs. Unless librarians understand what they are working with and looking for, they will not be able to make wise decisions as consumers.

As service providers, librarians have a responsibility to their clientele to provide quality services at a reasonable cost. Unless librarians understand how their MARC products have been produced and how their MARC systems work, they will not be able to use these products and systems to their patrons' advantage.

There are no formulas or model specifications that will fit all libraries or even two similar libraries. Each library's database or situation is quite different from that of any other library. Only a thorough, knowledgeable evaluation of where a particular library stands (in terms of its database, its financial situation, and other relevant factors) and where it wants to be (in terms of automation needs and goals) can provide information on specifically how the library should get there.

Practicing librarians are not by any means the only people who need more information on MARC. Library board members who want to better understand their library's major financial investments in MARC will also find an introduction and explanation to be beneficial in understanding the investments and plans they must judge. Vendor personnel, including account and marketing representatives, systems analysts, programmers, and others, often find themselves faced with questions and demands that have no easy answers and that involve a knowledgeable exploration of MARC possibilities. And, among other potential audiences, students of library science, as well as computer science, will find that an understanding of the theories and realities of MARC format and MARC systems will greatly expand their horizons and better equip them to deal with their career challenges.

Acknowledgments

I have been fortunate to have had the support of many knowledgeable and dedicated colleagues throughout the years and I am pleased to thank those who have had a direct influence on the creation of this book. Virginia Kuehn of Florida State University served as my "MARC mentor" many years ago. Ricky Johnson deserves my thanks for her enthusiasm and support for my professional work. I am grateful to Doug White of the Amigos Bibliographic Council, Gretchen Redfield of the Bibliographical Center for Research, and Terry Violette of the University of Colorado at Boulder for their reading of my manuscript and their feedback. Sandra Salazar Sternfield of the Bibliographical Center for Research has my appreciation for her ready technical assistance and encouragement. Annette Walker of the Amigos Bibliographic Council also deserves thanks for her assistance and consistent good humor.

The unsung hero of my work is my husband, Tim Byrne, who provided his unbounded support in every possible way. As head of the Government Publications Library at the University of Colorado, he has served as an invaluable resource person for the many documents that were vital to my research. And no one who knows Tim will doubt that his active dedication to our family made it possible for this career mother to have the time and energy to produce a book.

It has been my pleasure and good fortune to have had the support and assistance of the Libraries Unlimited staff, in particular David Loertscher, Rebecca Morris, and Susan Sigman. I have appreciated the work of all of those at Libraries Unlimited who have contributed their efforts to this book.

1

MARC Theory and Development

INTRODUCTION

The MARC (*Machine-Readable Cataloging*) format was developed by libraries as the solution to the problem of how to get the most out of a computer. The computer's ability to store massive amounts of data compactly and to perform complex routines speedily holds great promise for the improvement and expansion of library services. However, the computer hardware itself is only one part of a computer system. The computer's capacity and speed are useless without information (a database) to process and computer programs (software) to process that information. Within the library automation environment, the hardware and software have been and will continue to be primarily the responsibility of vendors, be they for-profit commercial organizations or not-for-profit corporations. The library's database, however, always has been and will continue to be the responsibility of the library. The MARC format was developed to assist libraries in the development, use, and maintenance of their databases. The MARC format has made shared cataloging a reality and has made library automation affordable for many libraries that otherwise would not be able to take advantage of the benefits of computers.

When the MARC format was developed, two very important design components gave MARC its value. One of these components is the structure of the MARC record. *Structure* is the form that the information takes in a computer record, such as the order of elements, lengths of fields, and how the fields are subdivided. The second important design component is that the MARC format is a standard for machine-readable records that can be used for all libraries. These design components of *record structure* and *standardization* are highlighted in figure 1.1.

The MARC format was not a pioneering effort just in regard to library applications. Among other innovations, libraries' entry into the data processing world introduced the first widespread use of variable-length records, variable-length fields, and an extended character set. The specifics of these innovations will be discussed later in this chapter. For the time being, suffice it to say that MARC-related research added finesse and culture to the world of computers.

Record structure

The structure of the MARC format provides for a comprehensive and flexible computer record, a record that can be the basis for a wide variety of library applications, both traditional and innovative. The structure of the record allows for expansion of library services through improvements in computer capabilities without having to input new information or restructure the records. This structure optimizes the value of the record for current and future uses. As enhancements are made in computer software and hardware, the structure of the MARC record can accommodate these enhancements without an additional investment by the library to enhance the database.

Standardization

The MARC format is a standard for all libraries to use. The standardization of a computer format for bibliographic records means that libraries can share records and that computer programs written for one library can be used by another library. The standardization of a record structure for library records means that vendors can design and develop computer programs for libraries to use for online systems and other purposes. If each library had to pay to have a computer system designed for its own individual record structure, the costs of development would be prohibitive for most of the libraries that currently use automated library systems that have been designed according to the MARC standard.

Fig. 1.1. Record structure and standardization are the two most important features of the MARC format.

PRE-MARC FORMATS

MARC research and development began during the mid-1960s. To understand what MARC is and how it works, it helps to understand the data processing environment at that time. Of course, computers were already being widely used for many types of applications, particularly in science and business. Scientific applications of computers involved such activities as research-related computations, which were completed by specially trained personnel. Business applications focused on the storage and retrieval capabilities of computers for maintaining financial accounts, inventory control, and customer records, among other uses. Business systems did not require their users to be as technically proficient as the scientific systems did; however, the business applications were not as sophisticated and complex either.

There were many library-related computer applications in the mid-1960s, but these were extremely limited in regard to both function and availability. Most library systems were circulation systems developed in-house and used only by the library that had developed them. The databases used in these systems followed the pattern used by the business systems of the day. Specifically, these records were fixed-length records containing fixed-length fields. They were designed for an extremely limited range of uses.

The term *fixed-length* means that each record or field includes a set number of characters. If the information to be used in the field or record actually consists of more than the set number of characters, then part of that information will be missing. For example, someone who lives in San Luis Obispo who is filling in a credit application form that includes a fixed-length "city" field of 12 characters will have to settle for living in

"San Luis Obi," at least as far as that account is concerned. People with compound (or very long) last names sometimes face a similar truncation problem in the "name" portion of a fixed-length record.

The use of fixed-length fields requires that the entire length of the field be used only for the information within that field, regardless of whether all of the reserved spaces are actually required to enter the information. If only part of the reserved spaces are used for the required information, then the remainder of the field or record is filled with blank characters. For example, if a person's last name is only 3 characters long, and the fixed-length field for "last name" is 15 characters, then the 3 letters of the person's last name will be entered in the first 3 spaces of the field, and the remaining 12 spaces in the field will be filled in with blanks. Although computers can accommodate the storage of large amounts of data, large numbers of unnecessary characters (such as valueless blanks that simply fill out a field) are doubly wasteful. They are a waste of computer memory (not inexpensive), and the excess characters (even if they are blank spaces) can slow down the operations of the computer.

The reason for using fixed-length fields for computer data records was that it was much simpler to write computer programs to manipulate fixed-length fields. When any of the information within a field needed to be located by the computer programs, the computer programs just looked for the required information within the spaces that were reserved for that information. For example, a computer program designed to sort customer records into zip code order for bulk mailing purposes simply needed to look at the portion of the record that included the zip code; it was always included within the same character positions on every customer record.

Even today, most records that are used for business and commercial purposes are a specified length, and are divided into fields of a specified length. A good example of this type of record is records that are used for checkout and inventory purposes by grocery stores. Generally speaking, these records are divided into three separate fields: one field contains the item number (usually the Universal Product Code or UPC); one field contains the item description; and one field contains the price of the item. These records are compiled into a database used by store staff to check out items when they are purchased by consumers. Also, the database is used by trained staff to provide current inventory information and for inventory procedures. Figure 1.2 includes examples of the type of record that might be used for a grocery story system.

8000012134JNSFRGRNBNS000.89

6999934562FRDSCNDCORN000.75

3004576540MOMSAPPLPIE002.89

Fig. 1.2. Examples of records that might be used in a grocery store system.

In figure 1.2, the fixed-length records of 27 characters include the item number in character positions 1-10, the item description in character positions 11-21, and the price in character positions 22-27. When a customer buys an item, the item number is entered into the computer, and the computer locates the item number in the database, prints out the item description and price on the checkout slip, and stores the item price to be totalled with other purchases at the end of the transaction. In some stores, the item description and price may also be displayed electronically and/or "spoken" by the system as each item is processed.

In these types of systems, the item number is the only "searchable" part of the record. In other words, the system is designed to "look for" only the characters 1-10, by comparing them with the characters that have been keyed in or scanned in by the scanner. The item description and price are used only for print, display, or calculation purposes, and they are found by the system only because they are connected with the item number. If the item number is not known, then the item description cannot be used to search for the item. The item description within such a system is designed to fit the limited amount of space available to identify the item on a checkout slip (or display monitor) and is not designed to be used as a searchable term. For example, in figure 1.2, the product *Jones frozen green beans* is described in the limited number of spaces in the record as "JNSFRGRNBNS"; the product *Fred's canned corn* is described as "FRDSCNDCORN"; and the product *Mom's apple pie* is described as "MOMSAPPLPIE." The descriptions are designed specifically to be printed or displayed within a limited amount of space, not to be searched through the system. Even if the computer programs were redesigned to search the item descriptions, by looking for character positions 11-21, the person searching the system would have to know the abbreviated item description that had been used in the record, which would be a hit-or-miss proposition. If the searcher described *Jones frozen green beans* as "JNFRZGRBNS" instead of "JNSFRGRNBNS," the system would not be able to locate that item through the alternate abbreviated description.

It should also be noted that, in addition to being focused upon a limited number of uses, such commercial systems are generally designed for use only by trained personnel, not by the public. Library systems do include many functions that are designed only for use by trained staff; a primary and essential focus of library systems is use by library patrons, not just trained personnel. A look at some of the earliest types of library systems, which were designed for very limited purposes and for use only by trained personnel, will further illustrate the pre-MARC environment and the deficiencies that MARC was designed to overcome.

PRE-MARC LIBRARY RECORDS AND SYSTEMS

Most early library systems, designed in the early to mid-1960s, were designed to serve as circulation systems. Specifically, these systems were used to maintain records of the items that were checked out by a patron and to produce overdue notices and other forms related to library circulation routines. They served a limited purpose within the range of library functions and were designed for use by trained library personnel. The records used with these systems were very much like the business and commercial systems described above. They were fixed-length records designed to fulfill a few simple functions, and they could not be used with much success for other purposes for which they had not originally been designed, such as online catalogs.

The length of pre-MARC library computer records was usually about 120 characters. The records were fixed-length records that included fixed-length fields for such elements of information as the author's name, the title, and the date of publication. As with other types of fixed-length field records, the amount of information that was to fit within the field might be either longer or shorter than the fixed number of character positions set aside in the record for that information. For example, a title might be longer than the number of character positions provided in the "title" field. In that case, only the first portion of the title would be included in the record. On the other hand, if a title was shorter than the number of characters in the prescribed field, the rest of the character positions would be filled in with blanks.

Because of the fixed-length record format, the computer programs could be very simple and could always locate the necessary information within the character positions set aside for that information. For example, if character positions 1-20 were the location for call number information, then the computer programs would always find the call number, and *only* the call number, within those character positions. An example of a fixed-length library computer record and its corresponding catalog card information are given in figures 1.3 and 1.4, respectively.

Field contents	Field description and length
F RANØØØØØØØØØØØØØØØØ	Call number - 20 positions
ØØØØØØØØØØØØØØØØØØØØ	Author - 20 positions
RAND MCNALLY BOOK OF	Title - 20 positions
Ø	Edition number - 1 position
CHICAGOØØØ	Publication place - 10 positions
RAND MCNAL	Publisher - 10 positions
1963	Date of publication - 4 positions
110 P	Pagination - 5 positions
63-11276ØØ	LC card number - 10 positions
ØØØØØØØØØØ	ISBN number - 10 positions

Fig. 1.3. Example of a typical fixed-length bibliographic record used in early, pre-MARC circulation systems.

The brief fixed-length circulation record illustrated in figure 1.3 represents the same item as described within the catalog card shown in figure 1.4.

```
F        The Rand McNally book of favorite
Ran          pastimes. Illustrated by Dorothy
         Grider. Chicago, Rand McNally [1963]
         110 p.  col. illus.  14 cm.

         1. Short stories. I. Title: Favorite
         pastimes.

                                    63-11276/AC
```

Fig. 1.4. Catalog card entry that corresponds to the brief computer record shown in figure 1.3.

The type of fixed-length circulation record shown in figure 1.3 was used for two primary purposes. One purpose was to link the circulation record for the item with a brief patron identification record when the item was checked out. In this way, the computer could provide information about what a patron had checked out. Although the brief circulation record was a scaled-down version of the complete catalog record, it usually provided enough information for the purpose of circulation records. Its second primary purpose was to print out overdue notices to be sent to patrons, when necessary. Again, although the information about the book was comparatively brief, it was generally enough to identify the book to the patron who had checked it out.

Although the brief fixed-length bibliographic record served its limited purposes well, when libraries began looking at such fixed-length records for use within online catalogs to be used by patrons, many deficiencies and problems became obvious. Some of the primary concerns about fixed-length records for complete catalog information are discussed in the list below.

1.   For an online catalog, the abbreviated information in the fixed-length fields usually would not provide enough information for patrons to successfully search for an item (e.g., by author or title). Even if patrons were able to search successfully for an item, the brief description often would not provide enough information to allow patrons to judge whether the item would fulfill their needs or was the specific item for which they were searching.

2.   Since subject headings, series entries, and other added entries (e.g., entries for joint authors or illustrators) were not necessary for circulation purposes, they were not included within the fixed-length circulation records. Thus, the records could not be searched by those access points, and important descriptive information was not available for patrons.

3.   The use of fixed-length fields and records meant that often information could not be entered in full text. As a result, abbreviations were often used, but they were rarely standardized. For example, the "publisher" field included fewer characters than were usually required for the full publisher name. In many cases, the abbreviation for the publisher's name differed from one record to the next. For example, *Jones & McGovern* might alternately be input as "JONES & MC," "JONES AND," "JONES&MCGO," or even "J & MC." Fixed-length fields that do not provide for entry of the full text of the information generally include such confusing variations for any given piece of information. Within short fixed-length records, the incompleteness of information and the lack of standardization illustrated the need for a record that could accommodate the full text of any field of information.

4.   In other cases, the information to be entered into a fixed-length field required far fewer character positions than were set aside for that information. In some cases, such as with title main entry (for which no author information was entered) or where no edition number was involved, the spaces had to be filled with blank characters, just so that the information to be located in the specified character positions could still be found there by the computer.

This problem is perhaps best illustrated by the call number field (see figure 1.3 in which 20 character positions were set aside for the call number). Because the call number is a very important and specific identifier, a reasonable number of positions need to be reserved for the full call number. A full call number might include a three-letter prefix (such as "Ref"), an eight- or nine-digit Dewey number plus decimal point, a four-character Cutter number, and a four-digit publication date, or even a location suffix (such as "Atlas"). A call number of this type required more than the reserved 20 characters; however, the 20 character positions accommodated the vast majority of call numbers. In fact, in most cases, the call number was much shorter than the reserved 20 positions and computer storage space was wasted with blanks used to fill out the 20 reserved spaces. Because the computer programs for fixed-length fields could identify and locate information only by the character positions occupied within the record, it was not possible to use the blank spaces within the call number field (characters 1-20) for the next piece of information to be entered, the author's name. Any information the computer located within characters 1-20 was considered as the call number because of its location within the record, regardless of whether it actually was call number information. Character positions within the record provided the computer's only means for determining what each piece of information in the record was.

5.   To save space and to avoid the misfiling of titles, initial articles (*a*, *an*, and *the*) could not be input as part of the title.

6.   During the mid-1960s, most computer applications and most computer records utilized very limited character sets, usually restricted to uppercase alphabetic characters, numeric characters, and a limited number of special characters, such as punctuation. Although this is not an inherent part of the use of fixed-length records, it was another aspect of the data processing environment that was to be enhanced through the research and development of MARC.

In practical terms, the reason for using a fixed-length record for library catalog records boiled down to the fact that a fixed-length record that could accommodate all possible necessary characters and fields (such as series titles and subject headings) would need to be several thousand characters long. This would be a very large fixed-length record, particularly in terms of the computer storage capacities and the data processing capabilities at that time. Furthermore, because many of the character positions would contain blank spaces for many items of information (e.g., works without series titles or fiction works that did not require subject headings), the use of these large fixed-length records would represent wasted computer storage. And, computer storage space was then, and still is, a comparatively dear commodity, a resource not to be wasted through the use of meaningless blank spaces.

It was clear to those who were researching the use of computers for online catalogs and other library purposes that another way to structure library records for computer use was needed. Rather than use a record structure in which the meaning of each specific character was implicit by its position in the record, there needed to be some other way to identify the information in a library computer record. Explicit codes that could identify each piece of information within a record would allow the computer to "recognize" each element of information (for searching, display, or other purposes). If the computer could recognize elements of information, such as the author, title, call number, and subject headings, through the use of explicit codes rather than from their position in the record (e.g., the call number contained in characters 1-20), then each record could be as long or as short as needed without the use of many meaningless blank characters. Coordinated international research focusing on explicit coding for a library computer record format began in 1965. This research culminated in the development of the MARC (*Machine-Readable Cataloging*) format.

MARC RESEARCH AND DEVELOPMENT: MARC I AND MARC II

The earliest MARC research focused on two primary factors: (1) the development of a machine-readable format (i.e., a type of record that computers could "understand") for library records and (2) the current and potential uses of library records within such an automated environment. As a national agency that created, used, and distributed more catalog records than any other organization, the Library of Congress was the obvious choice for facilitating, researching, and developing a machine-readable catalog format and its uses. In early 1965, the Library began its efforts to develop a format and research its functionality in automated systems.

Other libraries expressed interest in cooperating in this effort, and a number of test libraries that were using computers were chosen to participate in a pilot project. The pilot project included the development and use of the MARC I format. As the pilot project evolved and the Library of Congress distributed MARC I records to project members, a third aspect of the value and use of machine-readable catalog records became increasingly evident. MARC research included this third primary factor: that a machine-readable format could facilitate the transmission and sharing of catalog records between libraries. In other words, records previously distributed to libraries by the Library of Congress only in a print format (catalog card sets) could be distributed on magnetic tape in a machine-readable format that would eliminate re-keying of the information by libraries into their own computer systems.

As was noted above, MARC research included exploration of current as well as potential uses of library records within automated systems. The use of library records within computers presented opportunities and services that were not possible through the use of manual card catalogs. For example, library users could search for records within an automated catalog by using words or phrases that were not traditional access points in card catalogs, such as terms used in notes within the records or the format of materials desired (e.g., books or videocassettes). In addition to improvements in services to patrons, research in the use of a machine-readable format also focused on potential advantages to library administration, particularly in regard to management statistics. For example, a code in the format that indicates whether an item is fiction or nonfiction can provide for statistical analysis in regard to the proportion of fiction and nonfiction items. One piece of information considered for inclusion within the machine-readable format was the width of the item that was described in the catalog record. This information could have provided statistics in regard to the number of "linear" feet within a collection, which information could be used by library administration for planning purposes and for management statistics in regard to needed storage space and shelving. Although this piece of information was not actually included in the established format, it represents an example of the possibilities that were considered during initial MARC research.

The MARC I pilot project provided for input and research to establish a standard for machine-readable records. The MARC I format used during the pilot project was refined and expanded, beginning in March 1967, into the format known today as the MARC II communications format.

The history and theory of the MARC II format are expressed in the "Introduction" section of the Library of Congress document *The MARC II format: A communications format for bibliographic data*, prepared by Henriette D. Avram, John F. Knapp, and Lucia J. Rather, and published in January 1968. The introduction includes a discussion of the MARC Pilot Project, the MARC I communications format and the MARC II format, as follows:

The MARC (*Machine-Readable Cataloging*) Pilot Project was an experiment to test the feasibility of distributing Library of Congress cataloging in machine-readable form to a variety of users. This project grew out of the conviction of many librarians that automation was becoming necessary if libraries were to keep up with the rising tide of new materials and the mounting demand for rapid information. Although there were other library procedures which stood to profit from mechanization, it was felt that devising a method of recording bibliographical information in machine-readable form was basic to the solution of other problems.

There were a number of problems to be surmounted. Primarily, there was no established machine format, and there was lack of agreement among librarians as to what access points were needed in order to take full advantage of an automated system.

As the largest distributor of cataloging information, the Library of Congress was the obvious choice to develop an experimental bibliographical format. Work began early in 1965, and in June of that year the Library published the first draft of a format based on standard LC cataloging practices and suggestions from experts throughout the library field. This report was subjected to intensive review by both the Library of Congress and the library community.

Interest spread, and a number of libraries expressed willingness to participate in a pilot project to experiment in the use of machine-readable cataloging data. Using such criteria as computer equipment available, proposed utilization of cataloging data, geographical location, and type of library, sixteen participants were selected. The first tapes containing English-language titles with 1966 imprints were sent out in November 1966. Since the end of the Pilot Project in June 1967, the Library of Congress has moved into a new phase of development and testing which should culminate in an operational distribution service in 1968. In the interim, the Library is continuing its tape distribution to the original participants.

One immediate result of the distribution of the MARC tapes has been stimulation of interest in the concept of library data transmission. It has become evident that the MARC experiment has suggested to the library community the possibility that individual libraries can use a MARC-like system to contribute data from their own original cataloging for the use of others. Libraries will not only receive data from a centralized source like LC but also may send data, bringing a long anticipated concept of a network of libraries that can create and exploit a common data base much closer to reality.

Essential to such an exchange of data is a standardized "communications format." It is recognized that each institution may have an individualized local format tailored to its own needs. Many kinds of machines will probably be used. But if an institution is to send or receive data, only a single translation program should be necessary to convert the local format from or to the communications format.

One of the most important aspects of the MARC Pilot Project was the evaluation of the MARC I format. Having received a body of feedback from the MARC participating libraries as well as from the Library's MARC staff, the Library has used this material to design a new MARC format that will better serve the library community. At the same time we realized that the new MARC format should have enough built-in flexibility to serve as the standardized communications format for a wide variety of bibliographic data.

In March 1967, the MARC staff began work on a new format. The following steps were followed in developing this format:

1. Collection of more precise information about the data elements themselves, both as to the frequency of occurrence and numbers of characters in a defined element and/or field.

2. Analysis and evaluation of all reports from MARC participants and the Library's MARC staff.

3. Survey of machine formats for bibliographic data which have been designed for library applications in the United States and abroad and which have relevance to the MARC system.

4. Consultation with the National Agricultural Library and the National Library of Medicine.

5. Consultation with institutions which are active in library systems development and with those developing formats of their own.

6. Consultation with those departments of the Library of Congress which will be involved in the production of cataloging data or its use.

The communications format developed as a result of these procedures is designed to incorporate the following specifications:

1. Magnetic tape will be used as the storage and transmission medium. This does not preclude the use of other media in the future.

2. Transmission of the data between institutions will be accomplished by sending tape reels through the mails. It will be possible, however, to convert to other forms of transmission in the future.

3. The format will be flexible enough to allow a variety of local applications on a wide range of hardware configurations. Some of the criteria used to judge the flexibility and usefulness of the format were as follows:

    a. *Printing* — bibliographic data display in a variety of forms (3 × 5 cards, book catalogs, bibliographies, etc.).

b. *Catalog division* — e.g., personal names used as author and subject may be filed together in a separate catalog.

c. *Information retrieval* — i.e., retrieval of data from any part of the record. Since so little is known about how a bibliographic record will be used in machine-readable form for retrieval, it was only possible to anticipate future applications.

d. *Filing* — e.g., indicating the type of name so that similar headings can be arranged in a logical order. (This problem is not completely resolved. The Library's Technical Processes Research Office and the Information Systems Office are now engaged in a joint study of this problem.)[1]

There are two definitive characteristics of the MARC II format. One is its use of computer-readable codes to define elements within a record so that specific elements of information are recognized by the codes used rather than by their position within the record. The other characteristic is the fact that MARC II is a communications format. The primary use intended for the MARC format is to allow different libraries or organizations, with different systems, to transmit records to each other for use within an automated system for whatever purposes are desired. When the records are used in an automated system by a library or other organization, the records are generally restructured or reformatted for the specific uses for which they are intended at that point.

Today, the structure of the MARC format is formally defined within an internationally recognized standard, the American National Standards Institute (ANSI) standard Z39.2-1985, the standard for Bibliographic Information Interchange. ANSI standard Z39.2 defines the structure of the format, such as the types of codes to be used to identify elements of information; however, it does not define which specific codes are to be used to designate particular pieces of information. *Content designation*, the definition of specific codes to be used to identify specific elements of information in a record, is the function of the MARC II format.

MARC is not only an internationally recognized standard; it is also used by a number of nations around the world. For example, by 1985, 16 countries had national MARC tape services: Denmark, the Federal Republic of Germany, France, Italy, the Netherlands, Norway, Sweden, the United Kingdom, Japan, Malaysia, the Philippines, Taiwan, Canada, the United States, Australia, and New Zealand. At that time, another 17 national bibliographic agencies were planning to offer tape services.[2]

MARC FORMAT: FINESSE AND CULTURE

It was noted above that the development of a machine-readable format for library computer records represented some major advancements in the data processing world in general. In particular, the use of variable-length fields and records (as opposed to fixed-length fields and records) represented a departure from the norm in computer records. The use of explicit computer codes to identify elements within a record precluded the need for a fixed-length record in which elements were identified by their position within the record. This introduced a type of finesse in the formatting and use of computer records that had not been widely utilized previously.

In addition, libraries' needs for the use of alphabetic and special characters beyond those currently being used for data processing purposes introduced an element of culture into the world of computers. Given their important role in the preservation and purveyance of history and a myriad of cultures, libraries' use of machine-readable records required that the cultural limitations in the character set used by computers be expanded to include the use of diacritical marks used in non-English languages and special characters for scientific notations, as well as other special characters. An extended character set that included additional characters, which has traditionally been known as the "ALA character set," was developed and used. Today, this expanded character set is formally known as the "Extended Latin Alphabet Coded Character Set for Bibliographic Use," ANSI standard Z39.47-1985.

MARC II EVOLUTION: MARBI AND THE USMARC ADVISORY GROUP

The MARC II format is by no means a static or stagnant entity. As long as it has been in existence, the format has been subject to further refinement and enhancement to accommodate needs of libraries and their users. For example, the initial MARC format included codes defined only for use with catalog records for books. Eventually, codes and separate formats were designed for use with other types of materials, such as maps, sound recordings, and computer files. At this time, the MARC II format is undergoing revision that will culminate in the implementation of one integrated format for all materials. The projected implementation date for MARC format integration (which is discussed in more detail in a separate section, below) is 1993.

Changes to the MARC format include such factors as the addition of codes for additional pieces of information, the revision or clarification of definitions presented in the MARC II documentation, and ongoing research regarding the use and utility of MARC. The Library of Congress coordinates MARC research and proposals, as well as serving as the ultimate authority over the MARC formats and as the publisher of USMARC documentation. Two other organizations that have a strong influence on MARC development are the American Library Association committee commonly known as "MARBI" and the USMARC advisory group. The MARBI (*Ma*chine-*R*eadable *B*ibliographic *I*nformation) committee (the official name of which is the Representation in Machine-Readable Form of Bibliographic Information committee) is an interdivisional committee of the American Library Association that includes representatives from three different ALA divisions: the Association for Library Collections and Technical Services (formerly the Resources and Technical Services Division), the Library and Information Technology Association, and the Reference and Adult Services Division. These three organizations represent the catalogers who initially create and use MARC records, the systems personnel and others who coordinate the use of MARC records within automated systems, and the users of MARC-based automated systems in libraries. The mission of MARBI is basically to establish and maintain a mechanism for the development, review, and evaluation of needed standards for the representation, in machine-readable form, of bibliographic information and to maintain formal communication with appropriate parties within and outside ALA regarding such standards.[3]

In regard to the MARC format, MARBI assists in coordinating, facilitating, and overseeing the evolution of the MARC format. MARBI meetings (at ALA midwinter and summer conferences) serve as a forum for discussions focusing on MARC, within which many other organizations take part in the development and use of the MARC format. In many instances, MARBI performs or oversees formal studies of factors impacting upon or impacted by MARC and its use.

MARBI is the primary component of the USMARC advisory group, which also includes representatives from the Library of Congress and national libraries in the United States and Canada, as well as representatives from the bibliographic utilities (OCLC, RLIN, WLN, and Utlas), and from national groups representing various specializations of librarianship (e.g., the Music Library Association). Some of the more specialized groups may play a greater or lesser role depending upon the topics under consideration. For example, when the Archival and Manuscripts Control format was under development, the Society of American Archivists played a major role in MARBI activities and MARC development.

VARIATIONS OF MARC FORMAT

Although MARC format is considered as a standard that is usable by all MARC users, it should be noted that most vendors, bibliographic utilities, and national agencies have made some types of changes in the MARC formats, generally to facilitate their library users' use of the formats. For example, USMARC is the standard used by the Library of Congress within records created and distributed by the Library of Congress. OCLC-MARC, which is essentially the same format, contains additional fields (such as the 049 holdings field and the subfield ≠ w for heading fields in bibliographic records) that facilitate use of the records by OCLC users. National agencies in other countries that use MARC also have implemented changes within the USMARC format; such formats are generally identified by a distinctive name, such as CANMARC (for records created by the National Library of Canada) and UKMARC (for records created by the British Library).

Within any given country, and sometimes internationally, the changes to MARC format have generally been limited to the addition of fields or subfields and they have not included alternative uses or changes to established USMARC codes. Nevertheless, it is important for libraries to be aware of deviations from USMARC format and to make record processors (e.g., tape processing vendors and automated system vendors) aware of the deviations when the records are to be manipulated in any way. Often, the deviations are documented by the organization that devised them. For example, the OCLC document *OCLC-MARC tape format* was published by OCLC to assist libraries and record processors in using OCLC-MARC records.[4]

The ANSI standard Z39.2 was originally issued as the *American national standard for bibliographic information interchange on magnetic tape*. Magnetic tape (computer tape) was the focus largely because the transmission of MARC records was initially accomplished through the use of magnetic tape, well before microcomputers and floppy disks came into use. The revision of ANSI Z39.2, which was implemented in 1985, excluded the words *on magnetic tape*. The abstract includes the following information:

> This standard specifies the requirements for a generalized interchange format.... It describes a generalized structure designed specifically for exchange of data between processing systems and not necessarily for use as a processing format within systems. It may be used for the communication of records in any media.[5]

Today, the transmission and storage of MARC records take place through a variety of media, such as magnetic tape, floppy disk, and electronic transmission. Many libraries that did not previously use MARC records are now taking advantage of MARC-based automation through the use of microcomputer-based systems. Although it is possible to use a tape drive to load records to micro-based systems, this is generally not done because the number of records loaded to such a system at any one time is usually minimal. Floppy disks are generally used for microcomputer systems, instead of tape.

MARC FORMAT INTEGRATION

MARC formats for different types of materials have been developed at different times. The format for books was the first to be developed, with formats for maps, serials, audiovisual materials, music, archival and manuscript materials, and computer files being developed at later points. Although all of the formats have been developed according to the same principles, there are some inconsistencies between the formats for different types of materials. MARC format integration has been discussed and studied as a way to bring different formats into conformity with each other so that the people who use MARC format and the software that manipulates MARC records can work with a more standardized, easier-to-use record structure. The document *Format integration and its effect on the USMARC bibliographic format*, prepared by the Library of Congress Network Development and MARC Standards Office, provides the following explanation:

> Format Integration has been a recurring topic of discussion regarding the USMARC bibliographic format since the separate format documents began appearing in the late 1960s and early 1970s. While coordination across forms of materials, especially of core data elements, has always been a format development principle, the final step of establishing validity of all data elements for all forms required careful consideration. In the mid 1980s the work was finally undertaken....[6]

> The possibility of having an "integrated" USMARC bibliographic format has been discussed with increasing frequency over the years, particularly as an outgrowth of the 1978-79 review work carried out because of the adoption of the *Anglo-American cataloguing rules*, 2nd edition (AACR2), the consolidation of the bibliographic formats into one document in 1980, the MARC format review conducted by the Library of Congress in 1980-81, and the development of the USMARC statement of underlying principles in 1982-83.
>
> In August 1983, specific proposals for achieving format integration were set forth in Discussion Paper No. 7, "Integration of USMARC Bibliographic Formats." General discussion of the topic took place at a 1983 meeting of the American Library Association RTSD/LITA/RASD Committee on Representation in Machine-Readable Form of Bibliographic Information (MARBI), and the Library of Congress meetings with the Networks. At the January 9, 1984, meeting of the USMARC advisory group, of which MARBI is the principal component, the question was again discussed and ... agreement resulted....[7]

Format integration is the validation of data elements for all forms of material, thus removing restrictions on data elements that currently make them valid only for specific forms of material. The result is a single bibliographic format that contains data elements that can be used to describe many forms of material. It also provides the means for describing the serial-related aspects of any of these items as well as any archival characteristics present, regardless of the medium or form of material.

Integrating the USMARC formats also inevitably requires addressing the inconsistencies, ambiguities, and redundancies that result when all fields, sub-fields, and indicators are extended across all forms of materials.[8]

The preceding paragraphs illustrate not only the process involved with MARC format integration in particular but also the ongoing process of MARC development in general. The projected implementation date for MARC format integration is 1993. A more specific discussion of the impact of MARC format integration on the structure of MARC format is discussed at the end of chapter 2, MARC Format Structure and Content Designation. The impact of MARC format integration on specific MARC codes is discussed at the end of chapter 4, Major MARC Bibliographic Codes.

MARC REALITIES: TWENTY YEARS LATER

Many of the uses of MARC format that were only "hopes" in 1968 have become everyday realities in the more than 20 years since then. Cooperative and resource-sharing ventures, made possible by the creation of MARC, are a major force in library automation activities in the United States and around the world. Reports given at the American Library Association Annual Conference in June 1989 included information on a number of cooperative efforts. These cooperative ventures, which included participation by the Library of Congress, many individual libraries, OCLC, RLG (Research Libraries Group), and the Council on Library Resources, involved the creation of bibliographic records for monographs and serials, as well as name and series authority records.

Activities mentioned include National Coordinated Cataloging Operations (NACO); the Linked Systems Project (LSP), a nationwide multilibrary cooperative effort involving the creation of MARC authority records; the National Coordinated Cataloging Program (NCCP), in which other libraries add bibliographic records to the Library of Congress MARC database; and the Cooperative Online Serials Program (CONSER), which is a multilibrary effort focusing on the creation of MARC bibliographic records for serial publications. The extent and diversity of these activities is evidenced in the excerpts of the Library of Congress report that follow.

Library of Congress staff members reported on a broad range of activities at the Library for participants of NACO (National Coordinated Cataloging Operations)....

... through the end of May [1989] some 350,000 name authority records, 5,000 series, and 80,000 bibliographic records had been contributed through the [NACO] project....

... There are now eight RLG libraries and nine OCLC participants [in the Linked Systems Project]; through the end of May almost 31,000 new name authority records have been contributed via the link, 750 new series authorities, 8,000 changes to names, and 500 changes to series....

... One year into its operation the [National Coordinated Cataloging Program (NCCP)] project, involving eight libraries contributing full bibliographic records to the Library of Congress database, is at the halfway mark....

... An evaluation plan has been put into motion at the Library ... in addition to the comprehensive evaluation being undertaken by the Council on Library Resources, major sponsor of the project....

... CONSER (the Cooperative Online Serials Program) is very much in the cataloging business with more than 400,000 authenticated records contributed over the years.[9]

In many ways, the dreams of 20 years ago have been realized. Yet, in other ways, today's activities are fledgling efforts that only hint at the possibilities that the future holds. Some of those possibilities, and the paths that lead to them, are presented within the remaining chapters of this book.

NOTES

1.   Henriette D. Avram, John F. Knapp, and Lucia J. Rather, *The MARC II format: A communications format for bibliographic data* (Washington, D.C.: Library of Congress, 1968), 1-4.

2.   "Joint meeting of the Sections on Bibliography, Cataloguing, Classification and Subject Cataloguing, Information Technology, and National Libraries [of the International Federation of Library Associations]," *Library of Congress information bulletin* 44 (June 24, 1985): 145.

3.   *ALA handbook of organization 1988/1989* (Chicago: American Library Association, 1988), 136.

4.   Online Computer Library Center, *OCLC-MARC tape format*, 2d ed. (Dublin, Ohio: OCLC, 1989).

5.   *American national standard for information sciences – bibliographic information interchange* [ANSI Z39.2-1985] (New York: American National Standards Institute, 1986), [3].

6.   Network Development and MARC Standards Office, Library of Congress. *Format integration and its effect on the USMARC bibliographic format* (Washington, D.C.: Library of Congress Cataloging Distribution Service, 1988), 3.

7.   Ibid., 5.

8.   Ibid., 5.

9.   Suzanne Liggett, "Report from ALA meeting of the LC/NACO participants," *Library of Congress information bulletin* 48 (October 16, 1989): 367-68.

RELATED READINGS

Avram, Henriette D. *MARC, its history and implications.* Washington, D.C.: Library of Congress, 1975.

Avram, Henriette D. *The MARC pilot project: Final report on a project sponsored by the Council on Library Resources, Inc.* Washington, D.C.: Library of Congress, 1968.

Hagler, Ronald, and Peter Simmons. *The bibliographic record and information technology.* Chicago: American Library Association, 1982.

Rather, Lucia J., and Beacher Wiggins. "Henriette D. Avram: Close-up on the career of a towering figure in library automation and bibliographic control." *American libraries* 20 (9): 855-61 (October 1989).

2

MARC Format Structure and Content Designation

INTRODUCTION

The *USMARC format for bibliographic data*, published by the Library of Congress, describes USMARC records as being composed of three elements: record structure, content designation, and content. The official definition given in that publication is as follows:

A USMARC record is composed of three elements: the record structure, the content designation and the data content of the record. The **record structure** is an implementation of the American National Standard for *Bibliographic information interchange* (ANSI Z39.2). The **content designation** — the codes and conventions established explicitly to identify and further characterize the data elements within a record and to support the manipulation of the data — is defined by each of the USMARC formats [*USMARC format for bibliographic data*, *USMARC format for authority data*, and *USMARC format for holdings data*]. The **content** of the data elements that comprise a USMARC record is usually defined by standards outside the formats such as the *International standard bibliographic description* (ISBD), *Anglo-American cataloguing rules*, 2nd edition (AACR2), *Library of Congress subject headings* (LCSH), or other rules and codes used by the organization that creates a record. The content of certain coded data elements is defined in the USMARC formats (e.g., the Leader, field 007, field 008).[1]

Structure, content designation, and content are each briefly described below. This chapter focuses on the structure and content designation of the USMARC format. Content designation and content are further discussed in chapter 3, Patterns in the MARC Format and chapter 4, Major MARC Bibliographic Codes.

MARC Record Structure

The structure of the format involves the types of codes that are used to identify elements of information in a record. For example, fields of information (such as an author heading) are identified by three-character numeric codes called "tags." (The USMARC tag for a personal author main entry is 100.) Elements within a field of information, called "subfields," are identified within the field through the use of "subfield codes," which consist of a single letter or number immediately preceded by a "delimiter" sign ($\neq$). The **delimiter sign** is used so that the letter or number will not be mistakenly interpreted as part of the text of the field. An example of a USMARC subfield is the Name of publisher subfield, which is usually the second subfield of the Publication, distribution, etc. (Imprint) field. Within this field of a MARC record, the name of the publisher would be preceded by a $\neq b$.

MARC Content Designation

Content designation within the USMARC format involves the meaning of each code used to identify elements within a catalog record. Although the structure of the format designates the types of codes (e.g., three-character numeric tags to identify each field of information) to be used and the arrangement of the codes (e.g., one-character codes to be used to identify elements within a field), the structure does not designate what each code means. Content designation involves the definition of specific codes (e.g., three-character field tags and one-character subfield codes) to be used to identify specific pieces of information within a record.

MARC Record Content

The third part of MARC record composition is the data content. In regard to a bibliographic record, this basically refers to the catalog record that is being coded using the MARC format. A MARC record is created by first creating the catalog record according to cataloging rules (creation of a catalog record is not dependent upon the use of the MARC format) and then using MARC codes to identify the information within the catalog record. The MARC format does not stipulate which pieces of information should be included within a catalog record; it simply identifies those pieces of catalog information so that they can be recognized by a computer.

STRUCTURE AND CONTENT DESIGNATION

As was explained above, the three elements of a MARC record are record structure, content designation, and content. The content of the record is determined by cataloging rules and standards, not by the MARC format. Record structure and content designation are provided by the MARC format.

The USMARC bibliographic format consists of three main components, the Leader, the Directory, and the Variable Fields. They are described within the *USMARC format for bibliographic data* as follows:

Leader — Data elements that provide information for the processing of the record. The data elements contain numbers or coded values and are identified by relative character position. The Leader is fixed in length at 24 character positions and is the first field of a USMARC record.

Directory — A series of entries that contain the tag, length, and starting location of each variable field within a record. Each entry is 12 character positions in length. Directory entries for variable control fields appear first, sequenced by tag in increasing numerical order. Entries for variable data fields follow, arranged in ascending order according to the first character of the tag. The stored sequence of the variable data fields in a record does not necessarily correspond to the order of the corresponding Directory entries. Duplicate tags are distinguished only by the location of the respective fields within the record. The Directory ends with a field terminator character (ASCII 1E16).

Variable fields — The data in a USMARC bibliographic record is organized into variable fields, each identified by a three-character **numeric tag** that is stored in the Directory entry for the field. Each field ends with a field terminator character (ASCII 1E16). The last variable field in a record ends with both a field terminator and a record terminator (ASCII 1D16).

There are two types of variable fields:

Variable control fields — The 00X fields. These fields are identified by a field tag in the Directory, but they contain neither indicator positions nor subfield codes. The variable control fields are structurally different from the variable data fields. They may contain either a single data element or a series of fixed-length data elements identified by relative character position.

Variable data fields — The remaining variable fields defined in the format. In addition to being identified by a field tag in the Directory, variable data fields contain two **indicator positions** stored at the beginning of each field and a two-character **subfield code** preceding each data element within the field.[2]

Although they involve only one of the three components of a MARC record, the variable fields are by far the most complex fields. The variable fields are the fields that are most used within cataloging functions and for automated systems used by library patrons. Each MARC record contains only one Leader and one Directory; the majority of the fields within any MARC record are the variable fields. The variable fields include the text of the catalog record and other information. The Leader, Directory, and Variable Fields are discussed briefly in this section, followed by a more comprehensive and detailed discussion of the Variable Fields.

Leader

The Leader includes encoded or full text information that designates such features as the type of material being cataloged and the length of the record. Most of this information is provided automatically by the computer when the record is entered onto tape. In most cases, it does not have to be entered by the cataloger.

Directory

The Directory is constructed automatically when the record is entered onto tape. It does not require any calculation or data entry by the cataloger. The Directory provides a way for a computer to find particular fields within the MARC record by indicating the starting position of each MARC field. The Directory is not used by catalogers or library patrons. In some cases, the Directory is used by systems analysts for troubleshooting problems in the use of the record; however, the Directory is generally not provided for other system users. The Directory includes one fixed-length entry for each variable field in the MARC record. The fixed-length entry consists of 12 characters, divided into three groups of character positions. The first three character positions include the MARC tag (the three-character numeric code used to identify a variable field within the MARC record). The next four characters include the length of the field (i.e., the total number of characters in the field) and the next five characters give the starting character position of the field within the record (i.e., the character position within the MARC record at which that particular variable field begins). An example of the elements contained within a Directory entry is given in figure 2.1.

```
                            Starting
                Field       character
     Tag       length       position

     050       0012         00056
```

Fig. 2.1. Elements of a Directory entry.

Figure 2.1 shows the tag number for an LC call number (050), the length of the field (12 characters) and the starting character position within the record for that field (the 57th character). Because the numbering of character positions within the Directory begins with the number *0* instead of *1*, the number *56* actually indicates that the field begins with the 57th character in the record. Directory entries do not contain any spaces, so the elements illustrated in figure 2.1 would be contained within the Directory as a string: 050001200056.

Variable Fields

Variable data fields are described within the *USMARC format for bibliographic data* as follows:

The variable data fields are grouped into blocks according to the first character of the tag, which with some exceptions identifies the function of the data within the record. The type of information in the field is identified by the remainder of the tag.

0XX	Control information, identification and classification numbers, etc.
1XX	Main entries
2XX	Titles and title paragraph (title, edition, imprint)
3XX	Physical description, etc.
4XX	Series statements
5XX	Notes
6XX	Subject access fields
7XX	Added entries other than subject or series; linking fields
8XX	Series added entries, etc.
9XX	Reserved for local implementation

Within the 1XX, 4XX, 6XX, 7XX, and 8XX blocks, certain parallels of content designation are usually preserved. The following meanings, with some exceptions, are given to the final two characters of the tag of fields in these blocks:

X00	Personal names
X10	Corporate names
X11	Meeting names
X30	Uniform titles
X40	Bibliographic titles
X50	Topical terms
X51	Geographic names

Within variable data fields, the following two kinds of content designation are used:

Indicator positions — The first two character positions in the variable data fields contain values which interpret or supplement the data found in the field. Indicator values are interpreted independently, that is, meaning is not ascribed to the two characters taken together. Indicator values may be a lowercase alphabetic or a numeric character. A blank (ASCII SPACE), represented in this document as a ƀ, is used in an undefined indicator position. In a defined indicator position, a blank may be assigned a meaning, or may mean "no information provided."

Subfield codes — Two characters that distinguish the data elements within a field which require separate manipulation. A subfield code consists of a delimiter (ASCII 1F16), represented in this document as a ≠, followed by a data element identifier. Data element identifiers may be a lowercase alphabetic or a numeric character. Subfield codes are defined independently for each field; however, parallel meanings are preserved whenever possible (e.g., in the 100, 400, and 600 Personal Name fields). Subfield codes are defined for purposes of identification, not arrangement. The order of subfields is generally specified by standards for the data content, such as the cataloging rules.[3]

The variable fields are the most complex fields in the MARC record and they are the fields most used by catalogers in creating the records and by library staff and patrons in using the records in automated systems. They also constitute the majority of the information found within any MARC record. The remainder of this chapter is devoted to explanation and discussion of the MARC variable fields.

MARC VARIABLE FIELDS

As was discussed above, there are two types of MARC variable data fields: variable control fields and variable data fields. These two types of fields are explained and discussed below.

Variable Control Fields

Variable control fields are nine separate fields identified by the MARC tags 001 through 009. Unlike variable data fields, variable control fields contain neither indicator positions nor subfield codes. Generally speaking, variable control fields include information expressed through the use of codes, as opposed to variable data fields, which generally include textual data. Control fields do not require subfield codes (i.e., codes that designate different pieces of information within a field) because they contain only one piece of information (such as the record number in the 001 field) or a series of fixed-length data elements that are identified by their character position(s) in the field. For example, the first character position within the 007 field (Physical description fixed field) includes a single-character code, such as *m* for "motion picture," which indicates the type of material being described within the 007 field.

The term *MARC fixed field* is widely used to refer to the MARC 008 field. OCLC and other utilities or vendors may also include elements from the MARC Leader within their definition of the fixed field, and those elements need to be supplied by the cataloger (e.g., the Bibliographic level code, which indicates whether an item is a monographic or serial publication, such as a journal). Because this definition of the MARC 008 field and other codes is so widely used, the term *fixed field* is used in some cases in this book to refer to those codes.

Fixed field codes, such as those included in the MARC 007 and 008 fields, are brief, encoded pieces of information. The fixed fields differ from variable fields in that they are not full-text information that has been transcribed verbatim. Generally speaking, fixed field codes are letters or numbers, individual or grouped, that tell something about the item cataloged, such as whether it is a reprint, or the primary language of the work. The codes have been devised according to four types of patterns, as discussed in chapter 3, Patterns in the MARC Format.

There are several MARC variable control fields that are fixed length fields, including the 005 field (Date and time of latest transaction), the 007 field (Physical description fixed field) and the 008 field (Fixed-length data elements). *Fixed length* means that the fields are a set number of characters in length. Each position within a fixed-length field has been defined to contain a specific piece of information, which is usually a code of some type. The 29th character in the Books 008 field, for example, includes the Government publication code, which indicates whether or not the item is a government publication and which type of government publication it is. The 32nd character in the Books 008 field is the Index code, which is set to *1* if the item contains an index to its own contents or a *0* if there is no index.

Some of the information in the variable control fields can also be found in the variable data fields of the MARC record. The illustration statement is one example of such information; the country of publication is another. Within the variable data fields, the information is included as full-text information for library patrons to read, and it may be expressed in an implicit, ambiguous, or verbose manner that is difficult for a computer to decipher or understand. The coded information in the fixed field expresses the information explicitly and succinctly. This allows a computer to recognize the information and use it efficiently and effectively. For example, if a library patron searching an online catalog specifies that the material being searched is a government publication produced by the state of California, then the computer can identify such a publication by checking the fixed field codes for country (or state) of publication and for government publications. This is much easier and faster for the computer to do than to check other pieces of information within the text of the record in the variable data fields and try to interpret the data, which may or may not explicitly state that an item is a California state publication. The country (or state) of publication, may only be implied within the text of the variable data field, or it may be stated in one of a number of different languages. Inclusion of a two- or three-letter place of publication code within the fixed field provides for a recognizable and unambiguous statement that can be easily located and recognized by the computer.

Another example of the utility of fixed field codes involves illustration statements within a record. An illustration statement, for example, can be dealt with much more speedily and handily by the computer when it is expressed as the four-letter fixed field code *ahij* than when it is stated as *ill. (some col.), coats of arms, facsims., geneal. tables.* Since most databases involve thousands or even millions of records that must be handled by the computer, the time saved can be substantial. Also, within the variable data field statements, there is a much greater possibility of spelling or transcription errors, which make the statements literally unrecognizable by the computer.

It should be noted that, although the variable control fields are included as strings of characters within the MARC record, many utilities and vendors have rearranged or enhanced the way in which the fixed field data is displayed within a catalog record when it is used for cataloging purposes. This has been done to assist catalogers in correctly supplying fixed field codes. For example, the cataloging system may include a fixed field section within each catalog record that explicitly identifies, through the use of displayed terms, the fixed field code to be supplied and provides a particular position on the screen where the cataloger is to input the information. This is obviously much easier for the cataloger than having to input a string of 40 codes according to character position. The displayed terms used to identify the fixed field codes on the cataloging screen do not become part of the MARC record when it is placed on magnetic tape. When the record is placed on tape, only the codes, in their correct order, are placed on the tape.

Variable Data Fields

Within any MARC records, most of the fields will be variable data fields. Variable data fields differ from variable control fields in that they do not contain a set number of characters. In most cases, variable data fields include full-text data, the catalog record information that is used to provide information to library patrons in a form they can understand. A record will contain as many fields as are necessary to describe the item being cataloged. And, the fields can be as long or as short as required by their contents. For example, a contents note (505 field), which includes a listing of, say short stories within a book, may be one or two lines long, or it may require several thousand characters. Another example is the title statement (245 field), which may involve only a one- or two-word title and a brief author statement with the sole author's name. In other cases, the title statement may include a lengthy title proper, subtitle and parallel title, plus information on several authors, editors, illustrators, and/or translators.

Within MARC records, there are varying numbers of variable data fields from one record to the next and varying numbers of characters within these fields. The computer cannot recognize or locate any particular piece of information within the record by its position relative to other pieces of information, as can be done within fixed-length fields. For this reason, explicit codes, supplied by the cataloger when the record is created, are used to identify the specific elements within the variable data fields. The three types of codes used within variable data fields are tags, indicators, and subfield codes.

MARC tags are three-character numeric identifiers (ranging from 001 to 999) that identify fields of information within a MARC record. For example, the tag 110 identifies a corporate name main entry, such as "Ferris State University." Another example is the tag 245, which identifies the field in which the title, subtitle, and author statement are included. A 650 field includes a topical subject heading, such as "Dogs."

Figure 2.2 includes an example of a partial MARC record (variable data fields only) with the MARC tags highlighted.

010		‡a 81–43004
040		‡a DLC ‡c DLC
020		‡a 038517616 : ‡c $9.95
050		‡a PR6067.U347 ‡b D4 1981
100	10	‡a Quest, Erica.
245	10	‡a Design for murder / ‡c Erica Quest.
260	0	‡a Garden City, N.Y. : ‡b Published for the Crime Club by Doubleday, ‡c 1981.
300		‡a 184 p. ; ‡c 22 cm.

Fig. 2.2. Partial MARC record (variable data fields only) with MARC tags highlighted.

Indicators are one-character numeric codes that either provide instructions to the computer for processing the information in the field or provide explicit information about the contents of the field. For each MARC field, there are two indicator positions, which are used independently of each other. The use of indicators within the field is defined according to the field tag that has been used. In some fields, indicator positions are both defined as blanks because there is no information to be provided. In other fields, either the first or the second indicator may be defined as a blank. In still other fields, both indicator positions contain numeric indicators.

An example of an indicator used to provide instructions to the computer for processing purposes is the indicator officially described as the "number of nonfiling characters present" but more widely referred to as the "filing indicator." The filing indicator is used within fields, such as title fields, in which an initial article (such as *a*, *an*, or *the*) should be disregarded for purposes of filing the field in a catalog. The filing indicator is set to the number of characters (including spaces) at the beginning of the field that should be disregarded when the field is filed or searched in an online catalog or for other purposes. For example, for the title *The computer user's manual*, the filing indicator would be set to *4*. The computer interprets this to mean that filing should begin with the fifth character (the letter *c* in the word *computer*). The filing indicator may be either the first or second indicator in the field, according to the tag that is used.

An example of an indicator used to provide explicit information about the contents of a field is the first indicator within the MARC 100 field (Personal name main entry), which provides information about the type of name used within the field. A first indicator *0* indicates that the name is a forename only; a first indicator *1* indicates that the name in the field includes a single surname; a first indicator *2* indicates that the field includes a compound surname (such as "Fitzgerald-Jones").

Figure 2.3 is an example of a partial MARC record (variable data fields only) with the indicators highlighted.

```
010        ‡a 81-43004
040        ‡a DLC /=c DLC
020        ‡a 038517616 : ‡c $9.95
050 ⌀      ‡a PR6067.U347 ‡b D4 1981
100 10     ‡a Quest, Erica.
245 10     ‡a Design for murder / ‡c Erica Quest.
260 0      ‡a Garden City, N.Y. : ‡b Published for the Crime Club
              by Doubleday, ‡c 1981.
300        ‡a 184 p. ; ‡c 22 cm.
```

Fig. 2.3. Partial MARC record (variable data fields only) with MARC indicators highlighted.

Subfield codes are used to identify individual elements within each MARC field. Subfield codes are one-character codes (most of which are lowercase alphabetic characters, but in a few cases, a single number is used) that are immediately preceded by a delimiter sign (‡). Subfield codes are supplied according to the tag used to identify the entire field. For example, the subfield code *a* in the 260 field (Publication, distribution, etc. (Imprint)) is used to identify the place of publication, while the subfield code *a* in the 245 field is used to identify the title proper (as opposed to the subtitle, which is included in field 245, subfield ‡*b*).

Figure 2.4 is an example of a partial MARC record (variable data fields only) with the subfield codes highlighted.

```
010        ‡a 81-43004
040        ‡a DLC ‡c DLC
020        ‡a 038517616 : ‡c $9.95
050 ⌀      ‡a PR6067.U347 ‡b D4 1981
100 10     ‡a Quest, Erica.
245 10     ‡a Design for murder / ‡c Erica Quest.
260 0      ‡a Garden City, N.Y. : ‡b Published for the Crime Club
              by Doubleday, ‡c 1981.
300        ‡a 184 p. ; ‡c 22 cm.
```

Fig. 2.4. Partial MARC record (variable data fields only) with MARC subfield codes highlighted.

Figure 2.5 is an example of a MARC record for a book, taken from the *USMARC format for bibliographic data.*

```
LDR     *****cam♭♭22*****♭a♭4500
001     <control number>
005     19870504050512.0
008     | 820305 | s1982♭♭♭♭ | nyua♭♭♭ | ♭♭♭♭♭♭ | ♭00110♭ | eng♭d |


020     ♭♭‡a0442281536 :‡c‡15.95
040     ♭♭‡a<NUC symbol>‡c<NUC symbol>
050     14‡aTX745‡b.S49 1982
082     04‡a641.8/6‡219

100     10‡aShakespeare, Margaret N.
245     14‡aThe meringue cookbook /‡cMargaret N. Shakespeare.
260     0♭‡aNew York :‡bVan Nostrand Reinhold,‡c1982.
300     ♭♭‡a240 p. :‡bill. ;‡c25 cm.
500     ♭♭‡aIncludes index.
650     ♭0‡aCookery (Meringue)
```

Fig. 2.5. Example of a MARC record for a book.

OTHER ASPECTS OF RECORD STRUCTURE

Other aspects of MARC record structure that are prescribed by the USMARC format are field and subfield repeatability, display constants, and national level requirements. Each of these factors is discussed below.

Field and Subfield Repeatability

The *USMARC format for bibliographic data* provides the following instructions in regard to the repeatability of MARC fields and subfields within a bibliographic record:

> Theoretically, all fields and subfields may be repeated. The nature of the data, however, often precludes repetition. For example, a bibliographic record may contain only one 1XX main entry field; a field 100 may contain only one subfield ≠a (Personal name) but may contain more than one subfield ≠c (Titles and other words associated with a name). The repeatability/nonrepeatability of each field and subfield is specified in the [USMARC bibliographic] format.[4]

As was noted above, the informational content of a bibliographic record is not prescribed by the MARC format but by the cataloging rules and other standards used by the cataloger. The repeatability or nonrepeatability of informational fields is noted within the MARC format documentation, which would seem to place the MARC format in a "prescriptive" role in regard to the contents of catalog records. The repeatability information included as part of the MARC format documentation is based upon the cataloging rules; there is no conflict between established cataloging rules and the MARC format.

Display Constants

Display constants are elements of information or punctuation that can be provided automatically by a computer when they are required, rather than input manually by a cataloger. For example, "Summary:" is used as the first word of a summary note within a catalog record but does not have to be included in the catalog record because the MARC coding instructs the computer to print or display this text whenever the note is printed. The use of display constants saves staff time because the information or punctuation does not have to be written down or input as part of the record. The use of display constants also decreases the amount of database storage necessary to accommodate a library's records, because fewer characters are included within the records. The *USMARC format for bibliographic data* provides the following instructions in regard to the use of display constants with bibliographic records:

A display constant is a term, phrase, and/or spacing or punctuation convention that may be system generated under prescribed circumstances in order to make a visual presentation of data in a record more meaningful to a user. In the bibliographic format, certain field tags (e.g., field 770, Supplement/Special Issue Entry), indicators (e.g., fields 511, Indicator 1, Display constant controller) and subfield codes (e.g., the subject subdivision subfields ≠x, ≠y, and ≠z in a subject added entry), may be used to generate specific terms, phrases, and/or spacing or punctuation conventions for the display of a record. The use of display constants is determined by each organization or system [which uses the MARC records]. Examples of display constants are provided under "Input Conventions" in the field descriptions [in the *USMARC format for bibliographic data*]. The general convention of displaying a subfield code as a space in the display of a record is not highlighted in the display constant examples.[5]

National Level Requirements

The *USMARC format for bibliographic data* provides guidelines for full-level ("complete") and minimal-level ("brief") catalog records. Cataloging standards (specifically, the *Anglo-American cataloguing rules*, 2d ed. revised) provide for varying levels of completeness of a catalog record, with some applicable items of information being omitted when lower levels are followed. In the *USMARC format for bibliographic data*, the documentation for each data element includes instruction as to whether the element is necessary for inclusion within a catalog record if the record is to be considered as a full level record. The *USMARC format for bibliographic data* includes the following information in regard to full level and minimal level records:

Full level machine-readable bibliographic records that are contributed to a national database must follow the content requirements specified by the codes in the "Format/NLR" columns in the listing of content designators defined for each field [in the *USMARC format for bibliographic data*]....

There are four national level requirement codes used in the bibliographic format: M (Mandatory), A (Mandatory if applicable), O (Optional), and U (Unused).

M — Mandatory

Mandatory means that the data element must be present in a full level national level record....

A — Mandatory if applicable

Mandatory if applicable means that the data element must be present if it is appropriate and the information is available....

O — Optional

Optional means that the use of the data element is optional....

U — Unused

Unused means undefined or not used because of the nature of the material, the nature of the content designator, or the practices of an authoritative agency, etc.

National Level Record requirements for minimal level records are given in Appendix A of [the *USMARC format for bibliographic data*].[6]

MARC FORMAT INTEGRATION

MARC format integration, which is scheduled to be implemented in 1993, will rectify inconsistencies within the MARC format structure and content designation. The inconsistencies have arisen largely because different formats have been developed for different types of material at different times. Format integration will involve standardizing the use of codes, regardless of the type of material being described. Although the MARC bibliographic formats for different types of materials are very similar and generally do contain the same types of codes for the same types of information, there are conflicts and discrepancies. Such discrepancies include the use of different codes to designate the same element of information within different records, depending upon the type of material being described. MARC format integration will provide more uniformity within content designation, resulting in a coding scheme that will ultimately be easier for people (and computers) to use.

The following description of format changes resulting from integration is provided by the Library of Congress:

The basic change with format integration is the extension of the validity of all data elements to all forms of material ... a few content designators were deleted and added and a larger number were made obsolete.

Deletes

Several content designators had been reserved for a number of years but not fully defined. Rather than extending the reserved tag or subfield to all forms of material, these content designators were deleted from the format....

Unused content designation

A number of content designators had been defined but were not used, seldom used, or not used under current (post 1980) cataloging conventions. Rather than defining these for additional forms of material, most of them were made obsolete....

Criteria for specialized note fields

Many specialized note fields, applicable to only one form of material, have been defined in USMARC. In order to help identify unnecessary note fields that should be made obsolete rather than being defined for all types of material, criteria for establishing special note fields were developed.... Several note fields were made obsolete because they did not meet these criteria....

Unclear definition of content designators

In a few cases, the application of content designators had never been clearly defined and the practices of users thus varied. Several of these ambiguous values were made obsolete.

Brief record provisions

Several content designators ... had been established primarily to assist in creating brief records. Since they are not used for that or other purposes, continuing to code them and validating them for other forms of material seemed inappropriate, thus they were made obsolete.

Overlapping field content

In several instances, the same type of data was present in different fields for different forms of material. This meant that with format integration, the same data could be placed in more than one field. These situations were reconciled and one place established for the data in each case....

Name changes

The name of a content designator was not clear, in some cases, when it became valid for additional forms of material.... Such names were adjusted to clarify the appropriate data content.[7]

THE USMARC FORMATS — UNDERLYING PRINCIPLES

First prepared by John Attig of Pennsylvania State University in 1981, the document "The USMARC Formats — Underlying Principles" has been considered and revised by the USMARC advisory group. The principles are a relatively concise explanation of the structure and characteristics of the formats. The version presented below was approved by MARBI in 1982 and was published in the May 9, 1983, issue of *Library of Congress information bulletin* (pp. 148-52). Although the basic premises still stand, the document has unfortunately not been kept current. More up-to-date information or, in some cases, explanatory comments, have been provided in brackets at appropriate points within the text of the document. The "Underlying Principles" serve to reinforce and review the information provided in chapters 1 and 2 of this book, as well as to provide some previews of discussions in the following chapters.

Preface

The following statement of underlying principles is intended to reflect those principles which account for the current state of the USMARC formats and to constitute a provisional set of working principles for further format development. The statement will be included as prefatory material in *MARC formats for bibliographic data* [now *USMARC format for bibliographic data*] and *Authorities: A MARC format* [now *USMARC format for authority data*] and will be revised as necessary in the future. [The "Principles" have not been included in either the earlier or current versions of the documents.]

1.   Introduction

1.1.   The USMARC Formats are standards for the representation of bibliographic and authority information in machine-readable form. [In 1990, a format for holdings data will be published by the Library of Congress.]

1.2.   A MARC record involves three elements: (1) the record *structure*, (2) the *content designation*, and (3) the data *content* of the record.

1.2.1.   The structure of USMARC records is an implementation of the *American national standard for information interchange on magnetic tape* (ANSI Z39.2-1979) [now, *American national standard for information sciences - bibliographic information interchange* (ANSI Z39.2-1985)] and of *Documentation — Format for bibliographic information interchange on magnetic tape* (ISO 2709-1973) [now, ISO 2709-1981].

1.2.2.   Content designation — the codes and conventions established to explicitly identify and further characterize the data elements within a record and to support the manipulation of that data — is defined in the USMARC Formats.

1.2.3.   The content of those data elements which comprise a traditional catalog record is defined by standards outside the formats — such as the *Anglo-American cataloguing rules* or the *National Library of Medicine classification*. The content of other data elements — coded data (see section 9 below) — is defined in the USMARC Formats.

1.3.   A MARC format is a set of codes and content designators defined for encoding a particular type of machine-readable record.

1.3.1.   At present, USMARC formats have been defined for two distinct types of records. *MARC formats for bibliographic data* [*USMARC format for bibliographic data*] contains format specifications for encoding data elements needed to describe, retrieve and control various types of bibliographic material. *Authorities: A MARC format* [*USMARC format for authority data*] contains format specifications for encoding data elements which identify and/or control the content and content designation of those portions of a bibliographic record which may be subject to authority control. [As noted above, a third format for holdings information, such as the location of an item and the number of copies or volumes held, will be published in 1990 — (*USMARC format for holdings data*].

1.3.2.   The *MARC formats for bibliographic data* are a family of formats defined for the identification and description of different types of bibliographic material. USMARC bibliographic formats have been defined for Books, Films, Machine-Readable Data Files, Manuscripts, Maps, Music and Serials. [*USMARC format for bibliographic data* includes the same categories, but different terminology: Books, Visual Materials, Computer Files, Archival and Manuscripts control, Maps, Music, and Serials.]

1.3.3.   The USMARC Formats have attempted to preserve consistency of content designation across formats where this is appropriate. However, as the formats proliferated and became more complex, definitions and usages have diverged. While complete consistency has not been achieved, a continuing effort is being made to promote consistent definition and usage across formats. [The major focus of MARC format integration, which is to be fully implemented in 1993, is to provide consistency within the formats, regardless of the type of material involved.]

2.   General Considerations

2.1.   The USMARC Formats are communications formats, primarily designed to provide specifications for the exchange of records between systems. The communications formats do not mandate the internal formats to be used by individual systems, either for storage or display. ["Full-MARC" output, regardless of the storage or display format used within a system, has become increasingly recognized as an important system capability.]

2.2.   The USMARC Formats were designed to facilitate the exchange of information on magnetic tape. In addition, they have been widely adapted for use in a variety of exchange and processing environments.

2.3.   The USMARC formats are designed for use within the United States. An attempt has been made to preserve compatibility with other national formats. However, lack of international agreement on cataloging codes and practices has made complete compatibility impossible.

2.4.   The USMARC Formats serve as a vehicle for bibliographic and authority data of all types, from all agencies. Historically and practically, the formats have always had a close relationship to the needs and the practices of the library community. In particular, the formats reflect the various cataloging codes applied by American libraries.

2.5.   Historically, the USMARC Formats were developed to enable the Library of Congress to communicate its catalog records to other institutions. National agencies in the United States and Canada (Library of Congress, National Library of Canada, National Agricultural Library, National Library of Medicine, and Government Printing Office) are still given special emphasis in the formats, as sources of authoritative cataloging and as agencies responsible for certain data elements.

2.6.   The institutions responsible for the content, content designation, and transcription accuracy of data within a USMARC record are identified at the record level, in field 008, byte 39, and in field 040. This responsibility may be evaluated in terms of the following rule.

2.6.1.   Responsible Parties Rule.

a)   Unmodified records: The institution identified as the transcribing institution (field 040 ǂc) should be considered responsible for content designation and transcription accuracy for all data. Except for agency-assigned data (see section 2.6.2.1. below), the institution identified as the cataloging institution (field 040 ǂa) should be considered responsible for content.

b)   Modified records: Institutions identified as transcribing or modifying institutions (field 040 ǂc,d) should be considered collectively responsible for content designation and transcription accuracy. Except for agency assigned and authoritative-agency data (see section 2.6.2. below), institutions identified as modifying or cataloging institutions (field 040 ǂa,d) should be considered collectively responsible for content.

2.6.2.   Exceptions.

2.6.2.1.   Certain data elements are defined in the USMARC formats as being exclusively assigned by particular agencies (e.g., International Standard Serial Number, Library of Congress Card Number). The content of such *agency-assigned* elements is always the responsibility of the agency.

2.6.2.2.   Certain data elements have been defined in the USMARC Formats in relation to one or more *authoritative agencies* which maintain the lists or rules upon which the data is based. Where it is possible for other agencies to create similar or identical values for these data elements, content designation is provided to distinguish between values actually assigned by the authoritative agency and values assigned by other agencies. In the former case, responsibility for content rests with the authoritative agency; in the latter case, the Responsible Parties Rule applies, and no further identification of source of data is provided. Authoritative-agency fields are:

050   Library of Congress Call Number

060   National Library of Medicine Call Number

082   Dewey Decimal Classification Number
       (DDC is maintained by the Library of Congress)

2.7.   In general, the USMARC Formats provide content designation only for data which is applicable to all copies of the bibliographic entity described.

2.7.1.   Information which applies only to some copies (or even to a single copy) of a title may nevertheless be of interest beyond the institutions holding such copies. The USMARC Formats provide limited content designation for the encoding of such information and for identifying the holding institutions (see, for example, subfield ≠5 in the 7XX fields).

2.7.2.   Information which does not apply to all copies of a title, and is not of interest to other institutions, is coded in local fields (such as field 590).

2.8.   Although a MARC record is usually autonomous, data elements have been provided containing information which may be used to link related records. These linkages may be implicit, through identical access points in each record, or explicit, through a linking field. Linking fields (76X-78X) may contain either selected data elements which identify the related item or a control number which identifies the related record. An explicit code in the Leader [byte 19] identifies a record which is linked to another record through a control number [however, this capability is rarely used; the code usually appears as a blank].

3.   Structural Features

3.1.   The USMARC Formats are an implementation of the *American national standard for information interchange on magnetic tape* (ANSI Z39.2-1979). They also incorporate other relevant ANSI standards, such as *Magnetic tape labels and file structure for information interchange* (ANSI X3.27-1978).

3.2.   All information in a MARC record is stored in character form. USMARC communication records are coded in Extended ASCII, as defined in Appendix III.B of *MARC formats for bibliographic data*. [This information has not been included within the *USMARC format for bibliographic data*. Instead, it is included in a separate publication, *USMARC specifications for record structure, character sets, tapes*.]

3.3.   The length of each variable field can be determined either from the "length of field" element in the directory entry or from the occurrence of the "field terminator" character. Likewise, the length of a record can be determined either from the "logical record length" element in the Leader or from the occurrence of the "record terminator" character. (In the past, the field terminator of the last field was omitted, and the record terminator identified the end of that field.) The location of each variable field is explicitly stated in the "starting character position" element in its directory entry.

4.   Content Designation

4.1.   The goal of content designation is to identify and characterize the data elements which comprise a MARC record with sufficient precision to support manipulation of the data for a variety of functions.

4.2.   For example, MARC content designation is designed to support such functions as:

(1)   Display — the formatting of data for display on a CRT, for printing on 3" × 5" cards or in book catalogs, for production of COM [computer-output microform] catalogs, or for other visual presentation of the data.

(2)   Information retrieval — the identification, categorization and retrieval of any identifiable data element in a record.

4.3.   Some fields serve multiple functions. For example, field 245 serves both as the bibliographic transcription of the title and statement of responsibility and as the access point for the title.

4.4.   The USMARC Formats provide for display constants (text which implicitly accompanies particular content designators). For example, subfield ≠x in field 490 (and in some other fields) implies the display constant "ISSN," and the combination of tag 780 and second indicator value "3" implies the display constant "Superseded in part by:." Such display constants are not carried in the data [of the MARC record] but may be supplied for display by the processing system.

4.5.   The USMARC formats support the sorting of data only to a limited extent. In general, sorting must be accomplished through the application of external algorithms [e.g., filing rules coded as computer programs] to the data.

5.   Organization of the Record

5.1.   A MARC record consists of three main sections: (1) the Leader, (2) the Directory, and (3) the Variable Fields.

5.2.   The *Leader* consists of data elements which contain coded values and are identified by relative character position. Data elements in the Leader define parameters for processing the record. The Leader is fixed in length (24 characters) and occurs at the beginning of each MARC record.

5.3.   The *Directory* contains the field identifier ("tag"), starting location and length of each field within the record. Directory entries for variable control fields appear first, in tag order. Entries for variable data fields follow arranged in ascending order according to the first character of the tag. The order of fields in the record does not necessarily correspond to the order of directory entries. Duplicate tags are distinguished only by location of the respective fields within the record. [In some cases, MARC indicators have been mistakenly interpreted as an indication of the order of multiple occurrences of the same tag within a single record. However, the order duplicate tags should retain is the order in which they appear in the record.] The length of the directory entry is defined in the Entry Map elements in the Leader. In the USMARC Formats, the length of the directory entry is 12 characters. The Directory ends with a "field terminator" character.

5.4.   The data content of a record is divided into *Variable Fields*. The USMARC Formats distinguish two types of variable fields: *Variable Control Fields* and *Variable Data Fields*. Control and data fields are distinguished only by structure (see section 7.2. below). [In this book and within other environments, the term *fixed field* is used to refer to some of the Leader codes and variable control fields that are "fixed-length" fields.]

6.   Variable Fields and Tags

6.1.   The data in a MARC record is organized into fields, each identified by a 3-character tag.

6.2.   According to ANSI Z39.2-1979, the tag must consist of alphabetic or numeric basic characters (i.e., decimal integers 0-9 or lower-case letters a-z). To date, the USMARC Formats have used only numeric tags.

6.3.   The tag is stored in the directory entry for the field, not in the field itself. [In the vast majority of cases in which MARC records are used for cataloging and bibliographic maintenance purposes, the tags have been displayed with their respective fields. However, in many cases, on tape or other media, the Directory, not the field, contains the tag number.]

6.4.   Variable fields are grouped into blocks according to the first character of the tag, which identifies the function of the data within a traditional catalog record (e.g., main entry, added entry, subject entry). The type of information in the field (e.g., personal name, corporate name, title) is identified by the remainder of the tag [the last two characters].

6.4.1.   For bibliographic records, the blocks are:

0XX = Variable control fields, identification and classification
        numbers, etc.

1XX = Main entry

2XX = Titles and title paragraph (title, edition, imprint)

3XX = Physical description

4XX = Series statements

5XX = Notes

6XX = Subject added entries

7XX = Added entries other than subject, series

8XX = Series added entries

9XX = Reserved for local implementation

6.4.2.   For authority records, the blocks are:

0XX = Variable control fields, identification and classification
        numbers, etc.

1XX = Heading

2XX = General see references

3XX = General see also references

4XX = See from tracings

5XX = See also from tracings

6XX = Treatment decisions, notes, cataloger-generated references

7XX = Not defined

8XX = Not defined

9XX = Reserved for local implementation

6.5.   Certain blocks contain data which may be subject to authority control (1XX, 4XX, 6XX, 7XX, 8XX for bibliographic records; 1XX, 4XX, 5XX for authority records).

6.5.1.   In these blocks, certain parallels of content designation are preserved. The following meanings are generally given to the final two characters of the tag:

X00 = Personal name

X10 = Corporate name

X11 = Conference name [now called "Meeting name"]

X30 = Uniform title heading

X40 = Bibliographic title

X50 = Topical subject heading

X51 = Geographic name

Further content designation (indicators and subfield codes) for data elements subject to authority control are consistently defined across the bibliographic formats and in the authorities format. These guidelines apply only to the main range of fields in each block, not to secondary ranges such as the linking fields in 760-787 or the 87X fields. [There have been numerous exceptions to the consistency of content designation, many of which have been addressed within format integration.]

6.5.2.   Within fields subject to authority control, data elements may exist which are not subject to authority control and which may vary from record to record containing the same heading (for example, subfield ≠e, Relator). Such data elements are not appropriate for inclusion in the 1XX field in the authorities format.

6.5.3.   In fields not subject to authority control, each tag is defined independently. However, parallel meanings have been preserved whenever possible.

6.6.   Certain tags have been reserved for local implementation. Except as noted below, the USMARC Formats specify no structure or meaning for local fields. Communication of such fields between systems is governed by mutual agreements on the content and content designation of the fields communicated. [In other words, libraries that use locally defined fields, such as 59X or 9XX fields, should have documentation regarding the use of those fields to give to any processing agency or system vendor that will need to understand or manipulate the fields.]

6.6.1.   The 9XX block is reserved for local implementation.

6.6.2.   In general, any tag containing the character "9" is reserved for local implementation within the block structure (see section 6.4. above).

6.6.3.   The historical development of the USMARC Formats has left the following exceptions to this general principle:

009   Physical description fixed field for archival collections

039   Level of bibliographic control and coding detail

359   Rental price

490   Series untraced or traced differently

6.7.   Theoretically, all fields (except 001 and 005) may be repeated. However, the nature of the data often precludes repetition. For example, a bibliographic record may contain only one title (field 245) and authority record, only one entry (1XX fields). The repeatability/nonrepeatability of each field is defined in the USMARC Formats.

7.   Variable Control Fields

7.1.   00X fields in the USMARC Formats are variable control fields.

7.2.   Variable control fields consist of data and a field terminator. They do not contain either indicators or subfield codes (see section 8.1. below).

7.3.   Variable control fields contain either a single data element or a series of fixed-length data elements identified by relative character position.

8.   Variable Data Fields

8.1.   Three levels of content designation are provided for variable data fields in ANSI Z39.2-1979:

(1)   a three-character tag, stored in the directory entry;

(2)   indicators stored at the beginning of each variable data field, the number of indicators being reflected in the Leader, byte 10; and

(3)   subfield codes preceding each data element, the length of the code being reflected in the Leader, byte 11.

8.2.   All fields except 00X are variable data fields.

8.3.   *Indicators*

8.3.1.   Indicators contain codes conveying information which interprets or supplements the data found in the field.

8.3.2.   The USMARC Formats specify two indicator positions at the beginning of each variable data field.

8.3.3.   Indicators are independently defined for each field. However, parallel meanings are preserved whenever possible.

8.3.4.   Indicator values are interpreted independently—i.e., meaning is not ascribed to the two indicators taken together.

8.3.5.   Indicators may be any lower-case alphabetic or numeric character or the blank. Numeric values are defined first. [This means that an alphabetic character will be defined for use as an indicator only if all numbers 0-9 have already been defined for a particular indicator. Thus far, only numeric indicators have been defined.] A blank is used in an undefined indicator position, or to mean "no information supplied" in a defined indicator position.

8.4.   *Subfield codes*

8.4.1.   Subfield codes in the USMARC Formats consist of two characters— a delimiter [≠] followed by a data element identifier. Identifiers defined in the USMARC communications formats may be any lower-case alphabetic or numeric character.

8.4.2.1.   In general, numeric identifiers are defined for parametric data used to process the field, or coded data needed to interpret the field. (Note that not all numeric identifiers defined in the past have in fact identified parametric data.)

8.4.2.2.   Alphabetic identifiers are defined for the separate elements which constitute the data content of the field.

8.4.2.3.   The character "9" and the following graphic symbols are reserved for local definition as subfield identifiers: !"#$&'()* + ,-./:;<=>?

8.4.3.   Subfield codes are defined independently for each field. However, parallel meanings are preserved whenever possible.

8.4.4.   Subfield codes are defined for purposes of identification, not arrangement. The order of subfields is specified by content standards, such as the cataloging rules. In some cases, such specifications may be incorporated in the format documentation.

8.4.5.   Theoretically, all data elements may be repeated. However, the nature of the data often precludes repetition. The repeatability/nonrepeatability of each subfield code is defined in the USMARC Formats.

9.   Coded Data

9.1.   In addition to content designation, the USMARC Formats include specifications for the content of certain data elements, particularly those which provide for the representation of data by coded values.

9.2.   Coded values consist of fixed-length character strings. Individual elements within a coded-data field or subfield are identified by relative character position.

9.3.   Although coded data occurs most frequently in the Leader, Directory and Variable Control Fields, any field or subfield may be defined for coded-data elements.

9.4.   Certain common values have been defined:

    ƀ = Undefined

    n = Not applicable

    u = Unknown

    z = Other

    ¦ = Fill character [i.e., no information provided]

Historical exceptions do occur in the formats. In particular, the blank (ƀ) has often been defined as "not applicable," or has been assigned a meaning.

NOTES

1.   Library of Congress, Network Development and MARC Standards Office, *USMARC format for bibliographic data* (Washington, D.C.: Cataloging Distribution Service, Library of Congress, 1988), Introduction, 1.

2.   Ibid., 3.

3.   Ibid., 4.

4.   Ibid., 5.

5.   Ibid., 5.

6.   Ibid., 6-7.

7.   Library of Congress, Network Development and MARC Standards Office, *Format integration and its effect on the USMARC bibliographic format* (Washington, D.C.: Cataloging Distribution Service, Library of Congress, 1988), 9-10.

RELATED READINGS

Library of Congress, Network Development and MARC Standards Office, *USMARC specification for record structure, character sets, tapes* (Washington, D.C.: Library of Congress, 1987).

"The USMARC formats: Underlying principles." *Library of Congress information bulletin* 42 (19): 148-52 (May 9, 1983).

3

Patterns in the MARC Format

INTRODUCTION

The comprehensive and detailed nature of the MARC format makes it an extremely powerful and flexible tool when used by a computer. Nevertheless, the features that make MARC useful for a computer are the same characteristics that sometimes make it very difficult for humans to grasp. The sheer number and variety of elements within the format can seem overwhelming and can serve as a barrier to its effective use. Unfortunately, when humans cannot deal with the MARC format effectively, computers cannot either. That is because the success of the computer depends upon specifications, programs, and database records that are prepared by people. (And, by the way, "computer error" is usually a human error that shows up in computer programs and data.)

The good news is that there are patterns within the MARC format that make the format much easier to understand, remember, and use. The patterns include such features as alphabetical and numerical order, abbreviation, and repetition. These arrangements of codes and information involve a logic that makes the format easier to understand. The patterns also serve as mnemonic devices to make the details of the format easier to remember. And, the easier it is to understand and remember the format, the easier it is to use it effectively.

This chapter assumes an understanding of the concepts of fixed fields, fixed field codes, variable fields, tags, indicators, and subfield codes, which were introduced in chapter 2, MARC Format Structure and Content Designation. Fixed field code patterns are discussed first, followed by an explanation of the patterns of variable field tags, indicators and subfield codes. It should be noted that there are significant exceptions to all of the patterns discussed; however, the patterns still serve as useful guides to the logic and order of MARC coding.

FIXED FIELD CODES: BASICS

For the purposes of this chapter, the term *fixed field codes* refers to the characters in the MARC Leader and variable control fields (e.g., 007 and 008 fields) that are defined by their relative position within the field.

Fixed field codes are generally assigned to answer a question about characteristics of the material, for example, "Is this a conference publication?" or "What type of government document is this material?" Positive responses are indicated by numbers greater than zero or by alphabetic characters. Negative responses are indicated by a *0* or by blanks. For example, to indicate whether an item is a conference publication, a *0* is used to indicate "no" and a *1* is used to indicate "yes." Another example, for government documents: If the item is not a government publication, the correct code is a blank (*b̸*). If the item is a government publication, any of a number of alphabetic characters may be used to indicate the particular type of government publication, such as *f* for a "federal" publication.

In some cases, there are more character positions reserved for a fixed field code than are necessary for the item being described. For example, the Nature of contents code has four positions reserved to indicate types of reference materials (such as statistics and bibliographies) that might be found in one book; however, sometimes fewer than four types are involved. When the number of applicable codes is less than the number of reserved character positions, then alphabetic characters are left-justified with trailing blanks (e.g., *bsb̸b̸*). Numeric characters are right-justified with leading zeros (e.g., *0003*).

The use of abbreviation is notable throughout fixed field codes. Sometimes, codes are the first letter, the first few letters, or other abbreviation of the terms they represent. For example the code for the language *English* is *eng*.

FIXED FIELD CODES: PATTERNS

Fixed field codes generally conform to one of four patterns: (1) single numeric characters, (2) single alphabetic characters, (3) combinations of two or more alphabetic characters, or (4) combinations of four to six numeric characters. Each of these code patterns is discussed below, with examples.

Single Numeric Characters

A one-character numeric code, either a *0* or a *1*, indicates whether or not the item falls within a particular category. For example, within the character position defined for Conference publication information in the 008 field, a *0* indicates that the item is not a conference publication, while a *1* indicates that the item is a conference publication. Similarly, within the position defined for Fiction information, a *0* indicates that the item is nonfiction, while a *1* indicates that the item is fiction. In the USMARC Formats documentation, these single character fixed field codes (*1* — "on" or *0* — "off") are referred to as indicators. Fixed field indicators differ from variable data field indicators in that variable data field indicators range from 0 to 9 and often provide information beyond a "yes" or "no" indication.

Single Alphabetic Characters

While the single numeric characters *0* and *1* are used to indicate only whether or not an item has a certain characteristic, single alphabetic characters are used to provide even more specific information. For example, the character position for the Government publication code in the 008 fixed field may contain one of several alpha characters, depending upon the level of government that is involved. Figure 3.1 provides examples of a few of the Government publication codes.

Type of government publication	Fixed field code
Federal/national publication	f
State publication	s
Local publication (city, etc.)	l
Not a government publication	ƀ

Fig. 3.1. Examples of single alpha character codes (Government publication codes).

Some of the single character alpha codes are abbreviations, in that they are the same as the first letter of the characteristic they describe. Three of the alphabetic codes defined for the Biography code position in the 008 fixed field are abbreviations; the fourth one is not. A blank indicates that the book is not a biography. The biography codes are given in figure 3.2.

Type of biographical material	Fixed field code
Autobiography	a
Biography (Individual)	b
Collective biography	c
Contains biographical material	d
No biographical material	ƀ

Fig. 3.2. Examples of abbreviations (Biography codes).

Some single-character alphabetic codes may be used in groups of two or more. An example of this type of grouping can be found in the Illustration code section of the 008 field. Up to four alphabetic characters may be used within this section to indicate the types of illustrations that are found in an item. (Four blanks mean that there are no illustrations.) The alpha characters a through p have been defined to represent specific types of illustrations. Although the codes must be in alphabetical order within the section, there is no other relationship between the alpha characters in a group. The presence of a character in this portion of the 008 field is not dependent upon the presence or absence of any other particular character. Figure 3.3 provides examples of the illustration codes and how they appear in the 008 field.

Type of illustration	Alphabetic code	Fixed field code
maps, photographs	b,c	bcƀƀ
charts	d	dƀƀƀ
musics, facsimiles, forms	g,h,k	ghkƀ
maps, charts, plans, plates	b,d,e,f	bdef
none	ƀ	ƀƀƀƀ

Fig. 3.3. Examples of grouped single-character codes (Illustration codes).

Grouped single-character codes such as the illustration codes differ from the combination codes discussed in the next two sections. Combination codes are alphabetic or numeric characters used in predesignated combinations.

Combinations of Two or More Alphabetic Characters

For some fixed field codes, two or more alphabetic characters are used together. Combination codes were devised for those situations in which it is necessary to have a substantial number of different codes to represent a characteristic of an item. The use of alpha combinations provides for many more codes than does the use of single letters.

The three-letter codes defined for the Language code in the 008 field are good examples of combination alpha codes. The Language codes are three-character codes that are often abbreviations, in that they are the first three letters of the words that they represent. In some instances, however, such as when appropriate alpha combinations have already been used for other languages, the codes may not have such an obvious connection to the language they represent.

Figure 3.4 provides examples of Language codes.

Language	Fixed field code
English	eng
French	fre
Spanish	spa
Arabic	ara
Aramaic	arc
Arapaho	arp
Armenian	arm

Fig. 3.4. Examples of combined-character alpha codes (Language codes).

Combinations of Four to Eight Numeric Characters

Within the fixed fields, groups of four or more numerics are used together to represent dates or times. In the Dates portion of the 008 field, for example, four numerics are used together to indicate a year related to the publication of an item. The form in the fixed field is simply the year in direct order, such as 1983.

Six-character and eight-character codes for dates are used in the Leader and the 005 field, respectively. To represent the date September 5, 1978, the six-character code in the Leader is *780905*. The eight-character code in the 005 field would be *19780905*. In the 005 field, the time is represented by 8 characters, using a 24-hour clock. For example, 6:35 P.M. is expressed as *183500.0*. Although there are enough positions to record time to the tenth of a second, generally, the last position simply contains a zero.

VARIABLE DATA FIELD PATTERNS: GENERALITIES

Several types of patterns have been used within the MARC format variable data fields (MARC fields 010 through 999). Tags, indicators, and subfield codes often involve a logical, predictable design. Tag, indicator, and subfield code patterns are discussed as outlined in figure 3.5.


```
                       Tag patterns
                       Tag groups
            Numerical order and other orders
                     The "9" tags
         Function and form patterns (repetition)

                    Indicator patterns
                      Repetition

                 Subfield code patterns
                   Alphabetical order
                     Abbreviation
                      Repetition
```

Fig. 3.5. Outline of MARC variable field patterns (tags, indicators, subfield codes).

Tag Patterns: Tag Groups

The MARC tags are divided into nine groups, according to the type of information involved. These groups are indicated by the first digit in the tag, as shown in figure 3.6.


```
Tag                      Tag group
0XX    Control Fields and Classification Numbers
1XX    Main Entry
2XX    Body of Catalog Entry
3XX    Physical Description Field
4XX    Series Statement
5XX    Notes Fields
6XX    Subject Headings
7XX    Added Entries
8XX    Series Added Entry--Traced Differently
9XX    Local Information Fields
```

Fig. 3.6. MARC tag groups (identified by first digit in the tag)

To refer to any one of the nine tag groups generically, the characters *XX* are used in place of the last two digits of the tags. Subject heading tags are referred to as "6XX" tags, for example, instead of naming any one or all of the tags to represent the entire group.

Tag Patterns: Numerical Order and Other Orders

The numerical order of the tag groups generally follows the same order as the information found in a catalog record. For example, the main entry fields are the 1XX fields, just as the main entry is the first piece of information in a catalog record. The 6XX fields (subject access) precede the 7XX fields (Added entries) just as subject headings precede added entries in the tracings on a catalog card.

Individual tags within tag groups (for example, 500, 501, and 502 in the 5XX group) may or may not be numbered according to their correct placement within a catalog record. For individual tags, the correct order within a MARC record may be determined by some other criteria. Often, the correct order is specified in applicable cataloging rules (e.g., *AACR2*) and does not relate to the numerical values given to the tags. In these cases, reordering the fields according to numerical order of the tags would destroy the appropriate order of the fields.

The discussion that follows focuses on the numerical order of the individual tags in relation to the order of the fields when used in a MARC record or on a catalog card.

0XX Tags (Control and Call Number Fields)

0XX tags are not numbered in the order that they are found on a catalog card. Some 0XX fields are not included in a traditional catalog record, such as the 041 field, for language information. Other 0XX fields are found in various places within a catalog record. The 010 field (LC card number) generally is found in the lower right corner of a catalog card. The 015 field (foreign bibliography number) is found after the 4XX field (Series statement) within a catalog entry. The 020 field (ISBN) follows the last 5XX field (Notes) on a catalog card.

Although 0XX tags are not numerically in the order that they are found within a catalog record, two other kinds of patterns exist for the 0XX group:

1. The 0XX tag group includes fields that are composed mainly of numbers, such as LC card numbers, call numbers, music publisher numbers, ISBNs, and so forth.

2. The 0XX tag group also includes fields that are composed mainly of coded information not generally found on a catalog card, such as language codes and chronological codes.

1XX Tags (Main Entries)

No more than one 1XX field (Main entries) is allowed within a given record, so the numerical order of specific 1XX tags in relation to their order in a MARC record or on a catalog card is not a consideration.

2XX Tags (Body of Entry)

The 2XX tags are generally in numerical order as the fields are found in a catalog entry. For books, these tags include the 240 field (uniform title), the 245 field (main title), the 250 field (Edition statement), and the 260 field (imprint information).

3XX Tags (Physical Description)

For books, there is only one 3XX field.

4XX Tags (Series Statement)

In a MARC record or on a catalog card, 4XX fields should be arranged in order according to cataloging rules, not in numerical order according to their tag number. The only stipulation for order of series in *AACR2* is that they should be named in order of specificity (*AACR2* 1.6J), giving the more specific series first (e.g., a series on a specific type of art should be noted before a series on the arts in general). Therefore, the MARC tags are not necessarily in numerical order according to their placement on a catalog card.

5XX Tags (Notes)

The numerical order of the individual note (5XX) tags is not the same order in which they should be placed within a catalog entry or MARC record. In other words, a MARC record that includes fields 500, 501, 502, and 504 will not necessarily include those fields in that particular order.

The order of notes in a MARC catalog record should follow the specified order within the "Notes" section of *AACR2*. Some of the types of notes for books are listed in figure 3.7 in their specified order according to *AACR2*. Each note type is followed by its MARC tag.

AACR2 rule	Type of note	MARC tag
2.7B3	Source of title proper	500
2.7B6	Statement of responsibility	500
2.7B9	Publication, distribution, etc.	500
2.7B13	Dissertation	502
2.7B17	Summary	520
2.7B18	Contents	500/504/505
2.7B20	Copy being described	590
2.7B21	"With" note	501

Fig. 3.7. Sample list of notes for books in correct order (correct order is by cataloging rules, not number of tag).

6XX Tags (Subject Headings)

Subject headings should be listed in order of their predominance in the item being cataloged, a strictly judgmental decision that is not related in any way to tag numbers. The classification number for an item is devised according to the first subject heading, since it is the primary subject of that item. Therefore, it is important that the order of subject headings not be rearranged (either manually or by computer) once it has been set by the cataloger.

7XX Tags (Added Entries)

The individual tags for added entries are generally in numerical order according to their proper order in the tracings of a catalog record. Added entries are arranged within the tracings in the following order:

1. Personal name added entries (700 tags)

2. Organizational name added entries

    Corporate added entries (710 tags)

    and/or

    Conference added entries (711 tags)

3. Title added entries

    Uniform title added entries (730 tags)

    and/or

    Title added entries (740 tags)

The two kinds of tags listed in 2 and 3 above may or may not be found in numerical order in the tracings of a catalog record. For example, a conference added entry (711 field) may precede a corporate added entry (710 field), depending on the individual catalog record. But, a title added entry (730 or 740) should not precede an organizational added entry (710 or 711). And, personal name added entries (700) should always be listed before the other types of added entries.

8XX Tags (Series Added Entry—Traced Differently)

The only stipulation for order of series in *AACR2* is that they should be named in order of specificity. Therefore, the MARC 8XX tags are not necessarily in numerical order according to their placement on a catalog card.

9XX Tags (Local Fields)

Most 9XX tags have been devised locally by libraries, system vendors, MARC cataloging service providers, and others for use in automated systems and for other purposes. Generally, the order of these fields within a MARC record would be locally defined.

Tag Patterns: MARC "9" Tags

The number *9* within a MARC tag has been used to indicate a "local" field. The *9* may appear in the first, second, or third position of a tag. "Local" information may refer to the particular copy of an item owned by a library. "Local" information could also be subject headings used only by a particular library or specially formatted information to be loaded into a library's automated circulation system.

Not all MARC tags that include a *9* are local use fields, but most of them are. A list of *9* fields that include local information is given in figure 3.8.

Tag   Local-use field

049   Local holdings information
09X   Locally-supplied call numbers
59X   Local notes
69X   Local subject headings
9XX   Local-use miscellaneous (vendors)

Fig. 3.8. List of MARC local use fields.

The 490 field (for series statement, untraced or traced differently) is a major exception to the *9* rule, since it is a general use field, not for library-specific information.

Tag Patterns: Function and Form (Repetition)

The MARC tags have one other major pattern that involves repetition of the first character and the second two characters within tags for similar types of information. All the tags that relate to the traditional access points (main and added entries and subject headings) share a pattern in which the first digit of the tag indicates the *function* of the field (such as main entry) and the last two digits of the tag indicate the *form* of the field (for example, personal or corporate name heading). The first digit of each tag, of course, follows the "tag group" patterns that were noted above. The last two digits of some tags are repeated according to another pattern.

The second two characters of some MARC tags are used repetitively throughout the MARC format for the various types of access points, including main and added entry headings and subject headings. For example, MARC tags for personal name headings always end with *00*. When a personal name heading is used as a main entry heading, the MARC tag is 100. For a personal name heading that is used as an added entry, the MARC tag is 700. By the same token, the tag for a corporate name subject heading is 610 and, for a uniform title series entry, 830. The digits used and the headings that they specify are shown in figure 3.9.

Tag	Type of heading
X00	Personal name heading
X10	Corporate name heading
X11	Conference name heading
X30	Uniform title heading
X40	Alternate title heading
X45	Main title heading
X50	Topical subject heading
X51	Geographical subject heading

Fig. 3.9. MARC tag patterns for types of headings (identified by last two digits of tag).

Indicator Patterns: Repetition

Patterns for tags and subfield codes are more easily recognized than patterns for indicators. The primary pattern that MARC indicators follow is one of repetition. The same indicators are repeated within similar types of fields. Another way of thinking of this repetitive pattern is that *indicators follow tags*. This is not simply a reference to their physical location in the MARC record. This statement also correctly implies that "like tags will be followed by like indicators."

All X00 tags (personal name headings), for example, are followed by a first indicator that indicates whether the name heading includes a forename only (first indicator *0*), or a single surname (first indicator *1*), or a compound surname (first indicator *2*).

Another example is that all nonlocal subject headings (tags 600-651) have a second indicator that is set according to the subject heading list being used. Second indicator *0* is for LC subject headings, *2* is for MeSH headings, and *8* is for Sears headings, to name a few. Yet another pattern of repetition: tags for title fields, the X30 and X4X tags, are followed by a filing indicator in either the first or second indicator position.

Subfield Code Patterns: Repetition

As is the case with indicators, the use of subfield codes is also part of a larger pattern. Subfield codes for a given MARC field are related to the tag and indicators for the field. And, the same subfield codes are repeated within the same types of fields.

For example, within all personal name fields (MARC tags 100, 600, 700, and 800) that include a single surname form of name (first indicator *1*), the subfield codes *a*, *b*, *c*, and *d* are used to indicate a person's name, number (e.g., "II"), title (e.g., "Sir") and dates (of birth and death), in that order.

Another example occurs within all subject heading fields (600-690), where the subfield ǂa includes the subject heading. For all of these fields, subfield codes *x*, *y*, and *z* indicate the three types of subject heading subdivisions: general, chronological, and geographic.

Subfield Code Patterns:
Alphabetical Order

Within many MARC fields, the correct order of some or all of the subfield codes, when used in a MARC record or on a catalog card, is alphabetical order. The primary example of this alphabetical scheme is that within every MARC record, almost every field begins with subfield ≠a.

The first three codes within the MARC 260 field (Publication distribution, etc.) provide another commonly found example of the alphabetical order of MARC subfield codes. Subfield ≠a includes the place of publication; subfield ≠b includes the publisher's name; and subfield ≠c contains the publication date.

Often, not all possible types of subfields will be found within a MARC field. In those cases, the subfield codes used may still follow alphabetical order, with the omission of some letters. In some cases, the use of abbreviation patterns (see below) takes precedence over alphabetical patterns. In other cases, the subfields are not arranged in alphabetical order but follow some other logic.

Subfield Code Patterns:
Abbreviation

The mnemonic device of abbreviation is useful for identifying and remembering some MARC subfield codes. Some subfield codes are the first letter of the element of information they precede. For example, titles of publications are generally included in subfield ≠t when they are not the first element of information within a field (in which case they are assigned a subfield code a).

Any subfield that contains a person's dates (birth and/or death) is coded with a *d*. Two additional examples of abbreviation, both of which are found in title fields, are the use of subfield code *l* for the language of a work and subfield code *n* for the number of a part or section of a work.

4

Major MARC
Bibliographic Codes

INTRODUCTION

This chapter includes an ordered listing of the primary MARC codes for books (as well as a few selected codes used for nonbook materials), with an explanation of each and examples of uses, as well as caveats where appropriate. Given that books involve only one of a multitude of media types and given that there are hundreds of MARC codes, this may seem to be a minimalist approach. There is, however, no practical way to discuss all possibilities or eventualities.[1] So, the goal of this chapter is to do the next best thing. The most-used codes and the most familiar types of materials illustrate principles and provide background. Such information will serve as a solid foundation for readers' further acquaintance with and use of the MARC format codes.

It should be noted that the most-used books codes are often, though by no means always, used in the same way for other types of materials. For comprehensive information in regard to MARC format codes for all types of materials, consult the *USMARC format for bibliographic data*, published by the Library of Congress.

Successful use and understanding of this chapter requires a knowledge of the information provided in chapter 2, MARC Format Structure and Content Designation. Familiarity with the concepts presented in chapter 3, Patterns in the MARC Format, is also helpful.

Major codes for books are generally discussed in the numerical order of the MARC format, with one major exception. That exception is that the MARC 008 field is discussed in the same section as the Leader information, prior to other MARC variable control fields (i.e., 001-007). This arrangement has been used because the combination of Leader and 008 codes into a grouping known as the "MARC fixed field" is a very familiar concept to users of OCLC, RLIN, and other systems.

For each MARC field (or code, in the case of the Leader and variable control fields) discussed, the definition from the *USMARC format for bibliographic data* is presented. This formal definition is followed by a discussion that provides further description, information on potential uses for the field or code, and caveats in regard to the use of the field or code. The description is less technical and more informal than the *USMARC* definition, and provides more historical information. The discussion of potential uses for the field or code includes some uses that have already been implemented, and many others that have not yet been fully explored. The caveats include background information regarding possible problems that may present themselves because of inappropriate use or application of the fields or for other reasons.

The last section of this chapter focuses on changes to the MARC codes that will be affected by MARC format integration.

MARC FIXED FIELD

The grouping of codes known as the MARC fixed field includes some of the Leader information and codes and the 008 fixed-lengh data elements and field codes. The major fixed field codes are presented in numerical order, below.

MARC Leader Information

USMARC Definition

The Leader is the first field of a bibliographic record. It is fixed in length at 24 character positions (0-23). The Leader consists of data elements that contain numbers of coded values that define the parameters for the processing of the record.

The Leader contains no indicators or subfield codes; the data elements are defined by their relative position within the field. Because character positions start at byte 0, the character position is always one number less than the actual numbering of each character in the field. For example, character position *0* holds the first character in the field and character position *1* holds the second character in the field. The term *offset character* indicates the character number, with the first character in the field being offset character 0.

Major Leader Codes

Record Status (Offset Character 5)

USMARC Definition

The Record status character position contains a one-character alphabetic code that indicates the relationship of the record to a file for file maintenance purposes.

Description, Potential Uses, Caveats

This one-character code provides information about a record's status in a particular database. This character may be used in varying ways depending upon the database processor.

The Library of Congress codes new records with the code *n* for "new." Even records that were added to the database 20 years ago are still coded as new if they have not been changed in the meantime.

Code *c* stands for "corrected or revised." This code indicates that an addition or change has been made to the record. The change may involve the correction of a typographical error or similar correction. Additional material may have been added to the record for an additional volume of a multivolume set, or other such reason. When the Library of Congress sends out the MARC Distribution Service tapes to vendors and other organizations, corrected records are included with the new records. Usually, when the tapes are added to vendor-maintained databases, the records are matched up by Library of Congress card number (and possibly other keys) and the corrected record replaces the previous record. Corrections generally are not made manually to LC records in vendor-maintained databases.

Code *p* is another commonly occurring Record status code in Library of Congress records. This code is used to indicate the record is an upgraded or completed record that replaces an incomplete CIP (Cataloging in Publication) or NSDP (National Serials Data Program) record.

OCLC also uses code *n* for new records to the database. Code *c* is used for changed or corrected records, including *c* records that have been distributed by the Library of Congress. These codes have meaning only in regard to the OCLC master database, however, and they are not necessarily significant in regard to an individual library's OCLC database. An individual library's use of the record does not effect a change in the status code, either within the OCLC master database or in the library's records on tape.

For example, if an OCLC record coded *n* is used by a library twice, which places the record on the library's archival tape twice, the code will remain *n* in each case, regardless of whether the library has changed or corrected the record. On the other hand, if the library's first use of a record is made after the record status has been changed from *n* to *c* in the OCLC database, then the status code will be *c* in the library's archival file also, even though it is new to the library's database.

Libraries receiving records from other MARC distributors should check documentation provided by the vendor or request information from the vendor in regard to the use of the Record status code within the vendor's database. If the vendor cannot provide adequate information, then it may be possible to determine the vendor's practice by checking records in the library's database to detect status code patterns.

Type of Record (Offset Character 6)

USMARC Definition

The Type of record character position contains a one-character alphabetic code that specifies the characteristics and defines the components of the record.

Microforms, whether original or reproductions, are not identified by a distinctive Type of record code. The type of materials characteristics described by the codes take precedence over the microform characteristics of the item.

Description, Potential Uses, Caveats

The type of record code identifies a type of material in generic terms. More specific identification of a material type is included in other codes in the Leader and/or in the variable control fields. For example, for a book, the Type of record code is *a*, which is defined for "language material." Books are more specifically defined in the Bibliographic level code, another Leader code, as a "monograph." The term *monograph* includes one-volume items as well as multivolume monographs, such as encyclopedias and any other works that are intended to be complete within a finite number of volumes. By comparison, another type of language material is a serial, which is issued in successive parts, but which, unlike a multivolume monograph, is intended to be continued indefinitely. Serial publications, which include journals, magazines, and other periodical publications, are distinguished from monographic publications through the use of a separate Bibliographic level code, not through the Type of record code.

For microform materials, the Form of item code in the variable control field 008 is used for books (and some other types of materials) to indicate that the item is in microform.

The specific Type of record codes are listed below.

a — Language material

Code *a* indicates that the content of the record is for language material. Microforms of language material also use code *a*.

b — Archival and manuscripts control

Code *b* indicates that the archival control of the material is being emphasized over the distinguishing features of the format or medium.

c — Printed music

Printed music or a microform of printed music.

d — Manuscript music

Manuscript music or a microform of manuscript music.

e — Printed map

Printed map or a microform of a printed map.

f — Manuscript map

Manuscript map or a microform of a manuscript map.

g — Projected medium

Motion picture, videorecording, filmstrip, slide, or transparency, as well as material specifically designed for overhead projection. Includes archival projected items where the distinguishing features of the format or medium are emphasized.

i — Nonmusical sound recording

Recording of nonmusical sounds (e.g., speech).

j — Musical sound recording

Musical sound recording.

k — Two-dimensional nonprojectable graphic

Two-dimensional nonprojectable graphic, such as activity cards, charts, collages, computer graphics, drawings, duplication masters, flash cards, paintings, photonegatives, and so forth, and reproductions of any of these. Also includes archival graphics where the distinguishing features of the format or medium are emphasized.

m — Computer file

A body of information encoded in a manner that allows it to be processed by a computer. The information in the computer file may be numeric or textual data, computer software, or a combination of these types. Although a file may be stored on a variety of media (such as magnetic tape or disk, punched cards, or optical character recognition font documents), the file itself is independent of the medium on which it is stored.

o — Kit

A mixture of components from two or more of the Type of record categories defined for Leader/06, no one of which is identifiable as the predominant component of the item. This category includes the packages of material called laboratory kits, and packages of assorted materials, such as a set of K-12 social studies curriculum material (books, workbooks, guides, activities, etc.), or packages of educational test materials (tests, answer sheets, scoring guides, score charts, interpretative manuals, etc.). This includes archival items where the distinguishing features of the format or medium are emphasized.

r — Three-dimensional artifact or naturally occurring object

A three-dimensional artifact or a naturally occurring object. This includes manmade objects such as models, dioramas, games, puzzles, simulations, sculptures, and other three-dimensional artworks, exhibits, machines, clothing, toys, and stitchery. It also includes naturally occurring objects, such as microscope specimens (or representations of them) and other specimens mounted for viewing. This includes archival items where the distinguishing features of the format or medium are emphasized.

The Type of record code is one of the most significant single characters in a MARC record. One of its most powerful capabilities is the potential for substantially enhancing almost any type of search or selection from a MARC bibliographic file. A few examples follow.

For online searching, this single code can be used as a basis for including or excluding particular types of media. If a searcher is interested only in certain types of materials, say films, then using the Type of record code can effectively narrow down a search by eliminating the step of going through a list of items manually and selecting out films. On the other hand, the searcher can also use the code to exclude one or more types of materials during any given search.

For printed lists, say a list of new materials, a library can use the Type of record code to divide the materials into separate sections by type or to simply generate an explicit identifier (a letter, word, or graphic representation) in the margin next to the item entry or in a specified point within the entry.

For inventory and statistics purposes, say when a library is required to present an inventory of materials by type or wants to present a statistical comparison by type, the Type of record code can be used to produce statistics for various types.

There are precautions that should be kept in mind for the use of the Type of record code. One point to consider is that the Type of record code used for any given item or group of items is based on the cataloger's interpretation of that item, and there is much room for individual judgment in making such a determination. For example, one primary criterion for determining how an item is to be described is "predominance." If, in the cataloger's estimation, one of several types of material is predominant, then the item will be cataloged and coded as that type of material, with other types of material being listed as "accompanying material" in the Physical description field (MARC tag 300) or in a note.

Consider, for example, a book and a sound cassette that are produced as two components of a set. If the book contains more material than the sound cassette and the cassette contains only a few spoken exercises, then the item would be cataloged as a book, Type of record code *a*. If, on the other hand, the cassette includes songs and a narrative and the book contains only the lyrics to the songs, then the item would probably be cataloged as a sound recording, either Type of record code *i* or *j*, depending upon the predominance of the spoken material. A third possibility is that the book and the sound cassette are simply print and audio versions of the same text. In that case, the set may be considered either as a book (code *a*), with accompanying material, or as a kit (code *o*), depending on the cataloger's judgment or the prevailing practice or local policy.

Another point to consider is that the Type of record code provides only general information in regard to the type of material. More specific information is included in other parts of the record. For example, for film materials, the 008 field includes a Type of material code that identifies such specific types as filmstrips, motion pictures, and videorecordings. And, the 007 field indicates such specifics as whether, for example, a videorecording is Beta, VHS, or a laser optical videodisc.

Encoding Level (Offset Character 17)

USMARC Definition

The Encoding level character position contains a one-character alphanumeric code that indicates the fullness of the bibliographic information and/or content designation in the bibliographic record.

Description, Potential Uses, Caveats

In practical terms, the purpose of this code is to indicate whether an item has received complete cataloging or less-than-complete cataloging. Many libraries have policies regarding categories of materials that do not receive full cataloging, either because they are not priority materials or because the cataloging is not based on examination of the item itself, but on some secondary source.

For example, because economic and other considerations do not allow the Library of Congress to provide full cataloging for all materials received, certain categories of materials receive "minimal level" cataloging (Encoding level 7) — a compromise based on the belief that an incomplete record is better than no record at all. Encoding level 8 is used for prepublication cataloging done as part of the Cataloging in Publication program and the National Serials Data Program. In both cases, the catalog record is based on the publisher's description, galley proofs, or other prepublication information, which, by its very nature, does not provide all of the information necessary to make a complete bibliographic description.

Other libraries, besides the Library of Congress, have policies regarding minimal-level cataloging for such items as ephemeral materials (that receive only cursory description) and dissertations. Because of the sheer number of such items that require cataloging, a compromise may involve leaving out subject headings or other standard portions of a catalog record.

OCLC and other MARC database providers have developed their own Encoding level codes to reflect the needs of system users.

The three most-used Library of Congress encoding level codes are listed below.

𝑏 — Full level

Code 𝑏 indicates the most complete USMARC record. The information used in creating the record is derived from an inspection of the physical item. For serials, at least one issue of the serial is inspected.

7 — Minimal level

Code 7 indicates a minimal-level cataloging record that meets the National Level Bibliographic Record minimal-level cataloging specifications. Such a record is considered a final record by the creating agency. Any headings have been checked against an authority file and reflect established forms to the extent that such forms were available at the time the minimal-level record was created.

8 — Prepublication level

> Code *8* indicates a prepublication level record. This includes records created in the Cataloging in Publication (CIP) program and serial records created by the National Serials Data Program (NSDP).

OCLC accommodates all the LC-defined Encoding level codes; however, other codes that more clearly reflect the situations of OCLC user libraries have been defined for those users. Two of those codes are listed below.

I — Full-level cataloging input by OCLC participating library

> Encoding level *I* identifies a record that was entered by an OCLC participating library and that conforms to OCLC's Level *I* input standard. The Level *I* input standard represents full or complete cataloging. For details, refer to [OCLC] *Bibliographic input standards*. Use code *I* when transcribing LC or NLM copy.

K — Less-than-full cataloging input by OCLC participating library

> Encoding level *K* identifies a record that was entered by an OCLC participating library and that conforms to OCLC's Level *K* input standard. The Level *K* input standard represents less-than-full cataloging. For details, refer to [OCLC] *Bibliographic input standards*.

The Encoding level code can be valuable to users of a cooperative cataloging system. It can provide a concise explanation for why a particular catalog record looks the way it does. Without the code, a less-than-full level record may be somewhat confusing or even misleading. The code is useful for catalogers and for other users of cooperative cataloging databases. Such users as acquisitions staff (who use the database for preorder verification) and interlibrary loan staff (who use the database to verify ILL requests), can use the encoding level as a helpful clue when trying to verify a nebulous or incomplete citation. For example, assume that an interlibrary loan staff member is trying to verify a generic-sounding title for a nonfiction item. The only citation that the staff member has is the short title, which matches a number of other titles in the database being searched. The only other definitive clue that the searcher has is that the item is nonfiction, which indicates that the record for that item in the database should include a call number and subject headings. However, a database record without a call number or subject headings could be a nonfiction item that has received minimal-level cataloging. Subject headings are required for full-level nonfiction records, so the less-than-full encoding level within a record that does not include subject headings is a valuable clue (although not a confirmation) that the item is actually a nonfiction item. This allows the user to take into consideration a record that may have otherwise (erroneously) been excluded as irrelevant.

Another way in which the Encoding level code can be used is for processing databases that have been acquired through a batch conversion process. Batch conversion involves "blind searching" of a cataloging database by running a tape of search keys against the bibliographic records and selecting out the bibliographic records that match the search keys. The process is completely automated and involves no human intervention. It is very likely that a number of incomplete records (minimal-level LC, CIP, less-than-full level OCLC records, etc.) will be included in the database; it is also likely that the library will want to upgrade such records. Records that are candidates for upgrading can be easily identified and listed using a simple computer program that "looks for" specific coding levels.

There are many possible fields and subfields within any given catalog record; however, it is important to recognize that not all of them are required or mandatory for an item to qualify for "full" status. A full record may still lack a great deal of desirable or valid information.

Another important aspect in regard to use of Encoding level codes is that there is generally no double-check built into a cataloging system. There is nothing that will prevent a minimal-level record being input to a system coded as full level, or vice versa.

Descriptive Cataloging Form (Offset Character 18)

USMARC Definition

The Descriptive cataloging form character position contains a one-character alphanumeric code indicating whether the record was cataloged according to the *Anglo-American Cataloguing Rules*, 2nd Edition (AACR2), *International Standard Bibliographic Description* (ISBD), or conventions that do not follow ISBD. Subfield ≠e (Description conventions) of field 040 (Cataloging Source) allows for further information on the cataloging rules used.

Description, Potential Uses, Caveats

The three codes defined for this position are: ƀ for non-ISBD records, *a* for records that follow the *AACR2* rules, and *i* for records using ISBD. Practically speaking, the most obvious difference between non-ISBD and the other two descriptive forms is that non-ISBD form does not include the distinctive ISBD punctuation between fields and subfields.

The implementation of ISBD was notable for several reasons. As summarized by Wynar (1985), "ISBD facilitates the international exchange of bibliographic information by standardizing the bibliographic elements to be used in the bibliographic description, assigning an order to these elements in the entry, and specifying a system of symbols to be used in punctuating these elements."[2]

The example below shows a title statement with and without ISBD punctuation.

The detective short story, a bibliography by Ellery Queen

The detective short story : a bibliography / by Ellery Queen

The non-ISBD cataloging standards are primarily those that were used prior to the introduction of ISBD (in *AACR1*, rev. chap. 6) in 1974. These rules included the original *Anglo-American cataloguing rules (AACR1)*; *A.L.A. cataloging rules for author and title entries* (1949); *A.L.A. catalog rules, author and title entries* (1941); and *Catalog rules, author and title entries* (1908). Because the non-ISBD standards all predate ISBD, the terms *non-ISBD* and *pre-ISBD* are sometimes used interchangeably.

The primary differences between ISBD and *AACR2* are not so obvious to the casual observer. ISBD punctuation is actually part of the *AACR2* descriptive cataloging, but *AACR2* implies choice and form of entry decisions, among other factors, which are not part of the *International standard bibliographic description* conventions. For example, *AACR2* calls for the use of title main entry when the only other choice of main entry is editor. The editor's name would be given as an added entry. However, *AACR1* called for the use of editor main entry, with a title added entry. A catalog record that includes an editor main entry would thus be coded as "non-ISBD" if it did not include ISBD punctuation and "ISBD" if it did include that punctuation. A catalog record that includes a title main entry and editor added entry has been cataloged according to *AACR2*, of which ISBD punctuation is a part. In this case, the record would be coded as *AACR2*.

One potential use for the Descriptive cataloging form code is as a signal that the record may include obsolete forms of name headings or other obsolescent features. Any record that includes a ɓ or *i* would be a candidate for such evaluation. Although it is *not* generally recommended that libraries upgrade pre-*AACR2* catalog records to *AACR2* form in all respects, there are some types of disparities between *AACR2* and pre-*AACR2* cataloging that may cause difficulties for library patrons. Of course, conflicts that affect library service are much higher priority than the pursuit of conformity for its own sake. One example of such a conflict is an author's name that appears differently depending upon the cataloging rules used. Because the two (or more) forms of the same name will appear separately in an online catalog or other computer-generated file, library patrons will have to know all forms of the name to search for it; otherwise, they will miss all titles filed under variant forms of the name. (Chapter 6, MARC Database Processing includes a discussion of automated authority control.) Another example of a cataloging conflict is the case in which older editions of a book have been cataloged using editor main entry and newer editions have been cataloged under title main entry. Because the main entry usually affects the call number, and thus the placement of items on the shelves, different editions of the same item may be shelved in different places.

Another use of the Descriptive cataloging form code that has been used by OCLC and others involves the need for special punctuation between MARC fields in ISBD and *AACR2* records. The special punctuation, such as dashes that separate some fields, is generated automatically by the system when the code for either cataloging form is found in the record; it is not produced when the record includes the non-ISBD code.

The use of any set of cataloging rules involves many options and judgment calls. For example, two *AACR2* records for the same item could be quite different and each still be technically correct. The presence of a particular Descriptive cataloging form code does not necessarily provide specific guarantees in regard to what the record will look like.

It is also important to note that, although *AACR2* was implemented in 1981, there are still many pre-*AACR2* and pre-ISBD records being added to online databases. One reason for this is that printed catalog records for older items, from such sources as the *National union catalog, Pre-1956 imprints*, and old LC card sets, are being used as a basis for inputting the records to MARC databases. Use of an existing catalog record is usually less expensive and less time-consuming than devising original cataloging.

MARC 008 Fixed-length Data Elements

Although the MARC 008 field is actually a variable control field, it is presented separately because it is generally considered, along with some of the Leader characters, as part of the so-called MARC fixed field. The 008 field contains a series of codes that are all positionally defined. MARC subfield codes are not used to signify the presence or context of the codes within the 008 field. As in the Leader and other fixed-length fields, the character positions are numbered starting with 0 instead of 1; thus the second character position is 1, the third is 2, and so on.

USMARC Definition

This field contains 40 character positions (00-39) that provide coded information about the record as a whole and about special bibliographic aspects of the item being cataloged. These coded data elements are potentially useful for retrieval and data management purposes....

The data elements are positionally defined. Character positions that are not defined contain a blank (ƀ). All defined character positions must contain either a defined code or a fill character....

Major 008 Field Codes

Type of Date/Publication Status (008/06)

USMARC Definition

For books, archival and manuscript controls, monographic computer files, maps, music and visual materials, a one-character alphabetic code indicates the type of dates given in the 008/07-10 (Date 1) and 008/11-14 (Date 2). For serials, and serially-issued computer files, it indicates the publication status that also relates to the dates given in 008/07-10 (Beginning date of publication) and 008/11-14 (Ending date of publication).

The choice of code for 008/06 is made concurrently with a determination of appropriate dates for 008/7-14. For most records, data is derived from information in field 260 (Publication, Distribution, etc. (Imprint)), field 362 (Dates of Publication and Volume Designation), or from note fields....

Description, Potential Uses, Caveats

The Type of date code is used to provide information about the publication date(s) for an item. It is related to the 008 Date 1 and Date 2 fields (discussed below), either or both of which may include a year that is related to the publication of the item.

Examples of Type of date code values and their meanings are as follows:

b   No dates given; B.C. date involved

s   Single known date/probable date (One date)

c   Actual date and copyright date (Two dates)

m   Multiple dates

r   Reprint/reissue date and original date

q   Questionable date

With the exception of code *m*, the examples are fairly self-explanatory. Code *m*, when used for books, indicates that different volumes of a multivolume set were published in different years. In this case, the 008 Date 1 will contain the beginning year of publication and the 008 Date 2 will contain the last year of publication.

The Type of date code can be useful for explaining the relationship of different dates pertaining to the publication of an item. This is particularly useful because the dates in a bibliographic record that are indexed (for the purpose of qualifying a search) are usually the dates as found in the 008 field (Date 1, Date 2). These dates have been taken out of the context of the body of the record (in the publication area, notes, or other area) and may require the interpretation and clarification that the Type of date code provides.

In some cases, more than one Type of date code may apply to a record. The *USMARC format for bibliographic data* includes a table that stipulates the precedence of codes to be used when more than one is applicable.

Date 1/Beginning Date of Publication (008/7-10)

USMARC Definition

These character positions contain a date specified by the value in 008/06 (Type of date/Publication status code). For books, archival and manuscript control, monographic computer files, maps, music, and visual materials, 008/7-10 contain Date 1, generally a primary date associated with the publication, distribution, etc., of an item.

For serials, and serially-issued computer files, 008/07-10 contain the beginning date of publication (chronological designation). For reprints of serials, the beginning date of the original is input in these character positions. Dates are usually represented by four digits. Zeros, blanks, or the character 'u' may also be present in 008/7-10 when all or part of the date is unknown....

Description, Potential Uses, Caveats

Date 1 usually includes the most significant date pertaining to the publication of an item. This is generally either the actual publication date, the copyright date (if the publication date is not given on an item), or the first year that a multivolume item was published. For questionable dates of publication (008 Type of date code *q*), Date 1 includes the earliest probable date of publication.

In many cases, the date in the 008 Date 1 is the date that is used for indexing and searching by date. The reason for this is that dates found in other parts of the record may be difficult to locate or interpret. For some types of displays or lists, the 008 Date 1 may be used to indicate the date of publication as part of a truncated record. Particularly when all or part of the rest of the publication information (MARC field 260) is not part of the short entry record, use of the Date 1 data is a concise, predictable way of including the publication date.

In some MARC records, the Date 1 field is in error. This is more often true in the case of older non-LC records or records that have been modified from the original to use for another item. In many cases, when the records have been modified to produce catalog cards, the fixed field has not been updated to accurately reflect the modifications.

Date 2/Ending Date of Publication (008/11-14)

USMARC Definition

These character positions contain a date specified by the value in 008/06 (Type of date/Publication status code). For books, archival and manuscripts control, monographic computer files, maps, music, and visual materials, 008/11-14 contain Date 2, generally a secondary date associated with the publication, distribution, etc., of an item and the ending date of a collection. For books and visual materials, this may be a detailed date that represents a month and day.

For serials, and serially-issued computer files, 008/11-14 contain the ending date of the publication (chronological designation). For reprints of serials, the ending date of the original is input in these character positions. Dates are usually represented by four digits. Zeros, blanks, or the character 'u' may also be present in 008/11-14 when all or part of the date is unknown....

Description, Potential Uses, Caveats

Date 2 usually includes a secondary date pertaining to the publication of an item. When Date 1 includes the actual publication date, the copyright date (if given) is entered in Date 2. Among other types of dates, Date 2 may contain the latest year of publication for a multivolume item. For questionable dates of publication (008 Type of date code *q*), Date 2 includes the latest probable date of publication.

For various reasons, the date in the 008 Date 2 is not used nearly as often as the 008 Date 1 for indexing and searching by date. However, Date 2 could be used for some of the same purposes as Date 1.

In addition to the types of problems discussed under Date 1, Date 2 is sometimes erroneously omitted from the fixed field.

Place of Publication Code (008/15-17)

USMARC Definition

A two- or three-character alphabetic code indicates the place of publication, production, or execution. The place code is an authoritative-agency data element. The Library of Congress maintains the *USMARC code list for countries* and is the authoritative agency. Choice of a USMARC code is generally related to information in field 260 (Publication, Distribution, etc. (Imprint)), or in field 533 (Reproduction Note)....

Description, Potential Uses, Caveats

The Place of publication code is based upon the information that has been transcribed in the "place" element of the publication area within the catalog record. A code consisting of two letters followed by a blank is given for a country of publication. Three-letter codes are used to indicate a specific state or province within the United States, Canada, the Soviet Union, or the United Kingdom. In those cases, the third letter of the code represents the country, such as *u* for "the United States."

When more than one country of publication is involved, the first-named country is represented by the Place of publication code within USMARC and OCLCMARC records. However, UKMARC records often follow the policy of coding the first-named British place of publication, regardless of whether there are other places named first.

Examples of Place of publication codes are: *nyu* for an item published in New York (city or state); *cau* for an item published in California, and *jab* for an item published anywhere in Japan.

This code can be used to search a database for items published in a particular state or country. It can be used alone or as a qualifier to a subject heading, author's name, or other search parameter. Through the use of this code, statistics can be derived in regard to representation of various states and countries within a given collection or database.

By combining the code for a particular state with the government publications code for state publications, a checklist of state publications can be produced.

The provision of a Place of publication code is dependent upon the information found in the published item and entered into the publication area of the catalog record. In some cases, two, three, or more places are noted in the book itself, and it may be difficult to determine which is the most appropriate. For example, Golden Books regularly include two publication statements on the title page: one states "Western Publishing Company, Inc., Racine, Wisconsin" and the other one states "A Golden Book, New York." Depending upon the judgment (or guess) of the reader, either one of the places mentioned may be considered as the place of publication. For the purposes of searching a database or selecting records through a computer program, the best bet is to try all possible options.

Illustration Code (008/18-21)

USMARC Definition

One-character alphabetic codes indicate the presence of types of illustrations in the item represented by a books record. Information for this character position is usually derived from terms in field 300 (Physical description).

Up to four codes may be recorded, in alphabetical order. If fewer than four codes are assigned, the codes are left-justified and unused positions contain blanks (b̸). If more than four codes are appropriate to an item, only the first four are recorded.

Description, Potential Uses, Caveats

The Illustration code area may include from one to four single alphabetic characters that indicate the presence of certain types of illustrations in an item. If there is no illustrative matter, the Illustration code area includes four blanks. Codes are supplied according to the presence of certain terms in the physical description area of the catalog record. Codes are included in the code area in alphabetical order, regardless of the order of the types of illustrations in the physical description area in the catalog record. When more than four terms are involved, the codes that are the first four in alphabetical order are included in the Illustration code area.

The Illustration codes are as follows:

b̸	No illustrations	h	Facsimiles
a	Illustrations	i	Coats of arms
b	Maps	j	Genealogical tables
c	Portraits	k	Forms
d	Charts	l	Samples
e	Plans	m	Phonodisc, phonowire
f	Plates	o	Photographs
g	Music	p	Illuminations

The Illustration code holds a great deal of potential for fulfilling reference requests that may otherwise require lengthy manual searches or not be answered at all. The Illustration code provides direct access to the illustrative contents of books for the first time.

When used with other search parameters, this code can be particularly useful for requests that involve a particular type of illustration. For example, if a library patron is looking for a map of the United States during colonial times, then those three parameters can be combined as a single search. The search command might include the geographical subject heading with a chronological subdivision, "United States — History — Colonial period, 1600-1775," with an additional qualifier for "map."

The Illustration code has been applied inconsistently. Although the presence of a particular code within a record is usually a reliable indication that that particular type of illustration is included in the cataloged item, the converse is not necessarily true. In many cases, Illustration codes have been left blank even when illustrations are included in the item. In even more cases, the Illustration code has been recorded as the single generic code *a* despite the fact that one or more specific types are represented in the item. Generally speaking, time constraints are the primary reason that illustrations have not been accorded more exacting treatment in the physical description area and the 008 field.

Target Audience (008/22)

USMARC Definition

A one-character alphabetic code describes the intellectual level of the target audience for which the material is intended. This element is used only to distinguish juvenile materials from all others.

Description, Potential Uses, Caveats

This code was formerly known as the "Intellectual level" code. For books, this one-character code indicates whether or not the item is a juvenile item. A *juvenile* item is one that is intended for use by children and young people through the age of 15 or the 9th grade. The one-character code *j* indicates that the item is a "juvenile" item. The other possible Target audience code for books is *b̸*. A *b̸* indicates that the intellectual level of the target audience is unknown, or that the identification of the item as juvenile material is not applicable. For nonbook materials, such as films, age levels are noted more specifically and there are more defined codes.

One obvious use of this code is to limit a search in terms of age level, either including or excluding juvenile items. Another useful example would be combining the Target audience code *j* with a code for a particular foreign language to compile a listing of juvenile materials in that language. Through the use of the Target audience code, statistics may be provided on the proportions of juvenile and adult items in the collection.

There is no universal method for determining whether an item is geared towards a certain age group. One area of great inconsistency for Target audience determination is "young adult" materials. Another questionable area is picture books with sophisticated vocabulary.

The ƀ code can have one of two meanings—either the item is not juvenile or the item has not been evaluated for intellectual level. This ambiguous interpretation decreases the reliability of the code.

Form of Item Code (008/23)

USMARC Definition

A one-character alphabetic code specifies the form of material for the item in hand.

Description, Potential Uses, Caveats

This one-character code specifies several types of item form. The most-used codes are: *a* for microfilm; *b* for microfiche; *c* for microopaque; *d* for a large-print item; and *f* for a braille edition. This 008 code was formerly called the "Form of reproduction" code.

Among other uses, this code can be used to easily identify all large-print books in a collection. For users who need large-print materials, display terminals are not necessarily more readable than catalog cards. A selected database of large-print items could be used to produce a special large-print hardcopy catalog for patrons to use. Other possible uses of this code include qualifying a search for inclusion or exclusion of microforms.

This code has not been consistently used, particularly in the case of large-print items. There are often other clues in a MARC record that indicate a large-print item; however, such clues are not as concise or easy to locate as the Form of item code. There is often either a note (500 or other 5XX field) or a subject heading (650 or 690 field) that indicates that the item is large print or large type.

Nature of Contents Code (008/24-27)

USMARC Definition

One-character alphabetic codes indicate that an item contains certain types of materials. Generally, a specific code is used only if a significant part of the item is the type of material represented by the code. Information for these character positions is usually derived from other areas of the bibliographic record (e.g., field 245 (Title Statement), 6XX fields (Subject Added Entries), or 5XX (Note) fields).

Up to four codes may be recorded. Codes are recorded in the order of the list [in the *USMARC bibliographic format*]. If fewer than four codes are assigned, the codes are left justified and unused positions contain blanks (ƀ). If more than four codes are appropriate to an item, only the first four are recorded.

Description, Potential Uses, Caveats

Up to four one-letter codes are used to specify certain types of material used for reference purposes. There are codes for more than 20 types of reference materials, including the following: *b* for bibliography; *i* for index; *d* for dictionary; *e* for encyclopedia; and *s* for statistics.

These codes allow searchers to include or exclude specific types of reference materials or limit searches to a particular type of reference material. A valuable reference tool that can be produced through the use of this code is a printed list of each type of reference material (e.g., dictionaries, encyclopedias) within the library. These codes also can prove useful for collection management purposes when they are combined with the Date codes to obtain a listing of reference materials in a library's collection that were published prior to a given date. Weeding or acquiring items can be based in part on such an evaluation.

One potentially confusing aspect of the Nature of contents code is the way in which indexes are treated. The code *i* for "index" is used only if the item is an index to bibliographic material other than itself. If the item contains an index to its own contents only, then existence of the index is noted in a separate 008 code (Index).

Government Publication Code (008/28)

USMARC Definition

A one-character alphabetic code indicates whether or not the item is published or produced by or for an international, national, state, or local government agency, or by any subdivision of such a body. The code also describes the jurisdictional level of the government agency associated with the item.

Description, Potential Uses, Caveats

Different levels of government are each represented by a one-letter code, including the following: *f* for federal/national; *i* for international intergovernmental body; *c* for multilocal; *l* for local; and *s* for state. Additional codes indicate that the item is not a government publication (*b̸*), that it is unknown if the item is a government publication (*u*), or that it is a type of government publication for which there is no specific code (*o*).

Governments at all levels are prolific publishers on a wide variety of topics. Unfortunately, a number of factors make specific government publications difficult to track down. One complicating factor is the vast number of agencies that issue research, legal, and other documents; another is the generic nature of both the agency names ("Office of ... ," "Department of ... ," etc.) and the publication titles ("Report on ... ," "Annual survey of ... ," etc.).

Through the use of the Government publication code, a search for a specific document or a document issued by a particular level of government can initially be narrowed down to government publications at one particular level. Searches can be further narrowed down to a state or country through the use of the Place of publication code.

In addition to including or excluding government publications from searches through the use of the Government publication code, the code can also be combined with other types of search parameters, such as keyword or subject, to locate records for government publications on a particular topic.

Conference Publication (008/29)

USMARC Definition

A one-character numeric code indicates whether a work consists of the proceedings, reports, or summaries of a conference.

The following types of publications are considered to be conference publications:

Proceedings, including collections or partial collections of papers (or of contributions, essays, etc., that are based upon papers) presented at a conference or meeting.

A partial collection, defined as a work containing two or more papers (or contributions, essays, etc., that are based upon papers) presented at a conference or meeting.

A collection of preprints of conference papers.

The following types of publications are not considered conference publications:

Works composed of or based on a single paper

Symposiums in print

Hearings of legislative bodies

Courses given in a school (except where the main entry is the name of the meeting

Description, Potential Uses, Caveats

The Conference publication code *0* means that the work is not a conference publication. Code *1* indicates that the work is a conference publication. Given the generic nature of conference titles and the large number that may be in a database, the Conference publication code can be extremely useful for combining with a keyword or subject term to search for conference publications with nonspecific or unknown titles.

The Conference publication code could also be used to facilitate the production of a printed list of recent conference publications acquired by a library, to be used as a reference tool. When a large number of conference publications is involved, such lists might be subarranged by subject heading, call number, or other categorization.

Festschrift (008/30)

USMARC Definition

A one-character numeric code indicates whether or not the work is a festschrift.

A festschrift is defined as a complimentary or memorial publication usually in the form of a collection of essays, addresses, or biographical, bibliographic, scientific, or other contributions. It often embodies the results of research, issued in honor of a person, an institution, or a society, as a rule, on the occasion of an anniversary celebration.

A true festschrift generally mentions the person, institution, or society it commemorates on the chief source of information (i.e., title page). The title of the work may or may not use the word *festschrift*. Other indications that an item is a festschrift include phrases such as: "papers in honor of," "in memory of," "commemorating," or their equivalents in foreign languages.

Description, Potential Uses, Caveats

Festschrift code *0* indicates that the work is not a festschrift; *1* indicates that it is. Because festschriften often have generic or lengthy, unmemorable titles, they can be much more easily searched through the use of the Festschrift code combined with a keyword for the person, institution, or society commemorated by the festschrift.

Index (008/31)

USMARC Definition

A one-character numeric code indicates whether or not an item includes an index to its own contents. Information for this data element is derived from mention of an index in another part of the bibliographic record (e.g., in the title, or in a note).

Description, Potential Uses, Caveats

The Index code is set to *0* if the work does not include an index to itself; a *1* indicates that the work does include such an index. Because indexes greatly add to the research value of an item, this is something that researchers may want to include as part of their search criteria when searching a database.

An Index code set to *0* may indicate that the item does not include an index; however, it may also simply mean that the Index code was ignored in the cataloging process. In some cases, the words *Includes index* or a similar phrase may be included in one of the notes in the catalog description, in which case this indication should be considered more authoritative than an Index code that indicates otherwise.

Fiction (008/33)

USMARC Definition

A one-character numeric code indicates whether or not the item is a work of fiction. The information for this data element may sometimes be derived from the presence of the subject subdivision "fiction" in a subject added entry field (6XX).

Description, Potential Uses, Caveats

The Fiction code is set to *0* for works that are not fiction, and to *1* for works of fiction. The Fiction code may provide information about an item that cannot be easily derived from other parts of a catalog record. Collection analysis procedures could include consideration of this code (in addition to or instead of call numbers) to determine counts and proportions of fiction and nonfiction items within a library or group of libraries. This code could also be used to include or exclude fiction or nonfiction items within a search.

The Fiction code can be particularly useful with keyword searches that may retrieve a number of irrelevant items. Because the searcher knows whether a fiction or nonfiction item is desired, the search can be narrowed to fiction or nonfiction and thus eliminate a significant number of false hits that just happen to have the keyword included somewhere in the record.

The Fiction code may not be totally reliable for two reasons. One reason is that many works defy categorization as fiction or nonfiction; the Fiction code will generally indicate the predominant nature of the work. Another reason is that the default code *0* has simply been left as is on OCLC (and other systems) and has not been changed to indicate the fictional nature of the work.

Biography (008/34)

USMARC Definition

A one-character alphabetic code indicates whether or not an item contains biographical material, and if so, what the biographical characteristics are.

Description, Potential Uses, Caveats

Biography codes have been defined for four different types of biographical material: *a* for autobiography; *b* for biography; *c* for collective biography; and *d* for a work that contains biographical information. The blank (*b̷*) code indicates that there is no biographical material.

A biography listing could be produced easily through the use of this field, regardless of how the items have been classified within the collection. This can allow for convenient access to biographical information that would not otherwise be easily accessed (particularly in the case of the d code).

The Biography code could also be used as a way to narrow down keyword searches for biographical works when a large number of materials are retrieved for a given name — for example, for an author whose name will retrieve all works *by*, as well as *about*, that person.

Language Code (008/35-37)

USMARC Definition

A three-character alphabetic code indicates the language of the item. The language code is an authoritative-agency data element. The Library of Congress maintains the *USMARC code list for languages* and is the authoritative agency. Choice of a USMARC code is based on the predominant language of the item. When an item contains text, etc., in more than one language, or is a translation, textual information regarding the language is usually given in field 500 (General Note) or field 546 (Language Note). If more than one language code is appropriate to an item, all appropriate codes are given in field 041 (Language Code) and the first one is recorded in 008/35-37.

Description, Potential Uses, Caveats

A three-letter code, such as *eng* for "English," indicates the primary language of an item. If more than one language is involved, then codes for all languages are included in the MARC 041 field, in addition to the code for the primary language in the 008 field Language code.

The Language code could be used for searching items that have been written in a particular language. Circulation statistics, collection analysis, and other management data could also be generated on the basis of the language of materials. The 008 Language code is generally used within computer programs for filing indicator correction (see chapter 6, MARC Database Processing).

For a variety of reasons, the 008 Language code in any given record may incorrectly include the code for English (*eng*) when the record is actually for an item in another language. The frequency of this type of error is not known; however, it is more likely to be found in older records, particularly those created prior to the late 1970s. It is much less common to find an English-language record incorrectly coded as another language.

VARIABLE CONTROL FIELDS

USMARC Definition

The control fields contain control numbers and other kinds of control and coded information that is used in the processing of machine-readable bibliographic records. These fields have no indicators or subfield codes. Content designation for some of the control fields has not been fully defined; only the field tag has been reserved.

For fixed-length fields with various kinds of coded information, specific data elements are positionally defined. A more detailed explanation of positionally-defined data elements can be found in the sections describing specific fields.

Field 009 is currently reserved for local use and is not described in [the *USMARC bibliographic format*].

001 Control Number

USMARC Definition

This field contains the control number assigned by the organization creating, using, or distributing the record. For interchange purposes, documentation of the structure of the control number and input conventions must be provided to exchange partners by the organization initiating the interchange. An organization receiving a record may move the control number of the distributing system from field 001 to field 035 (System Control Number) and place its own control number in field 001.

The structure of the Library of Congress control number is described in field 010 (Library of Congress Control Number). The control number in records distributed by LC is contained in field 001. An organization using an LC record may move the LC control number from field 001 to field 010 and place its own control number in field 001.

EXAMPLES

001   ƀƀƀ86104385ƀ

001   CAT84800045ƀ

001   IND84800595ƀ

001   RLINCSUZ76035-A

001   ƀƀƀ80692458ƀ/MAPS

Description, Potential Uses, Caveats

The 001 field is a mandatory MARC field. Every MARC record must include an 001 field. The format of the control number is usually dependent upon the system in which the MARC record is being created or maintained. Control numbers are usually system-generated; that is, they are not manually input but are automatically assigned by the system.

A control number can serve as a unique identifier within an online system. If control numbers are assigned to records in consecutive order, then it is possible to tell when a particular record was loaded to the system in relation to other records. This information can be of value for some types of database maintenance functions.

An article in *Library systems newsletter* focuses on the importance of the control number. Among other points, it is noted that:

A library's machine-readable data base represents a heavy investment of staff time and equipment expenditures, therefore it is important that the records be of high quality and integrity. A major aspect of record integrity is the treatment of unique identification numbers....

... When a library has access to a resource file of machine-readable cataloging records, a cataloger will often find a record for an item similar, but not identical to, the book in hand....

In most instances, the amendments required are minor—a change in publisher name, or place and date of publication, a change in edition, etc. However, after such changes, it is no longer valid for the amended record to retain the same control number.... The amended record represents a different bibliographic entity than that of the original record ... the new record should be assigned its own unique control number.

There are pressing reasons, other than concerns of bibliographic purity, why care should be taken to ensure that a "derived, but amended record" is assigned a unique control number....[3]

One of the most important aspects of a unique record identification number is that when a bibliographic record is changed in such a way that it no longer represents the item for which it was originally created, then the unique identification number is no longer valid. Among other differences, a different title, publisher, date of publication, or pagination generally signifies a separate edition. Changing, adding, or deleting call numbers, subject headings, notes, or other such information are not usually considered a change in the "bibliographic description" and usually do not warrant a separate bibliographic record.

Library of Congress guidelines for determining whether an item is simply another copy (for which the same bibliographic record can be used) or a separate edition (requiring a separate bibliographic record) are given in the *Cataloging service bulletin*. The guidelines are given as part of the "Library of Congress Rule Interpretations" ("LCRI") under "1.0 General rules — Edition or Copy" and are regularly updated with additional clarification. The guidelines given in the Summer 1989 *Cataloging service bulletin* are as follows:

Edition or Copy

When a new manifestation of an item reaches the cataloger, the question arises as to whether this is a copy of an earlier manifestation or an edition separate from the earlier manifestation needing its own bibliographic record. Consult the definition of "Edition" in Appendix D [of the *Anglo-American cataloging rules*, 2nd ed., rev.]. If, according to this definition, two items are known to be two different editions, create a separate record for each.

Also, consider that a new edition is involved whenever

1) there is an explicit indication of changes (including corrections) of content; or,

2) anything in the following areas or elements of areas differs from one bibliographic record to another: title and statement of responsibility area, edition area, the extent statement of the physical description area, and series area. (For an exception relating to CIP items, see below.)

Whenever the question relates to the publication, distribution, etc., area or to ISBNs, consider that the item is a copy if the only variation is one or more of the following:

1) a difference in the printing or copyright date;

2) a minor variation in an entity's name. There are relatively few examples of this phenomenon, which arises when a publisher uses multiple forms concurrently. For example, "Duckworth" and "G. Duckworth" and "St. Martin's" and "St. Martin's Press" have been used at the same time by these publishers. A genuine name change, even if minor (see below), should not be considered as a variation;

3) the addition, deletion, or change of an ISBN;

4) a difference in binding; or,

5)   a difference in the edition statement or the series whenever the item is a CIP book issued by the publisher in both a hardbound and a softbound version.

For variations in the publication, distribution, etc., area not covered by the preceding statements, consider that the item is a new edition. Noteworthy examples for the publication, distribution, etc., area are variations involving different places or entities transcribed or any difference in an entity's name that is suggestive of either a name change or a different entity. Examples of the latter case are the many instances of a sequence of names used, with one used for some time and another at some point replacing the first. For example, "Harper & Brothers" becomes "Harper & Row"; "Doubleday, Doran" becomes "Doubleday."

N.B. Rare books in general follow the same policy, with exceptions as necessary.[4]

Valid record control numbers, with a unique number for each individual edition of an item, are essential for duplicate resolution within a single institution's database, as well as for merging files of multiple institutions, among other types of database processing that rely upon the 001 field. Incorrect control numbers, especially duplicate control numbers for the two different editions of an item or two completely different items, will almost inevitably cause significant problems in the processing and subsequent use of MARC databases.

OCLC records added to an institution's archival tape between June 30, 1980, and June 26, 1983, included the date of use of the record as the last six characters of the 001 field, in the pattern YYMMDD (last two digits of year, two digits for the month, two digits for the day of the month).

005 Date and Time of Latest Transaction

USMARC Definition

This field contains 16 characters that specify the date and time of the latest record transaction. The date and time serve as a version identifier for the record.

The date is recorded according to *Representation for calendar date and ordinal date for information interchange* (ANSI X3.30). The date requires 8 numeric characters in the pattern "yyyymmdd" (4 for the year, 2 for the month, and 2 for the day).

The time is recorded according to *Representations of local time of the day for information interchange* (ANSI X3.43). The time requires 8 numeric characters in the pattern "hhmmss.f" (2 for the hour, 2 for the minute, 2 for the second, and 2 for a decimal fraction of the second, including the decimal point). The 24-hour clock (00-23) is used.

The date on which a record is first entered into machine-readable form is contained in field 008/00-05. The "Date entered on file" never changes.

EXAMPLE

005   19860901141236.0

[Sept. 1, 1986, 2:12:36 P.M.]

Description, Potential Uses, Caveats

The process of deduping (discussed in chapter 6, MARC Database Processing) relies heavily upon the date and time of use of a record. In most cases, the date and time of the use of the record are the local time of the host computer, which is not necessarily the same as that of the user library. Because most processing that relies on the 005 field uses the information to compare with other 005 fields, relative difference is all that matters.

The 005 field did not become a part of the USMARC format until 1982, so not all records in a library's database may contain an 005 field. In some cases, vendors used other fields to record this information. For example, OCLC records include the date of use information as follows:

Records used prior to June 30, 1980: date and time of use not included in record.

Records used between June 30, 1980, and June 26, 1983: date of use is recorded in the 001 field after the OCLC number, using the pattern YYMMDD.

Records used after June 26, 1983: the 005 field is included in records created after this point.

---

007 Physical Description Fixed Field

USMARC Definition

This field contains the physical characteristics of an item in a coded form. The physical characteristics are usually derived from information in other parts of the USMARC record especially from field 300 (Physical Description) and/or one of the 5XX note fields.

Field 007 has a generic tree structure, whereby values given in 007/00 (Category of material) determine the data elements defined for subsequent character positions.

Not all USMARC records contain field 007.

Field 007 is used in "books" records for microforms only. There is no 007 defined for textual material.

Field 007 is used in "archival and manuscript control" records for microforms.

Field 007 is used in "maps" records to describe maps, globes, and maps in microform.

Field 007 is used in "music" records for music in microform and sound recordings.

Field 007 is used in "visual materials" records for projected and nonprojected graphics, videorecordings, microforms, and motion pictures. It is also used for component parts of a kit that are any of the preceding media and to describe a sound recording, map, and/or globe when part of a kit (the specifications for sound recordings, maps, and globes are used, respectively, in such instances).

Field 007 is used in "serials" records for microforms only. There is no 007 defined for textual material.

Field 007 is not used for "computer files."

Description, Potential Uses, Caveats

For microforms and various other media, the 007 field includes encoded information about the physical characteristics. Most of the identifying characteristics noted are information that potential users would want to know or need to know to use the item properly. For example, the 007 field for motion pictures indicates the specific type of material (e.g., cartridge, cassette, reel), whether the film is color or black and white, the film emulsion, the width of the film, and other pertinent information. Although the physical characteristics are often noted in other parts of the MARC record, such as note fields, the encoded information in the 007 field allows a computer to locate and interpret the information much more quickly and with greater accuracy.

The encoded information in the 007 field can be used to search for a specific type of material or particular characteristics. Another possible use of the 007 information is to generate a printed or online description of materials according to the codes found in the 007 field.

Because the 007 field information is in code, rather than in a form more easily understood by humans, the field is not an easy one to input. For this reason, errors of omission or commission are not unusual. In such cases, manual correction of the field will generally be required before the field can be properly processed.

008 Field (Described in MARC 008 Field Codes Section Above)

009 Local Use Field (Not Described Herein)

VARIABLE DATA FIELDS

USMARC Definition

The remaining variable fields [010-999] defined in the format [as opposed to the variable control fields, 001-009]. In addition to being identified by a field tag in the Directory, variable data fields contain two indicator positions stored at the beginning of each field and a two-character subfield code preceding each data element within the field.

01X-09X Numbers and Codes

USMARC Definition

Fields 01X-09X contain standard numbers, classification numbers, codes, and other data elements pertaining to the record.

010 Library of Congress Control Number

USMARC Definition

This field contains unique numbers that have been assigned to a bibliographic record by the Library of Congress. The control number for USMARC records distributed by LC is an LC control number.

The LC control number is carried in field 001 (Control Number) in records distributed by LC's Cataloging Distribution Service. It may also be carried in field 010≠a. An organization using LC records may move the LC control number from field 001 to field 010 and use field 001 for its own control number.

An LC record may contain field 010 with a cancelled or invalid control number of a previously-distributed record. A record may be cancelled because it is a duplicate record for the same item. The structure of the cancelled/invalid control number is the same as that used by LC in field 001. Field 010 may or may not contain subfield ≠a with the control number from the field 001 in it.

Description, Potential Uses, Caveats

The Library of Congress Control Number (LCCN) is basically the same thing as the LC card number, which for decades has been the identifier for ordering catalog card sets from the Library of Congress. For MARC records distributed by the Library of Congress, most vendors and users transfer the LCCN from the 001 field into the 010 field. In MARC records that have not originated at LC (particularly pre-1968 records), libraries have transcribed LCCNs from LC card sets (either from cards the library has ordered, or from copies printed in the *National Union Catalog*) and from books, where the LCCN has been printed on the verso of the title page or elsewhere.

Library of Congress card numbers have not always been formulated in the same way. A discussion of variations in LCCNs, and instructions for entering such numbers in MARC records, are included in "Old style card numbers" in the *Cataloging service bulletin*: 1 (Summer 1978). One major difference between previous and current ways of formulating LC card numbers is that LC formerly assigned duplicate card numbers to various forms of media and differentiated between the numbers by assigning alphabetic prefixes to the numbers. The duplication and prefixes are not a part of current methods of assigning LCCNs. There are many types of "pseudo-LCCNs" that are currently used in the 010 field that include prefixes that signify their origin. For example, in UKMARC records used on OCLC, the British National Bibliography number is placed in the 010 field with the prefix *gb*.

One primary use of the LCCN is as a search key for online searching. The LCCN is also used as a search parameter for batch retrospective conversion projects: libraries use the LCCNs printed in their materials to match against a MARC database, retrieving the "matching" records to be used by the library for in-house automation. When using the LCCN as a search key, libraries should take into consideration the caveats provided below.

One significant disadvantage of using the LCCN from a book as a search key is that the LCCNs used by publishers are often incorrect. In some cases, the numbers have been printed with typographical errors or transposed numbers. In most cases, the publisher has simply reused an LCCN from one edition or title to print in another. Curiously enough, when users find that the LC card number in a book has retrieved a different record from what was expected, their reaction is that "the Library of Congress got the number wrong." In most cases, it is actually the publisher that has misprinted or misused the LCCN. Informal studies have shown that approximately 30 percent of the LCCNs printed by publishers in books are not the correct LCCN for the item.[5]

The implications of this situation should be given serious consideration by any library considering batch conversion. A significant number of incorrect records are likely to be retrieved by LCCNs taken from books (or other materials). These incorrect records will later need to be detected in the library's database, deleted, and replaced with the correct records; this can significantly impact upon the time and expense required to actually complete a database conversion.

020 International Standard Book Number

USMARC Definition

This field contains the International Standard Book Number (ISBN), the terms of availability, and any cancelled/invalid ISBN. Each field 020 contains all the information relevant to one ISBN, or if no ISBN exists, relevant to one item. Field 020 is repeated for multiple numbers that refer to different editions of a work (e.g., ISBNs for the hard bound and paperback editions).

The ISBN is an agency-assigned data element. ISBNs are assigned to monographic publications by designated agencies in each country participating in the program. An ISBN consists of ten digits comprising four groups separated by hyphens. (The tenth digit is a check digit used as a computer validity check; it consists of a number between 0 and 9 or an uppercase X (for the arabic numeral 10)). Procedures for validation of the ISBN by calculating the check digit and hyphenating instructions are in *Book numbering* (ANSI Z39.21). A description of the ISBN structure and guidelines for recording qualifying information are found in *Cataloging service bulletin*, no. 16 (Spring 1982), published by the Library of Congress.

Description, Potential Uses, Caveats

The ten digits of the ISBN all carry significance. Each ISBN is divided into four sections: the group identifier, the publisher identifier, the title identifier, and the check digit. The group identifier, which is the first one, two, or three digits in the ISBN, identifies the national, geographic, or other similar grouping of publishers. For example, the identifier *0* has been allocated to represent publishers in Australia, Canada, New Zealand, Rhodesia, South Africa, United Kingdom, and the United States. The publisher identifier identifies a particular publisher within a group. The length of the publisher identifier varies according to the publisher's output: the larger the output (titles published), the shorter the number. The title identifier is usually assigned by the publisher; this number identifies a specific title published by that particular publisher. The length of the title identifier depends upon the length of the publisher identifier. The check digit is one character that is derived from a calculation on the other nine digits of the ISBN and is used in computer systems to validate numbers as a means of checking against errors in transcription.

The ISBN has significant value as a search key in online systems. The ISBN can be used for searching for a specific title. It can also be used to search for the works of a particular publisher, by utilizing only the first two sections of the ISBN (the group identifier and the publisher identifier). The ISBN even has potential for identifying works published in specific countries or groups of countries, through the use of the group identifier.

Two factors negatively impact the value of the ISBN for searching. The first is that many publishers do not use ISBNs. The second is that many publishers that do use ISBNs apply them in an inconsistent or confusing manner. For example, it is not unusual to find that two or more ISBNs have been used for a single item, some of which may be printed in the item and some of which may be included in a MARC record. For this reason, an ISBN search that does not retrieve any records is not a conclusive search; the desired record may actually be in the database without an ISBN or with a different ISBN.

041 Language Code

USMARC Definition

This field contains three-character alphabetic codes for languages associated with an item when field 008/35-37 (Language code) is insufficient to convey full information for a multilingual item or a translation. The language code is an authoritative-agency data element. The Library of Congress maintains the *USMARC code list for languages* and is the authoritative agency....

This field is used in conjunction with 008/35-37 (Language code). If 008/35-37 does not contain all blanks (bbb), the code in 008/35-37 is also recorded as the first code in subfield ǂa of field 041....

Field 041 is used when one or more of the following conditions exist:

The work is or includes a translation

The text contains more than one language

The language of the summaries, abstracts, or accompanying material differs from the language of the text

The language of the table of contents differs from the language of the text

---

Description, Potential Uses, Caveats

The 041 field is included in the MARC record in one of two cases: when an item is in more than one language or when a translation is involved. The first indicator of the 041 field is set to *0* if the work is not a translation or does not include a translation. The first indicator is set to *1* if the work is or includes a translation. Subfield ǂ*a* includes the codes for the language or languages of the item, in order of predominance. Subfield ǂ*b* includes the language code(s) for summaries when the language is different from that of the text. Subfield ǂ*h* contains code(s) for the original language(s) of translated works.

The potential uses of the 041 field are basically the same as those for the 008 field Language code; however, the 041 field includes more information (and more specific information) that can be used for searching, generation of statistics, and other processing.

050-099 Call Numbers (Introduction)

A MARC record may contain one or more classification numbers or call numbers. The difference between a class (classification) number and a call number is that the class number is only one part of a call number. The same class number is assigned to all items on a particular topic; this serves to group related works on the shelf together. The call number is a combination of the class number and another line or lines of characters that are usually an abbreviation of the main entry of the book (this line is sometimes referred to as the "item" number, the "book" number, or the "Cutter" number). Using this system, books arranged together on the shelf by topic will usually be subarranged by the author's last name or the title of the book.

In many cases, not all call number information is included within the call number field. A call number prefix (such as "Ref" for reference or "CS" for computer software) is a primary example of one portion of a call number that may not be included in the call number field. For example, in an OCLC-MARC record, the most likely placement of such a call number prefix is within the OCLC-defined 049 field, as an "input stamp." The input stamp is enclosed in square brackets and is located directly before the library's OCLC holding symbol in the 049 field.

In some cases, call number prefixes are not found within the MARC record at all. Some prefixes are generated automatically by a computer program when the MARC record includes a specified signal. For example, OCLC system-generated prefixes or automatic stamps automatically print out the desired location prefix on cards without the text being input to a catalog record. For each four-letter OCLC collection code that must be input, the library may specify one or more lines of text that will print automatically above or below the call number. Some online systems also provide similar system-generated prefixes with record displays. Automatic text saves the keystrokes involved in inputting the location prefix with each record. Having the prefixes display automatically rather than inputting each one also allows for more flexibility. For example, if a location prefix is to be changed from "R" to "Ref," then only a few lines of the computer program will need to be changed, rather than changing each and every record that explicitly includes the prefix.

It is of the utmost importance that a library be able to specify exactly how call numbers are to be formulated when MARC records are processed or used within an online catalog. If information must be taken from fields other than the call number field or if the library relies upon system-generated information, then this must be stated very explicitly in the library's specifications. The library should keep in mind that current instructions for call number processing may not be the same as those used at an earlier time. A library's database will generally reflect the practices that were used at the time the records were added to the database; if practices have changed over time, then the changes and their effective dates should be documented.

Call number fields within a MARC record have great potential value aside from indicating the call number that has been assigned to a particular item. Many MARC records, particularly those that are devised by the Library of Congress, contain more than one type of call number. Deleting extra call numbers from a record is generally unnecessary and may actually decrease the value of the record. Because most systems select out only one particular call number, on the basis of library specifications, other call numbers can be left in the record without causing a problem.

One example of the potential value of different types of call numbers is for the purpose of collection analysis, which can be accomplished through the use of different classification systems, including Dewey and LC. The more different types of call numbers within a record, the more options a library has for this type of analysis. When collection analysis is being completed as part of a cooperative collection development program between several libraries, the inclusion of at least one common type of classification system within the MARC databases is very valuable.

For libraries that currently use one classification system but may change to another system in the future (for example, changing from Dewey to LC), the inclusion of that alternative type of call number within MARC database records can serve as the basis for a future batch reclassification procedure.

Libraries that are used to filing their call numbers manually, such as in a shelflist catalog, may be surprised by computer-filed call numbers. Some sort routines will file decimal numbers (such as in a Cutter number) as whole numbers, or vice versa, regardless of what the library has intended. In some instances, sort routines will be "case-sensitive," that is, upper-case and lower-case letters will file separately. Proper specifications drawn up by the library can help to avoid unwelcome surprises.

Often the sorting of call numbers includes a subsort on the main entry. If each call number is unique to one item, then a call number sort can produce proper filing order; however, when more than one item in a collection has the same call number, then a call number sort may not produce the desired results. A common example of non-unique call numbers is the use of the first two, three, or more letters of the main entry as the Cutter line (the last line of the call number); all items with the same class number and the same first few letters of the main entry will have the same call number. If the computer routines for the call number sort include a subsort on the main entry, this provides for correct filing when the Cutter line of the call number is based on the main entry. However, when the Cutter line is based on a subject heading or some element other than the main entry, then misfilings can result.

One case that often leaves libraries without a useful remedy is the case of materials classed as "biography," where the last line of the call number is based on the name of the biographee, not the main entry. If the call number sort includes a subsort on the main entry, a biography of George Washington (Cutter line *Was*) by Keene will sort before a biography of Booker T. Washington (Cutter line *Was*) by Smith. Likewise, a biography of Martha Washington by Abrams will file before the previously mentioned biographies of George and Booker T.

050 Library of Congress Call Number

USMARC Definition

This field contains a call or classification number assigned either by the Library of Congress or by other agencies using the *Library of Congress classification* or *LC classification — Additions and changes*. The second indicator values distinguish between content actually assigned by the Library of Congress and content assigned by an organization other than LC.

Description, Potential Uses, Caveats

The 050 field is used for call numbers that are assigned according to the Library of Congress classification system. The call numbers do not have to be assigned by the Library of Congress to be tagged with the 050 tag. The MARC 050 field first indicator position is one of the few cases in which a *0* signifies a positive condition (the item is in the Library of Congress collection) and a *1* indicates a negative condition (the item is not in the Library of Congress collection).

Two subfield codes have been defined for use with the 050 field. Subfield ≠*a* includes the classification number portion of the call number; subfield ≠*b* includes the item number portion of the call number. LC call numbers may include any of a variety of elements, and they may contain as few as three lines or as many as eight or more lines. In some cases, this makes it difficult to determine the correct placement of the subfield code *b*, particularly if the person supplying the MARC coding is not familiar with the way the call number was created. One rule of thumb is that the subfield code *b* should be placed in front of the last uppercase letter in the call number. If the last uppercase letter is directly preceded by a decimal point, then the subfield code *b* should precede the decimal point. This rule will produce satisfactory results in most cases, but not in all. The first five examples shown below are call numbers with which the rule can be used successfully; the last example illustrates an exception to the rule.

QC861.2 ≠b .B36

Z695.7 ≠b .B37 1980

Z6174.N3 ≠b L34 no. 9

JX1974.7 ≠b .M5

HF5549.5.R44 ≠b M35

M1001 ≠b .H3 op. 76, no. 3 .S3 1987

Incorrect subfielding of call numbers can produce undesirable results. Such results may include problems in searching and filing by call number and erroneous collection analysis statistics. If there is any doubt about proper placement of the subfield code *b*, classification schedules should be checked to determine where the class number ends and the item number begins.

082 Dewey Decimal Call Number

USMARC Definition

This field contains a call number assigned from editions of the Dewey Decimal Classification schedules....

Description, Potential Uses, Caveats

The three subfield codes defined for the 082 field are *a* for the classification number, *b* for the item number, and *2*, which includes the number of the edition of the Dewey classification schedules from which the classification was assigned. In comparison to the 050 call number field, the assignment of the *a* and *b* subfields for the 082 field is a fairly simple matter. With a few predictable exceptions, the class number portion of the Dewey call number is a three-digit number, which may be followed by one or more decimal characters; the item number portion of the call number begins with an alphabetic character and is followed by one or more numeric or alphabetic characters.

The subfield ≠2 information is most often included in MARC records produced by the Library of Congress. This subfield should not be used as part of a call number within a library catalog. It has been included as part of the LC records because Dewey class numbers may be assigned to entirely different subjects, depending upon the edition that has been used. A library that uses a different edition from the one noted in the subfield ≠2 will want to verify the appropriateness of the class number.

086 Government Document Classification Number

USMARC Definition

This field contains the classification number assigned to a government document by a government agency at any level (e.g., state, national, international). If a number can be characterized as both a stock number (field 037) and a classification number, the number is recorded in field 086. If the nature of the number is unknown, it is recorded in field 037 (Stock number)....

Description, Potential Uses, Caveats

The use of this MARC field has been broadened from its original one, which was the "Superintendent of Documents classification number," for call numbers of United States government publications. Through the use of the indicators or subfield *2* it is now possible to indicate a particular national, state, or other jurisdiction that assigned the government document number.

The Government document classification number can be used for the purposes of searching, collection analysis, and other statistical analysis. Even if a library does not use a particular government classification system, the 086 field should be maintained in the record for all of its potential uses. Some types of government classification numbers provide the most valuable access points for tracking down government publications. For example, the first part of the Superintendent of Documents number is usually an abbreviated or coded form of the name of the agency that published the item; this may be the most concise identifier available for searching materials published by that agency.

09X Local Call Numbers

USMARC Definition

Fields 090-099 are reserved for local call number use and local definition. For interchange purposes, documentation of the structure of the 09X fields and input conventions must be provided to exchange partners by the organization initiating the interchange.

Description, Potential Uses, Caveats

The 09X fields are used for call numbers devised according to classification systems other than those represented by specific USMARC tags. These may be locally developed classification systems or systems that are not as widely used as those specified by USMARC. For purposes of processing a library database for use in an online catalog, the 09X field generally takes precedence when more than one call number field is present.

1XX Main Entries

USMARC Definition

Fields 100, 110, 111, and 130 contain a name or a uniform title heading used as main entry. Except for differences in the definitions of indicator values, content designation in the 1XX fields is consistent across all formats.

The main entry is a traditional access point. Each 1XX tag is discussed individually, including the primary indicators and subfield codes, examples of coded headings, and the discussion section entitled "Description, Potential Uses, Caveats."

100 Main Entry — Personal Name

Primary indicators and subfield codes for personal name main entry are as follows:

1st indicator	Personal name entry element
0	Forename
1	Single surname
2	Multiple surname

2nd indicator	Main entry/subject relationship
0	Main entry/subject relationship irrelevant
1	Main entry is subject

Subfield code	Portion of field
a	Personal name
q	Fuller form of name
d	Dates associated with a name

Two examples of coded headings are shown below.

100 10 ≠a Fowler, T. M. ≠q (Thaddeus Mortimer), ≠d 1842-1922.

100 20 ≠a Fitzgerald-Jones, Sandra, ≠d 1938-

Description, Potential Uses, Caveats

A personal name main entry names the primary author or, in broader terms, the person chiefly responsible for the creative content of the work. There are two points regarding personal name main entry that often require clarification. One is the concept of "single surname" and the other is the main entry/subject relationship.

The first indicator for the 100 field identifies the type of name involved. The difference between a "single surname" and a "compound surname" is sometimes confusing because some surnames that include two or more words, such as "La Fayette" and "Del Mar," are actually single surnames. When prefixes that are prepositions (such as "De"), articles (such as "El"), or a combination of the two (such as "Del") are followed by only one word, the name is considered a single surname, not a compound surname.

The second indicator for the 100 field is set according to the main entry/subject relationship of the name. This concept is actually much simpler than it sounds. If the material is autobiographical and a subject heading for the author is desired, then that subject heading will be automatically generated by setting the second indicator to *1*. The purpose of the indicator is basically to save the inputter from having to enter the same text twice, once in the 100 field and once in the 600 field (personal name subject heading). Nevertheless, the second indicator *1* is not widely used. Generally, the text is just entered twice, once in each field, in which case the second indicator is set to *0* to avoid generating a second identical subject heading.

Within the environment of MARC-based automation, the most obvious use of a personal name main entry is for searching purposes. Personal name main entry is a traditional access point—access by an author's name is expected of any library catalog. A library will need to provide specifications for searching, display, and filing of the 100 field within an automated environment. The most significant part of the specifications process will be to decide which subfields should be indexed ("searchable"), which subfields should be included in the display of the field, and which should be considered in the filing of the field. Surprisingly, the answer is not the same in all cases, and it is generally not all subfields. For example, one subfield that is generally not searched or filed upon is the subfield e, which is a "relator term," such as "editor" or "illustrator." (The e subfield has been used primarily in pre-AACR2 records.) Another subfield that should not be included in searching, display, or filing is the OCLC-defined subfield ≠w, which includes a code that indicates whether or not the name is in AACR2 form. Libraries may want to specify that this subfield be deleted from the record or be displayed only as part of a MARC display of the record, not within a patron display.

One method for judging specification options is to devise sample files of names that represent as many different types of subfields as possible. Then determine how each would search, display, or file (on its own and with the rest of the names) with the inclusion or deletion of each subfield. It is also important to refer to printed and other resources, such as the ALA filing rules and other libraries that have had to devise—and live with—similar specifications.

110 Main Entry—Corporate Name

Primary indicators and subfield codes for corporate name main entries are as follows:

1st indicator	Corporate name entry element
1	Jurisdiction name
2	Name in direct order
2nd indicator	Main entry/subject relationship
0	Main entry/subject relationship irrelevant
1	Main entry is subject
Subfield code	Portion of field
a	Corporate or jurisdiction name
b	Subordinate unit

Two examples of coded corporate name headings are shown below.

110 10 ≠a United States. ≠b Court of Appeals (2nd Circuit)

110 20 ≠a AFL-CIO.

Description, Potential Uses, Caveats

The concept of "corporate name" in cataloging often requires clarification: a *corporate* entity can be one of a wide variety of groups and is by no means simply a business organization. *AACR2* basically defines corporate body as an organization or a group of persons with a particular name that may act or does act as a single entity.[6] This definition includes governmental agencies, private businesses, musical groups, schools and colleges, and many other entities. The *USMARC format for bibliographic data* identifies almost 200 ambiguous headings categories as corporate names, including named airplanes, bars, broadcasting stations, coal ash sites, communication satellites, racetracks, and warehouses.

Generally speaking, corporate name main entries serve the same purposes and require the same types of specifications as personal name main entries (100 field). Searching, display, and filing specifications must all be determined. For searching library databases that include a large number of federal government publications, a stoplist of commonly occurring words, such as that used by OCLC, may be a consideration. Because lengthy names of governmental (and other corporate) agencies may be identical except for the last few characters, filing routines should not be limited to a certain number or characters, but should file through all appropriate subfields. This will eliminate the possibility that such names will be listed in random order.

A common error in the MARC tagging of corporate names is the use of the tag 100 instead of 110. This can cause significant problems in the use of the records; however, identifying mistagged 110 (or other X10) fields can be accomplished fairly easily by searching corporate names (e.g., state names) as personal names. It is important that the tags be corrected.

111 Main Entry — Meeting Name

Primary indicators and subfield codes for meeting name main entries are as follows:

1st indicator	Meeting name entry element
2	Name in direct order

2nd indicator	Main entry/subject relationship
0	Main entry/subject relationship irrelevant
1	Main entry is subject

Subfield code	Portion of field
a	Meeting or jurisdiction name
d	Date of meeting
c	Location of meeting
n	Number of part/section/meeting

Two examples of coded meeting name headings are shown below.

111 20 ≠a Vatican Council ≠n (1st : ≠d 1969-1970)

111 20 ≠a Expo '70 ≠c (Osaka, Japan)

Description, Potential Uses, Caveats

The Meeting name field has been popularly known as the "conference name" field; however, the concept of a "conference" is very limited, compared to the types of activities that this field comprises. *AACR2* basically defines conferences as meetings devoted to discussion and/or action upon topics of common interest.[7] *USMARC format for bibliographic data* has a list of ambiguous headings that qualify as meeting names, including such categories as exhibitions, expositions, fairs, and festivals.

A meeting name that is entered subordinately to a corporate body is used in an X10 field, *not* an X11 field. An example of this type of heading is an entry for a political party convention, such as "Democratic Party (Tex.) State Convention (1857 : Waco, Tex.)."

The considerations for searching, display, and filing of the 110 field are much the same as those discussed above for the 100 and 110 fields. One additional point of deliberation: library staff and patrons will probably be required to define meeting names as "authors" (or "names"), as opposed to "titles," when determining specifications or when searching a computerized catalog. Traditionally many libraries have filed meeting names within the author section of a divided catalog. (According to *AACR2*, a *meeting* is a type of corporate body, and rules for meeting names are included as part of chapter 24, "Headings for corporate bodies.") Learning to look for a meeting name in a particular location (i.e., a specific section of a card catalog) does not involve the same mental processes as consciously determining that a meeting name is actually a name, rather than a title — particularly when a meeting name looks more like the title of a meeting than the name of a corporate author. In the grand scheme of library automation, this is actually a very minor point (some solid documentation works wonders in such cases); however, it is a good illustration of how an automated system can become somewhat user-hostile without the essential human touch.

The order of some of the elements in meeting names was different under pre-*AACR2* rules, as were some of the subfield codes. It is entirely possible that a library database includes some of these headings. Automated authority control (which is discussed in chapter 6, MARC Database Processing) may rectify some or all of the deviations. The primary difference in subfield codes is that the number of the meeting was previously coded as *b*, whereas the current code is *n*.

130 Main Entry – Uniform Title

Primary indicators and subfield codes for uniform title main entries are as follows:

1st indicator	Nonfiling characters
0-9	Number of nonfiling characters present

2nd indicator	Main entry/subject relationship
0	Main entry/subject relationship irrelevant
1	Main entry is subject

Subfield code	Portion of heading
a	Uniform title
n	Number of part/section of a work
p	Name of part/section of a work
l	Language of a work
s	Version

Three examples of coded uniform title headings are shown below.

130 00 ≠a San Francisco journal (1980)

130 00 ≠a Three little pigs.

130 00 ≠a Bible. ≠p N.T. ≠l English. ≠s Revised standard.

Description, Potential Uses, Caveats

Uniform title main entries are used for several different categories of materials in cases where the use of an author's name for main entry is either not possible or not appropriate. The three primary types of materials for which uniform title main entries are devised are: religious works, such as the Bible, the Koran, or the Talmud; anonymous works (particularly classics), such as *Beowulf*, *Chanson de Roland*, *Mother Goose*, or *Three Little Pigs*; and publications or productions such as newspapers and other serial publications, radio and television programs, and motion pictures.

The purpose of the uniform title is to provide a way for library users to find all of the different editions of a particular work through the use of one uniform title, rather than having to know all the possible variations of a title that may have been used. Consider, for example, the situation of a library patron who is interested in finding all the editions of Mother Goose tales in a library's collection. The editions of Mother Goose tales include a wide variety of titles, some of which include the words *Mother Goose* and some of which do not. Some of the titles are composed of familiar phrases, such as, "To market, to market." A number of different languages may be represented. In short, there is no common thread among the numerous editions that would allow a library patron to find all of them. Yet, through the use of the uniform title (in this case "Mother Goose") which is supplied by the cataloger, a library user can easily have access to all the editions of such an item. In many cases, the uniform title is used as a main entry, but it can also be used as a subject heading (630 field), a uniform title added entry (730 field), or in some cases a series added entry (830 field).

Uniform titles are used much more often in larger libraries than they are in smaller ones. Of course, larger libraries are more likely to have a wide variety of editions of an item, making the use of the uniform title a necessity. Nevertheless, uniform titles can be a valuable part of a smaller library's catalog as well. The cases in which a uniform title should be used are strictly a local decision. *AACR2*, chapter 25, provides guidelines for devising uniform titles; examples of uniform titles can be found in catalog cards and MARC records produced by the Library of Congress.

Specifications for the searching, display, and filing of uniform titles require many of the same considerations as those for other types of main entries (100, 110, 111 fields). One traditional approach to the use of uniform title main entry has been to leave the actual title-page title (245 field) untraced, that is, without access by the title found on the particular edition of a work. One reason for this was that one less card had to be typed and filed in the catalog. Given that any number of entries can be computer-generated and computer filed without any appreciable effort, providing access by the title-page title seems more than reasonable.

245 Title Statement

USMARC Definition

This field contains the title and statement of responsibility area of a bibliographic record. The Title statement field consists of the title proper and may also contain the general material designation (medium), remainder of title, other title information, and the statement of responsibility/remainder of title page transcription. The title proper includes the short title and alternative title, the numerical designation of a part/section and the name of a part/section....

Primary indicators and subfield codes for title statement are as follows:

1st indicator	Title added entry
0	No title added entry
1	Title added entry

2nd indicator	Nonfiling characters
0-9	Number of nonfiling characters present

Subfield code	Portion of field
a	Title
b	Remainder of title
c	Remainder of title page transcription
h	Medium

Three examples of coded title statements are shown below.

245 10 ≠a Build your own gazebo / ≠c by Amanda Blythe.

245 00 ≠a America ≠h [videorecording].

245 14 ≠a The dark of night : ≠b a novel / ≠c by John Rowe.

Description, Potential Uses, Caveats

The title statement field contains information that is usually transcribed directly from the title page, including the title proper (or short title), the subtitle (and other title information, such as the title in another language), and the statement of responsibility (formerly called the "author statement"). These three elements of the title field receive subfield codes ≠a, b, and c, respectively. Punctuation, capitalization, and the order of elements may be altered somewhat in the transcription process; however, they are usually not changed to a significant degree.

The use of the 245 field in an automated environment involves decisions regarding how the title field should be searched, displayed, and filed. For example, which subfields should be indexed (i.e., searchable)? The title and subtitle areas are obvious choices for indexing; however, the information found in the statement of responsibility (subfield ≠c) and the media designator (subfield ≠h) is usually found in another field that is better designed for computer retrieval. Usually, significant information in the statement of responsibility is included as a main or added entry (1XX or 7XX fields) and specific media information is encoded in the Type of record and/or Type of material Leader codes and/or the 007 field (Physical description field).

Some computer systems display a list of shortened entries, and users are required to select the desired entry to view the complete record. Because filing on only the first few words results in a random ordering of longer titles, it is desirable to file entries based on the full title and not just the section of the title that displays.

Generally speaking, the media designator (subfield ≠h) should not be included in the filing of the title field. Inclusion of the medium as part of the primary sort will cause serious filing errors. For example, the single-word title *America* should file before all other titles beginning with the same word, regardless of the media involved. However, if the word *America* is followed by the media designator *videocassette*, filing on the media designator will cause the title to file after almost all other titles beginning with the word *America* (e.g., *America at the turn of the century*, *America through the eyes of a child*, *America vaults ahead*). The most reasonable alternative is to perform a primary sort on the title and then a secondary sort on the media designator. This way all items with the same title will file together, and they will file in order by media designator.

One of the most common and obvious problems related to MARC coding of the 245 field is an incorrect filing indicator (2nd indicator). The purpose of the filing indicator is to enable the computer to disregard articles (*a*, *an*, and *the* and their foreign language equivalents) at the beginning of a field for purposes of filing. The filing indicator should be set to the number of characters that the computer should ignore at the beginning of the field. For example, if the title begins with the article *An*, the filing indicator will be set to *3*, which will allow the computer to skip the article and the space following it and begin filing upon the first nonarticle word. A filing indicator that does not include the correct digit will cause the field to misfile, which in most cases causes the entry to be irretrievable when searched correctly. Because incorrectly set indicators are most often caused by human error, they can be found in any database; however, for various reasons, MARC records devised and added to a database prior to 1976 are more likely to contain incorrect filing indicators. Special computer programs that have been designed to correct filing indicators are discussed in chapter 6, MARC Database Processing.

Since tables of initial articles are used for filing indicator correction, this may give the impression that filing indicators are unnecessary. Filing programs within some online systems (such as online catalogs) refer only to tables and not to the indicators. For example, a table including the English articles *a*, *an*, and *the* would be part of the filing program and the computer would consistently skip these words at the beginning of a title and begin filing on the next word. However, because not all uses of the characters *a*, *an*, and *the* are actually articles, this type of program does not work. The examples below illustrate some of the problems with this type of program.

Title in MARC record	Word under which title will file using table-driven programs
A to Z of gymnastics	to
A is for apple	is
A, B, C	B
A la carte [Title of an English-language work]	la
An the anteater	anteater

Since table-driven filing programs do not allow for exceptions, they are obviously not an improvement over incorrectly set filing indicators. Incorrectly set filing indicators can be corrected, but table-driven filing programs do not allow for exceptions.

250 Edition Statement

USMARC Definition

This field contains information relating to the edition of a work. What constitutes an edition statement is determined by applying various cataloging rules.

Primary indicators and subfield codes for an edition statement are as follows:

1st indicator   Undefined
    ƀ

2nd indicator   Undefined
    ƀ

Subfield code	Portion of field
a	Edition statement
b	Remainder of edition statement

An example of a coded edition statement is shown below.

250 ᵬᵬ ≠a 2nd ed., rev. and corr. / ≠b by Melanie Sandra.

Description, Potential Uses, Caveats

The edition statement includes information regarding the way a particular edition differs from other editions of the same work. In most cases, the edition statement is taken from explicit statements found in the item. The edition may be a different-numbered edition, or it may be a revised edition, illustrated edition, Book Club edition, abridged, unabridged, or any of a variety of other distinctions.

The edition statement generally displays in the same instances that the title displays, directly following the title. Although the edition statement generally is not used as a search parameter, it conceivably could be used to qualify or narrow down a search. Searching or indexing of the edition statement should take into consideration the formatting and abbreviations used within the field, according to *AACR2*.

The tagging of the edition statement can be somewhat confusing because the remainder of edition statement (which often takes the form of an author statement) is in subfield ≠*b*, whereas the actual author statement, which is found in the more familiar 245 field (Title statement), is included as subfield ≠*c* of that field. The two similar statements require two different subfield codes.

260 Publication, Distribution, Etc. (Imprint)

USMARC Definition

This field contains information relating to the publication, printing, distribution, issue, release, or production of a work....

Primary indicators and subfield codes for the publication, distribution, etc. (imprint) field are as follows:

1st indicator	Presence of publisher in imprint
0	Publisher, distributor, etc., is present
1	Publisher, distributor, etc., not present

2nd indicator	Undefined
ᵬ	

Subfield code	Portion of field
a	Place of publication, distribution, etc.
b	Name of publisher, distributor, etc.
c	Date of publication, distribution, etc.

An example of a coded publication, distribution, etc. (imprint) field is shown below.

260 0*b* ≠a New York : ≠b Elsevier, ≠c 1984.

Description, Potential Uses, Caveats

Of the MARC codes in the 260 field, the first indicator is the one most misunderstood and the subfield code *b* is the one most neglected. Fortunately, MARC format integration will make the 260 first indicator obsolete. The 260 first indicator is one of the few instances in the MARC format in which a *0* indicates the *presence* of something while a *1* indicates the *absence* of something.

For purposes of searching, the date of publication is often used as a qualifier to narrow down searches. Usually, however, the dates in the dates portions of the 008 field, not the 260 field, are used for indexing purposes. This is often the case as well for dates that are displayed as part of a truncated display — regardless of what is included as subfield ≠*c* of field 260.

Although the publisher name in the 260 field (subfield ≠*b*) is not usually a searchable element, it holds great value as a search parameter. The variations of publisher names and the ways in which they are transcribed would have to be taken into consideration in the searching and/or indexing of the publisher element of the record. For some publishers, there is also the possibility of using the publisher's ISBN prefix, as found in the 020 field, as a more concise, less ambiguous search key. This possibility is discussed in the 020 field section of this chapter.

For some unknown reason, the subfield code *b* in the 260 field is one of the codes most frequently omitted from MARC records. Many 260 fields that do include the name of the publisher do not contain the proper subfield code for the publisher — only a code *a* (for place) and *c* (for date) are present. In these cases, the computer considers the name of the publisher as part of the place of publication; in effect, the publisher name does not exist in that record.

300 Physical Description

USMARC Definition

This field contains the physical description of the item which consists of the extent of the item and its dimensions and that may also include other physical details of the item and information concerning accompanying material.

Primary indicators and subfield codes for the physical description field are as follows:

1st indicator   Undefined
     ƀ

2nd indicator   Undefined
     ƀ

Subfield code   Portion of field
     a   Extent
     b   Other physical details
     c   Dimensions
     e   Accompanying materials

An example of a coded physical description field is shown below.

300 ƀƀ ǂa 271 p. : ǂb ill., maps ; ǂc 21 cm. + ǂe 1 answer book.

Description, Potential Uses, Caveats

In regard to books, the more familiar terminology for the extent subfield is "number of pages"; for other physical details, it is "illustration statement"; and for dimensions, it is "height." The more generic terms provide for a broader application of cataloging rules and MARC format to materials of all types.

In some cases, particularly for truncated displays or short entries in a printed list or catalog, only subfield ǂa (pagination) is used. Although it is not currently widely used for purposes of searching, the pagination statement could be a useful qualifier, especially with the use of "greater than" or "less than" parameters.

For purposes of searching, specific types of illustrations are stated in coded form in the 008 field; indexing of the 300 subfield ǂb is unnecessary.

The OCLC card production system refers to the subfield ǂc to generate an "oversize" location prefix that prints above call numbers. According to a system user's profile, the oversize designation automatically prints when the height in centimeters is greater than a specified number.

4XX Series Statements

The concept of "series" is one of the most difficult aspects of cataloging for non-catalogers (and catalogers) to grasp. The proper use of the 4XX and 8XX MARC fields requires an understanding of the distinctions between "series statements," "series added entries," "untraced series," "traced series" and "series traced differently." The distinctions between these concepts are partially explained by the difference between the *description* of a cataloged item and *access* to the item. Description of an item generally requires adherence to the content and form of information found on the item being cataloged. Access points, however, may differ from the information found in the description of the item if adhering to the description would create difficulty in locating the item through the catalog. A further explanation of these dynamics is given in the next few paragraphs.

The way that the series is named on the book itself is used as a "series statement" in the catalog entry; it is usually transcribed verbatim as part of the description of that particular item. The series statement is included in the same paragraph on a catalog card as the physical description field. It is usually the last piece of information in that field and has traditionally been enclosed in parentheses, although the parentheses may not appear as part of an online display. Figure 4.1 is an example of a catalog card entry with a series statement.

```
F         Martin, Melanie.
Mar            Itsy-bitsy giant / written by
          Melanie Martin ; illustrated by Doug
          Cushman.--Mahwah, N.J. : Troll
          Associates, c1989.
               48 p. : col. ill. ; 23 cm.
          (Fiddlesticks)
```

Fig. 4.1. Example of a catalog entry with a series statement.

A series statement is part of the description of an item, but the presence of a series statement alone will not enable card catalog users to look up that series in the catalog. To provide access by the series title, a "series added entry" is used. A "series added entry" means that there is an additional card for the series, with the title of the series printed at the top, which is filed under (and enables users to access) the item by series title. Figure 4.2 is an example of a catalog card entry for a series added entry.

```
          Fiddlesticks
F         Martin, Melanie.
Mar            Itsy-bitsy giant / written by
          Melanie Martin ; illustrated by Doug
          Cushman.--Mahwah, N.J. : Troll
          Associates, c1989.
               48 p. : col. ill. ; 23 cm.
          (Fiddlesticks)
```

Fig. 4.2. Example of a catalog card entry for a series added entry.

In a card catalog or online catalog, a "traced series" is one that users can access by the series title. An "untraced series" has no access by the series title. A "series traced differently" is a series that has a series title used for searching that is different from the series statement used in the description of the item. This situation generally arises in one of two cases. One case is when a publisher has expressed a series title in an inconsistent manner from one volume to the next. The second case involves two or more series with the same title.

One example of the first case is a series that the publisher has sometimes called "Geophysics research series" and in other cases has referred to as the "Geophysical research series." (The series has not formally changed names; the publisher has simply been inconsistent in its use of the series title.) The series added entries for these two variations would file separately, with all volumes for the "Geophysical research series" filing before all those that included the "Geophysics research series" entry. For catalog users, this situation would be confusing at best, and it is entirely possible that users would not find those materials under a different title or mistakenly ignore them as being a different series altogether. Rather than provide access in an inconsistent manner, the general practice is for catalogers to choose one of the titles as the form that will be used to provide entries for all variations. This way, users will not have to know or search for all the variations of a series title. Generally, cross-references are provided in the catalog from variations of the title that have not been used as the added entry form.

When there are two or more series with the same title, cataloging practice calls for the cataloger to add to the title a qualifying term or phrase that will distinguish one series from another. Usually this phrase is the place of publication, but other qualifications may be used. For example, a series titled "Open doors," which is published by an architectural organization, needs to be distinguished from another series called "Open doors," which is published by a psychologists' association. The place of publication for the first is Tucson, Arizona, and for the second, New York, New York. The "series traced differently" for the first series would be "Open doors (Tucson, AZ)" and for the second, "Open doors (New York, NY)."

When a "series traced differently" is used, the series statement in the body of the catalog description is the actual text of the series title as taken from the book itself (even though it is not the form of the series title under which an added entry will be made). The series added entry is the form of the series title that has been established to allow for easier searching of works in a particular series.

The MARC 440 field is used for series titles that are traced in the same form as the series statement. The MARC 490 field includes series statements that are not traced at all (first indicator 0) or that are traced differently from the series statement (first indicator 1). For "series traced differently," the form of the series name that is used for added entries is entered in a MARC 8XX field. (MARC 8XX fields are discussed later in this chapter.)

440 Series Statement/Added Entry — Title

USMARC Definition

This field contains a series statement consisting of a series title alone. Field 440 is both a series statement and a series added entry. When a 440 field is present, a corresponding 830 field is not used since it would duplicate the 440 field.

Primary indicators and subfield codes for series statement/added entry – title are as follows:

1st indicator	Undefined
ƀ	
2nd indicator	Nonfiling characters
0-9	Number of nonfiling characters present
Subfield code	Portion of field
a	Uniform title
n	Number of part/section of a work
p	Name of part/section of a work
v	Volume number/sequential designation
x	International Standard Serial Number

Some examples of coded series statement/added entry fields are shown below.

440 ƀ0 ≠a Russian titles for the specialist, ≠x 0305-3741 ; ≠v no. 78

440 ƀ4 ≠a The Rare book tapes. ≠n Series 1 ; ≠v 5

440 ƀ0 ≠a Journal of polymer science. ≠n Part C, ≠p Polymer symposia ;
≠v no. 2

Description, Potential Uses, Caveats

The 440 field contains the title of a series and other related information, including a designation for the particular volume of the series (e.g., volume number) being described. The 440 field is used when the series statement is also an added entry; this implies that the series title will be indexed and displayed.

Probably the most commonly found problem in computer filing of series titles has to do with the volume designation, found in subfield ≠v. If the volume designation is not consistent for all volumes, then volumes will not file in numerical order. For example, if volume 5 has been designated as "vol. 5" and volume 6 has been designated as "v. 6," then volume 6 will file before volume 5, because *v.* files before *vol.* Other variations in the volume designation ("no.," "number"; "v.," "V.," etc.) can also cause entries to file out of order. One possible solution to this problem is to standardize designations. Another possible solution would be for filing routines to simply ignore the volume designation and file on the volume number itself; however, this resolution may not always bring about the desired results, particularly when unusual volume numbering or designation is involved.

490 Series Statement

USMARC Definition

This field contains a series statement for which no series added entry is to be made or for which the series added entry is in a form different from that which appears in the series statement. Unlike the other 4XX fields, field 490 does not serve as a series added entry. When field 490 is used and a series added entry is desired, both the series statement (field 490) and a corresponding series added entry (fields 800-830) are separately recorded in the bibliographic record....

Primary indicators and subfield codes for series statement are as follows:

1st indicator	Specifies whether series is traced
0	Series not traced
1	Series traced differently

2nd indicator	Undefined
b	

Subfield code	Portion of field
a	Uniform title
n	Number of part/section of a work
v	Volume number/sequential designation
x	International Standard Serial Number

Some examples of coded series statements are shown below.

490 0b ≠a Pelican books

490 1b ≠a Uniform crime reports

830 field also in record with 490 1b field:

830 0b ≠a Uniform crime reports (Washington, D.C.)

Description, Potential Uses, Caveats

The primary purpose of the 490 field is to state the form of the series title found on the item cataloged. The series will either not be used as an added entry or the added entry will be in a form different from the series title as found on the cataloged item.

Use of the 490 field implies that the series statement will not be searched or filed, although it will be displayed as part of the bibliographic record; however, use of the 490 field may change within an online environment. Within a card environment, the distinction between traced and untraced series has been made in order to give priority to more important series. This was necessary because sufficient resources were not available to type, file, and maintain cards for all series entries. Within an online environment, however, access to a series statement can be provided without any additional typing or filing. When designing specifications for an online catalog, libraries may be given the option of having all series fields indexed, regardless of the tag. If the library chooses to be able to search the 490 fields, the cataloging and MARC format background of this field should be fully evaluated in light of this change. For example, it should be noted that the 490 field does not include a filing indicator, as the 440 field does; this means that 490 field entries with initial articles will file on the article, not on the first significant word. Libraries would be better off simply tagging all series 440 (or 490 *1* with an 8XX field), rather than give an ambiguous meaning to the 490 field.

5XX Notes

USMARC Definition

Fields 500-59X contain bibliographic notes. Each note is entered as a separate 5XX field. General notes are recorded in field 500 (General Note). Specialized notes are contained in fields 501-585. In general, a specialized note field is defined when access to the data is needed and/or the note is introduced by a distinctive word or phrase.

Information that appears in the notes area on printed output or machine displays is not always recorded in a specially defined 5XX note field. Data is sometimes carried in a structured or coded form in another field (e.g., field 086 (Government Document Classification Number) or field 310 (Current Frequency))....

500 General Note

USMARC Definition

This field contains a note that provides general information for which a specialized note field (i.e., a specific 5XX field) has not been defined.

Description, Potential Uses, Caveats

The 500 field indicators are both undefined (ʬ) and the only commonly used subfield code is *a*.

Information to be included in the 500 field covers a broad range of topics. For example, explanations in regard to the bibliographic description of the item (e.g., source of the title proper, statements of responsibility, information about the publication or distribution of the item) are included in separate 500 fields. Unformatted information about the contents of the work is placed in field 500 (other types of contents notes are placed in field 505 or 520). Information regarding the language(s) of the work or bibliographic history (e.g., previous editions under another title) may also be included as a 500 note.

Although 500 fields are usually included in record displays, they are not usually indexed; however, the most valuable types of information contained within 500 field notes are also represented elsewhere in the record in a form that is more easily accessible or recognizable to the computer. For example, the 008 field and the 041 field both include encoded information about language(s) of the cataloged item. The 008 field indicates whether the item includes an index and includes information as to the content of the work, specifically, whether or not specific types of reference materials are involved (e.g., statistics, abstracts).

504 Bibliography Note

USMARC Definition

This field contains a note indicating the presence of a bibliography(ies), discography(ies), filmography(ies), and/or other bibliographic references in an item. It may also indicate the presence of a bibliography, etc., in accompanying material that is described in the record. For multipart items, including "serials," the note may pertain to all parts or to a single part or issue....

Description, Potential Uses, Caveats

The 504 field indicators are both undefined (ʬ) and the only commonly used subfield code is *a*.

Bibliography notes are formulated according to *AACR2*; they may simply note the existence of bibliographical references in a work. When bibliographical information is confined to a particular section of the book, then page numbers are usually noted as part of the bibliography note.

The 504 field is usually not indexed, but it is usually included as part of a bibliographic display. The Nature of contents code in the 008 field is a more appropriate field to use for access to works including bibliographies; the code could easily be used to narrow a search to works including bibliographies.

505 Formatted Contents Note

USMARC Definition

This field contains a formatted contents note. A contents note usually contains the titles of separate works, or parts of an item, and may also include statements of responsibility associated with the works or parts. Volume numbers and other sequential designations are also included in the contents note, but chapter numbers are generally omitted....

Unformatted contents notes are recorded in field 500 (General Note).

The note is usually displayed and/or printed with an introductory term or phrase that is generated as a display constant based on the first indicator value.

Description, Potential Uses, Caveats

The 505 field is basically a list of titles of separate works that are included in an item, such as short stories within a single volume or songs on a sound recording. The individual titles are separated in the note by a dash with a space on each side. The only commonly used subfield code in field 505 is code *a*.

Within an online environment, the contents note can be accessed through the use of keyword searching. The contents note is not a traditional access point. In a card environment, if the titles in a contents note were to be accessible, an individual added entry card had to be typed and filed for each title. Keyword searching has greatly increased the value of the contents note—individual entries do not need to be made.

Keyword searching of the contents note will be of the greatest value when the distinctions between a keyword search and a title search are clearly understood. In particular, it must be understood that the indexing of a contents note for keyword searching does not necessarily make the titles in that contents note accessible through a title search; generally they will only be accessible through a keyword search. For example, if the title of the short story "The gift of the Magi" is included in a contents note, but not as an added entry, then a keyword search will retrieve that title, but a title search will not. In most cases, a title will be retrievable through a title search only if it is included within a title field or title added entry field.

520 Summary, Abstract, Annotation, Scope, Etc., Note

USMARC Definition

This field contains an unformatted note that describes the scope and general contents of the described materials. This could be a summary, abstract, annotation, or only a phrase describing the material....

The text of the note is sometimes displayed and/or printed with an introductory term that is generated as a display constant based on the first indicator value.

Description, Potential Uses, Caveats

The summary note field is used to give an informal description of the contents or subject of a book in one or a few sentences. The most commonly used subfield in the 520 field is code *a*.

Along with the 505 (Contents) field, the 520 Summary field has been opened up to catalog users through the use of keyword searching. The information in the 520 field can offer access to the record through words or phrases not used elsewhere in the record (thus offering more access), and the information can also offer more specific access, when the note provides more detail than the subject headings in the record. Because the vocabulary in the 520 field is not controlled, use of the field for searching may result in many false hits. For example, use of the word *lime* in a keyword search will retrieve works that refer to lime as a color, a citrus fruit, and a type of rock. By comparison, controlled vocabulary, such as is used with subject headings, allows searchers to specify a particular meaning of the word. Controlled vocabulary helps to eliminate false hits.

6XX Subject Access Fields

USMARC Definition

The 6XX fields contain subject access entries and terms. Most of these fields contain subject added entries or access terms based on the lists and authority files identified in the second indicator (Subject heading system/thesaurus) or in subfield ≠2 (Source of subject heading or term). One field contains uncontrolled subject access data.

The MARC 6XX fields include subject headings of various types: personal, corporate and meeting names, uniform titles, topical, and geographical headings used as subjects.

The MARC coding for the 6XX fields is similar to that for other heading fields (e.g., 1XX, 7XX fields). There are two primary differences: in the 6XX fields the second indicator is used differently and there are three additional subfield codes that are used only with subject headings. The second indicator is defined to indicate which subject heading list or authority file has authorized the heading. For example, headings assigned according to the Library of Congress subject headings or the Library of Congress authority file are coded as second indicator *0*. Three subfield codes have been assigned for use with subject heading subdivisions: *x* for general subdivisions; *y* for chronological subdivisions; and *z* for geographical subdivisions. Examples of the use of these subdivisions and subfield codes are given in the sections for individual tags below.

Two precautions are given for use of the subdivision subfield codes. One is that the general subdivision covers many subdivisions that are designed for use with only one subject heading or one type of subject heading. The subdivisions are called "general" simply because they do not fit into either of the other two categories of "chronological" or "geographical"; in many cases, general subdivisions are actually quite specific and meant for use only in a narrowly defined manner. General subdivisions should not be confused with "free-floating" subdivisions, which can be used with any appropriate subject heading.

Another precaution involving the use of subdivision subfields involves the chronological subdivision subfield, y. In many cases, subfield ≠y includes only the date range of the chronological subdivision, such as 1960-1974; however, in other cases, the subfield includes textual information in addition to the dates, such as Revolution, 1775-1783. Both the ALA filing rules (Rule 8.7.2) and the Library of Congress filing rules (Rule 16.7.1) stipulate that such subdivisions file chronologically (numerically), disregarding the initial alphabetic characters for the purposes of filing. Nevertheless, many computerized filing systems erroneously file upon the alphabetic characters found in the y subfield. Filing upon the alphabetic characters not only separates those subject headings from the rest of the chronological file (where subdivisions include only numerics) but also causes those subject headings to file out of chronological order in relation to each other. Libraries should determine whether the system they rely upon files such subfields correctly, and, if not, they should request that the filing be corrected. If a vendor has advertised or agreed that the ALA (or LC) filing rules will be followed, such rectification should not incur an extra charge to the library.

Because the 6XX and 7XX fields look similar to each other and because they are both located in the same area of a catalog card or MARC record, the distinction between subject headings (6XX fields) and added entries (7XX fields) sometimes requires clarification. Subject entries (6XX fields) indicate the subject matter of a work, that is, what the work is about. Other added entries (7XX fields) name a person or a group of people that has been connected with the creation or issuance of a particular work; or, they name another title for the work (such as a subtitle) or the title of a related work (such as a previous edition).

600 Subject Added Entry—Personal Name

Primary indicators and subfield codes for personal name subject added entry are as follows:

1st indicator	Personal name entry element
0	Forename
1	Single surname
2	Multiple surname

2nd indicator	Subject heading system/thesaurus
0	LC subject headings/LC authority files
1	LC subject headings for children's literature
8	Sears subject headings [OCLC-defined indicator]

Subfield code	Portion of field
a	Personal name
q	Fuller form of name
d	Dates associated with a name
x	General subdivision
y	Chronological subdivision
z	Geographical subdivision

Two examples of coded personal name subject added entries are shown below.

600 10 ≠a Pushkin, Aleksandr Sergeevich, ≠d 1799-1837 ≠x Museums, relics, etc. ≠z Russian S.F.S.R. ≠z Moscow ≠x Maps.

600 00 ≠a Jesus Christ ≠x History of doctrines ≠y Early Church, ca. 30-600.

Description, Potential Uses, Caveats

The 600 field includes names of persons who are the subject of a work. Except for the second indicator (subject heading system used) and additional subfields (including *x*, *y*, and *z*), the description, potential uses, and caveats for the 600 field are quite similar to those of the 100 and 700 fields.

610 Subject Added Entry — Corporate Name

Primary indicators and subfield codes for corporate name subject added entries are as follows:

1st indicator	Corporate name entry element
1	Jurisdiction name
2	Name in direct order

2nd indicator	Subject heading system/thesaurus
0	LC subject headings/LC authority files
1	LC subject headings for children's literature
8	Sears subject headings [OCLC-defined indicator]

Subfield code	Portion of field
a	Corporate or jurisdiction name
b	Subordinate unit
x	General subdivision
y	Chronological subdivision
z	Geographical subdivision

Two examples of coded corporate name subject added entries are shown below.

610 10 ≠a United States. ≠b Army ≠x History ≠y Civil War, 1861-1865.

610 20 ≠a United Nations ≠z Africa.

Description, Potential Uses, Caveats

The 610 field includes names of corporate bodies that are the subject of a work. Except for the second indicator (which indicates the subject heading system used) and additional subfields (including *x*, *y*, and *z*), the description, uses, and caveats for the 610 field are quite similar to those of the 110 and 710 fields.

611 Subject Added Entry — Meeting Name

Primary indicators and subfield codes for meeting name subject added entry are as follows:

1st indicator	Meeting name entry element
2	Name in direct order
2nd indicator	Subject heading system/thesaurus
0	LC subject headings/LC authority files
1	LC subject headings for children's literature
8	Sears subject headings [OCLC-defined indicator]
Subfield code	Portion of heading
a	Meeting or jurisdiction name
d	Date of meeting
c	Location of meeting
n	Number of part/section/meeting
x	General subdivision

An example of a coded meeting name subject added entry is shown below.

611 20 ≠a Olympic Games ≠n (23rd : ≠d 1984 : ≠c Los Angeles, Calif.) ≠x Periodicals.

Description, Potential Uses, Caveats

The 611 field includes the name of a meeting that is the subject of a work. Except for the second indicator (which indicates the subject heading system used) and additional subfields (including *x*, *y*, and *z*), the description, uses, and caveats for the 611 field are quite similar to those of the 111 and 711 fields.

630 Subject Added Entry — Uniform Title

Primary indicators and subfield codes for uniform title subject added entry are as follows:

1st indicator	Nonfiling characters
0-9	Number of nonfiling characters present
2nd indicator	Subject heading system/thesaurus
0	LC subject headings/LC authority files
1	LC subject headings for children's literature
8	Sears subject headings [OCLC-defined indicator]
Subfield code	Portion of field
a	Uniform title
n	Number of part/section of a work
p	Name of part/section of a work
l	Language of a work
s	Version
x	General subdivision

Some examples of coded uniform title subject added entries are shown below.

630 00 ≠a Bible. ≠l English ≠x Versions.

630 00 ≠a Ukrainian weekly ≠x Indexes ≠x Periodicals.

630 00 ≠a Bible. ≠p N.T. ≠p Romans ≠x Geography ≠x Maps.

Description, Potential Uses, Caveats

The 630 field includes a uniform title for a work that is the subject of another work. Except for the second indicator (which indicates the subject heading system used) and additional subfields (including *x*, *y*, and *z*), the description, uses, and caveats for the 630 field are quite similar to those of the 130 and 730 fields.

650 Subject Added Entry — Topical Term

USMARC Definition

This field contains a topical subject used as a subject added entry. Topical subject added entries may consist of general subject terms including names of events or objects. Subject added entries are assigned to a bibliographic record to provide access according to generally accepted thesaurus-building rules....

A title (e.g., Bible and atheism), a geographic name (e.g., Iran in the Koran) or the name of a corporate body (e.g., Catholic Church in motion pictures) used in a phrase subject heading are also recorded in field 650.

Primary indicators and subfield codes for topical term subject added entries are as follows:

1st indicator	Nonfiling characters
ƀ	

2nd indicator	Subject heading system/thesaurus
0	LC subject headings/LC authority files
1	LC subject headings for children's literature
8	Sears subject headings [OCLC-defined indicator]

Subfield code	Portion of field
a	Topical term
x	General subdivision
y	Chronological subdivision
z	Geographical subdivision

Some examples of coded topical term subject added entries are shown below.

650 ƀ0 ǂa Kalmyk cattle.

650 ƀ0 ǂa Art ǂx Exhibitions.

650 ƀ0 ǂa Music ǂy 500-1400.

650 ƀ0 ǂa Real property ǂz Mississippi ǂz Tippah County ǂx Maps.

Description, Potential Uses, Caveats

The MARC 650 field includes subject headings that are not personal, corporate, or geographical names or titles. The subject headings included in the 650 fields are entered in the 650 subfield ǂa, and they may be further subdivided (specified) by general, chronological, or geographical subdivisions (subfields ǂx, ǂy, and ǂz respectively).

651 Subject Added Entry — Geographic Name

USMARC Definition

This field contains a geographic name used as a subject added entry. Subject added entries are assigned to a bibliographic record to provide access according to generally accepted cataloging and thesaurus-building rules....

Jurisdiction names alone or followed by subject subdivisions are contained in 651 fields. A name of a jurisdiction that represents an ecclesiastical entity is contained in a 610 field. A corporate name, a form subheading, a title of a work and/or a city section name entered under the name of a jurisdiction are contained in 610 fields. Geographic names used in phrase subject headings (e.g., Iran in the Koran) are contained in 650 fields.

Primary indicators and subfield codes for geographic name subject added entries are as follows:

1st indicator	Nonfiling characters
ƀ	

2nd indicator	Subject heading system/thesaurus
0	LC subject headings/LC authority files
1	LC subject headings for children's literature
8	Sears subject headings [OCLC-defined indicator]

Subfield code	Portion of field
a	Geographic name
x	General subdivision
y	Chronological subdivision
z	Geographical subdivision

Some examples of coded geographic name subject added entries are shown below.

651 ƀ0 ǂa Amazon River

651 ƀ0 ǂa Aix-en-Provence (France) ǂx Social life and customs ǂx Early works to 1800.

651 ƀ0 ǂa Greece ǂx History ǂy Geometric period, ca. 900-700 B.C.

651 ƀ0 ǂa United States ǂx Boundaries ǂz Canada.

Description, Potential Uses, Caveats

The MARC 651 field includes geographical names that are not being used as jurisdiction (e.g., governmental) names. Generally speaking, a geographical name heading that is followed by a subdivision other than x, y, or z is considered as a jurisdiction name and should be entered in a corporate name (X10, X11) field rather than the 651 field.

700-740 Added Entries

USMARC Definition

Fields 700-730 contain added entries that provide additional access to a bibliographic record from names and/or titles having various relationships to a work. Added entries are made for persons, corporate bodies, and meetings having some form of responsibility for the creation of the work, including intellectual and publishing responsibilities. The fields also contain added entries for other titles related to the work for which the record is made, such as other editions, etc. Field 740 contains variant titles for the work being cataloged. Added entries are assigned to records for persons, corporate bodies, meetings, and titles which are not given access through subject or series entries....

700 Added Entry — Personal Name

Primary indicators and subfield codes for personal name added entries are as follows:

1st indicator	Personal name entry element
0	Forename
1	Single surname
2	Multiple surname

2nd indicator	Type of added entry
0	Alternative entry
1	Secondary entry
2	Analytical entry

Subfield code	Portion of field
a	Personal name
q	Fuller form of name
d	Dates associated with a name
t	Title of a work
f	Date of a work

Some examples of coded personal name added entries are shown below.

700 10 ≠a Pickford, Mary, ≠d 1893-1979.

700 11 ≠a Shakespeare, William, ≠d 1564-1616. ≠t Hamlet.

700 12 ≠a Hazlitt, William, ≠d 1778-1830. ≠t On the fear of death.
≠l French & English. ≠f 1966.

Description, Potential Uses, Caveats

The MARC 700 field includes the name of a person involved with the creation or issuance of a work. Except for the second indicator (type of added entry) and some additional subfields, the description, potential uses, and caveats for the 700 field are quite similar to those of the 100 and 600 fields.

Author-title entries (more commonly found as 7XX fields than as 6XX fields) sometimes present a special filing problem. Although the title portion of the entry (subfield ≠t) sometimes begins with an article, which should be ignored for filing purposes, there is no filing indicator for titles that are embedded within a field (i.e., titles not included as subfield ≠a). When the initial article is included as part of the title subfield, most existing computer programs incorrectly file the title portion under the initial article, rather than skipping to the first non-article word. If the cataloger has omitted the initial article from the subfield ≠t, the field will file in the correct order, but it may alter the meaning of the title. Also, when a catalog includes entries both with and without the initial article, these entries will file separately within the catalog. Users will need to search both ways to find all entries.

710 Added Entry – Corporate Name

Primary indicators and subfield codes for corporate name added entries are as follows:

1st indicator	Corporate name entry element
1	Jurisdiction name
2	Name in direct order
2nd indicator	Type of added entry
0	Alternative entry
1	Secondary entry
2	Analytical entry
Subfield code	Portion of field
a	Corporate or jurisdiction name
b	Subordinate unit
t	Title of a work

Two examples of coded corporate name added entries are shown below.

710 11 ≠a United States. ≠b Dept. of State. ≠t Department of State bulletin

710 11 ≠a Brookfield (Conn.) ≠t Charter

Description, Potential Uses, Caveats

The MARC 710 field includes the name of a corporate body involved with the creation or issuance of a work. Although the indicators and some of the subfields may be different, the description, potential uses, and caveats for the 710 field are quite similar to those of the 700, 110, and 610 fields.

711 Added Entry — Meeting Name

Primary indicators and subfield codes for meeting name added entry are as follows:

1st indicator	Meeting name entry element
2	Name in direct order
2nd indicator	Type of added entry
0	Alternative entry
1	Secondary entry
2	Analytical entry
Subfield code	Portion of field
a	Meeting or jurisdiction name
d	Date of meeting

c	Location of meeting
n	Number of part/section/meeting
t	Title of a work

An example of a coded meeting name added entry is shown below.

711 21 ≠a IGU Symposium in Urban Geography ≠d (1960 : ≠c Lund, Sweden).
≠t Proceedings

Description, Potential Uses, Caveats

The MARC 711 field includes the name of a meeting that is related in some way to the creation or issuance of a work. Although the indicators and some subfields may be different, the description, potential uses, and caveats for the 711 field are quite similar to those of the 700, 111, and 611 fields.

730 Added Entry — Uniform Title

Primary indicators and subfield codes for uniform title added entries are as follows:

1st indicator	Nonfiling characters
0-9	Number of nonfiling characters present

2nd indicator	Type of added entry
0	Alternative entry
1	Secondary entry
2	Analytical entry

Subfield code	Portion of field
a	Uniform title
n	Number of part/section of a work
p	Name of part/section of a work
l	Language of a work
s	Version

Two examples of coded uniform title added entries are shown below.

730 00 ≠a Bible. ≠p O.T. ≠p Judges V. ≠l German ≠s Grether

730 00 ≠a People speak (Radio program)

Description, Potential Uses, Caveats

The MARC 730 field includes the name of a work that is related in some way to the creation or issuance of another work. Although the indicators and some subfields may be different, the description, potential uses, and caveats for the 730 field are quite similar to those of the 700, 130, and 630 fields.

The 730 field is one of the two primary title added entry fields, the other being the 740 field. One obvious question that arises pertains to the difference between the 730 field and the 740 field. The MARC tag 730 is used with added entries that are for a uniform title for another work; the 740 tag is for a variant title of the item being cataloged. An example of a use of a 730 field would be for a publication that is a supplement to another publication. The inclusion of each title in a 730 field within the record for the other title would be explained by a note within each record pertaining to the relationship between the two titles.

740 Added Entry — Variant Title

USMARC Definition

This field contains a form of title that is different from the title proper portion of the title statement (field 245 subfields ≠a, ≠n, and ≠p) but that is not the uniform title for the work. This kind of added entry is assigned according to various cataloging rules to give access to forms of a title which would otherwise not be possible. The form of title in a 740 field will often be explained in a note field (5XX).

Primary indicators and subfield codes for variant title added entries are as follows:

1st indicator	Nonfiling characters
0-9	Number of nonfiling characters present
2nd indicator	Type of added entry
1	Secondary entry
2	Analytical entry
Subfield code	Portion of field
a	Title
n	Number of part/section of a work
p	Name of part/section of a work

Two examples of coded variant title added entries are shown below.

740 01 ≠a History of the world. ≠n Part 1.

740 41 ≠a The Hielsdorfer Files. ≠p Chemical. ≠p Administrative.

Description, Potential Uses, Caveats

The MARC 740 field includes a title that is a variation of the title of the work being cataloged. In many instances, the variant title is a subtitle, which may be just as well known or better known than the title proper. In other cases, the 740 field includes the title of preceding or succeeding editions, sequels, or other such variations of an edition of a work. Usually, when the 740 includes a variant title other than a subtitle, the relationship is explained within a note field in the catalog record. Although the indicators and some subfields may be different, the description, potential uses, and caveats for the 740 field are quite similar to those of the 700, 130, 630, and 730 fields.

830 Series Added Entry — Uniform Title

USMARC Definition

This field contains a title series added entry in which the entry of the series is under uniform title. It is used when the added entry form of a series title is different from that in the corresponding series statement. When the 830 field is used, the series statement should be contained in a 490 field or a note concerning the series should be in a 5XX note field.

Primary indicators and subfield codes for uniform title series added entries are as follows:

1st indicator	Undefined
ƀ	
2nd indicator	Nonfiling characters
0-9	Number of nonfiling characters present
Subfield code	Portion of field
a	Uniform title
n	Number of part/section of a work
p	Name of part/section of a work
v	Volume number/sequential designation

Two examples of coded uniform title added entries are shown below.

830 ƀ0 ǂa Musica da camera (Oxford University Press) ; ǂv 72

490 1ƀ field also in record with 830 field:

490 ƀ1 ǂa Musica da camera ; ǂv 72

Description, Potential Uses, Caveats

The MARC 830 field includes a series added entry. The MARC 830 field is generally used in one of two situations. The primary instance is when the series title is traced in a different form from which it appears in the 490 field (490 field, first indicator *1*—series traced differently). The other instance is when a work has been published previously as part of a series, but in this edition (e.g., by another publisher) it has not been published as part of the same series. Usually, the relationship is explained in a note within the catalog record, and the record does not include a 4XX field for the series that is named in the 830 field.

There are two primary reasons for tracing a series title differently than it appears in a work. One is that the way in which the title appears in the work is a variation of the way it has usually appeared in other titles in the series. To maintain uniformity for the ease of catalog use, the predominant, "established" form of the series title is used as an entry in the catalog. The other reason for tracing a series title differently than it appears in a work is that several different series may be published under exactly the same title page title. To differentiate between these titles within a catalog, some additional identifying information (such as the place of publication) has been added to each series title.

Although the indicators and some subfields may be different, the potential uses and caveats for the 830 field are similar to those of the 700, 440, 730, and 740 fields.

MARC FORMAT INTEGRATION

MARC format integration involves the consolidation of the different formats for different types of materials into one format for all types of materials. Because of some existing conflicts and discrepancies among the different existing formats as they were originally developed, MARC users will find that the integrated format contains a few major differences in the way that certain fields are used.

Probably the two most significant differences between the existing MARC formats and the integrated MARC format are the implementation of the 006 field and a difference in the way that the 246 and 740 fields are used.

The 006 field is being introduced to accommodate the material characteristics of different types of materials that are part of an item being cataloged. This is especially valuable for multimedia items that include different formats of material. The 006 field includes coded information regarding characteristics of a specific type of material, such as whether an archival item is in microform or the form of composition of a musical score (such as "studies and exercises," "anthems," or "bluegrass music"). As many 006 fields may be included within a MARC record as are required to describe the different types of material that are involved.

The use of the 740 field, which has historically been used for variant titles of the item being described in the record, as well as some other related titles, will be much more limited under MARC format integration. Field 246 will be used to contain variant titles for all types of materials after MARC format integration takes place in 1993. Variant titles are usually shortened titles or subtitles of the work described in the catalog record that are likely to be used as access points by catalog users.

The changes that will be made to the MARC bibliographic format are discussed in more detail at the end of chapter 2, MARC Format Structure and Content Designation. Major changes will not go into effect until 1993, with less extensive changes being implemented much sooner. Format changes resulting from MARC format integration have been categorized into the following types:

1. Deleted content designators include codes that had been reserved for a number of years but not fully defined.

2. Obsolete content designators include codes that were seldom-used or not used under current (post-1980) cataloging conventions; some specialized notes fields; codes that had been unclearly defined, causing deviation in their use; and codes that had been established primarily to assist in creating brief records, but which had not been used for that or other purposes. These codes will continue to appear in USMARC bibliographic format documentation, but the documentation will state that the elements should no longer be used in records (new or retrospective) being input. The codes will appear, if used, in older records already input.

3. New content designators include several new codes to be added to the format.

4. Name changes include changing the names of some codes that were not clear, in some cases, when they became valid for additional forms of material beyond the one for which they were originally created. These names will be changed to clarify the appropriate data content.

5. New type-of-material validity for content designators includes new validation of some codes. Because MARC format integration basically involves extending the validity of all codes across all types of material, some codes that were originally created for use with one type of material will be validated for use with other types of material.

6. Other conventions used include changes in specific elements. When an element (either a fixed field code or a variable data field indicator) is "undefined," the element position contains a blank. The notation *b* is used to show the value *blank*.

NOTES

1.   For discussions on codes for other types of materials, see: Crawford, Walt, *MARC for library use: Understanding integrated USMARC* (Boston: G. K. Hall, 1989).

2.   Bohdan Wynar, *Introduction to cataloging and classification*, 7th ed. (Littleton, Colo.: Libraries Unlimited, 1985), 43.

3.   "Unique numbers in machine-readable cataloging," *Library systems newsletter* 8 (May 1988): 34-36.

4.   "Library of Congress rule interpretations," *Cataloging service bulletin* 45 (Summer 1989): 9.

5.   In working with dozens of libraries using LC card numbers for retrospective conversion searching, the author's "educated guesstimate" was that about one-third of the LCCNs printed by publishers in books were incorrect. This estimate was later upheld by a library that had documented the number of LCCNs in books that had resulted in receipt of the wrong card sets (e.g., cards for another edition or another title) when used to order cards from the Library of Congress; approximately 30 percent of the LCCNs were incorrect.

6.   *Anglo-American cataloguing rules*, 2nd ed. 1988 revisions (Chicago: American Library Association, 1988), 312.

7.   Ibid., 313.

RELATED READINGS

Aveney, Brian. "Tails wagging dogs." *Journal of library automation* 14 (1): 5 (January 1981).

Byrne, Deborah. "The much-misunderstood MARC fixed field." *Action for libraries* 13 (2)-13 (4) (February 1987-April 1987).

5

MARC Records on Magnetic
Tape and Floppy Disk

TAPE AND DISK: SOME
INTRODUCTORY COMPARISONS

Computer tape and floppy disk are the two most familiar and commonly used methods for transporting and storing MARC records. Traditionally, tape has been considered more as a mainframe-related storage device, and floppy disk has been connected more with microcomputers. However, advances in the technology and the blurring of differences between computers of all sizes are allowing users of all kinds of computers to avail themselves of the advantages of both types of magnetic media. Three primary differences between tape and disk are: their compactness (both in terms of storage and physical size), their durability, and the means of access to data they provide to users.

The average tape can hold over 20,000 MARC records, while the average floppy disk can hold a few hundred MARC records. For larger files of MARC records, tape is obviously the more compact storage method; however, for storage of just a few records, floppy disk is a more compact method, since a floppy disk is smaller than even the smaller size of tape reel. In general, tape is the more durable medium of the two, partly because of the way it is constructed and stored and partly because of the way it is used. Although both tape and disk can be damaged by environmental factors, tape is less vulnerable to some factors. Because only the outermost layer and edges of the tape are generally exposed, tape on a tape reel is comparatively well protected from dust, smoke, and other such environmental elements. On the other hand, some part of the "playing surface" of a floppy disk is exposed at all times, with several openings in the cover of the disk allowing a potential entry point for dust and other foreign material. To use records on a MARC tape, the tape is generally read into a computer where the records are loaded onto hard disk for use by the computer, and no further access to the tape itself is involved. On the other hand, to use records on floppy disk, records are accessed, read from, and written directly to the floppy disk as needed, making for a much more constant use of the disk. This, of course, affects the useful life of the disk.

The two methods for accessing records on magnetic media are called "sequential access" and "direct access." These access methods provide another means for comparing tape and disk. While tape provides only sequential access, disk can be used for either sequential access or direct access. The difference between these two types of access can be illustrated by comparing the computer media to two familiar audio counterparts: audiocassette tape and phonodisc. To reach a particular point on an audio-tape, it is necessary to move from the starting point, through all intervening tape, to the desired position on the tape. All entries (songs or other recorded material) on the audio-tape must be accessed in sequence; there is no way to skip from the first entry to the fifth without passing through the second, third, and fourth on the way. By comparison, to reach a particular point on a phonodisc, two methods of access are possible. One method is to begin at the starting point of the disk, and play all material in sequence until the desired point is reached. This is *sequential access*. The other method is to direct the playing arm to the desired point on the disc, skipping all intervening material. This is *direct access*, a method similar to direct access of files on a floppy disk.

TAPE AND DISK: SOME COMMONALITIES

Bits and Bytes

Both tape and floppy disk are constructed of a base, usually some type of plastic (such as mylar, polyester, or acetate), that is coated with magnetic particles. A computer reads or writes data through the use of magnetized spots that are arranged in a particular way on the tape or disk. Each magnetized spot represents a "bit," which is the smallest unit of information that a computer uses. The word *bit* is actually a contraction of the phrase *binary digit*. In binary notation, only two digits are used: zero and one. The two different bits are represented on tape by spots that are magnetized in two different ways. A spot magnetized one way sends one distinct type of electrical pulse to the computer, which the computer interprets as either a 0 or a 1.

A computer is programmed to look at a specific number of bits and then to interpret the arrangement of 0s and 1s as a coded representation of a letter, number, punctuation, or other type of symbol used by humans. For example, the bit arrangement of 01000001 represents the capital letter *A* and the bit arrangement of 01110000 represents the lower-case letter *p*.

A grouping of bits is referred to as a "byte." In some ways, the use of bits and bytes by a computer is comparable to humans' use of letters and words. The smallest unit of data for computers is a bit; for humans, a letter. Bits are grouped together in meaningful (to the computer) combinations known as bytes, and letters are grouped together in meaningful (to humans) combinations known as words. In fact, in relation to data processing, bytes are also sometimes referred to as words. One major difference is that, within any given context, bytes are limited to a specific number of bits per "word," while "human words" are regularly composed of a widely varying quantity of letters.

There are some common misconceptions about the way in which characters are represented on a computer tape or disk. One of these is that each character is simply a very miniaturized version of a human-readable character. And, because the interpretation of binary notation appears to be a rather tedious process, the question arises as to why such a complex method is used to represent characters to the computer. A primary reason for using binary encoding is that, compared to graphic characters (such as letters of the alphabet), binary notation is an explicit, specific, and unambiguous way of communication that can be easily understood. To illustrate the difference, one good example is the interpretation of the letter *c*. As with many letters of the alphabet, the only difference between an uppercase and lowercase *c* is the size of the letter. To interpret the letter *c* as uppercase or lowercase, it is necessary to compare that letter to other letters and/or to evaluate the context in which the *c* is used. Even to the human eye, interpreting a predetermined group of 0s and 1s as representing a specific letter is a much more reliable method than trying to judge the meaning of the graphic representation.

A byte of data is commonly expressed in groupings of six, seven, or eight bits. The difference is that the use of an 8-bit byte provides for the representation of many more characters through different arrangements of bits, 8-bit bytes can be presented in 256 different arrangements, while 7-bit bytes offer only 128 possible variations. A 7-bit code of representation thus accommodates uppercase and lowercase alphabet (52 characters), numbers (10 characters), as well as some common punctuation and other such symbols and special characters that are used to represent specific messages to the computer. An 8-bit code allows for a much more comprehensive and specific method of communication. An 8-bit code accommodates a fuller range of the symbols used in social and scientific languages, such as diacritical marks, Greek characters, and superscript and subscript characters. Examples of eight-bit binary combinations and the characters they signify are shown in figure 5.1.

Binary character combination	Character
00110001	1
00110010	2
00110011	3
00111010	: (colon)
01000001	A
01000010	B
01100001	a
01100010	b

Fig. 5.1. Examples of eight-bit binary combinations (ASCII) and the characters they represent.

ASCII, EBCDIC

Of course, the arrangement of bits in a byte is not arbitrary. In order for one computer to be able to read or write the data of another computer, an established coding scheme is necessary. There are two widely used standards for this purpose. One is EBCDIC (pronounced EB-suh-dik or EB-kuh-dik), which stands for *Extended Binary Coded Decimal Interchange Code*. This code was developed by IBM. The other coding scheme is ASCII (pronounced ASK-ee), which is an abbreviation for *American Standard Code for Information Interchange*. ASCII was developed through the American National Standards Institute (ANSI) and is the most widely used scheme of binary notation. Because ASCII is by far the most-used system of binary notation used for MARC records, this discussion will focus primarily on ASCII.

The development of 8-bit coding schemes came about when it became obvious that the use of 7-bit bytes (158 different characters) did not provide for all of the characters that were desired for any given application. Within ASCII, 8-bit codes include all of the established notations from the 7-bit code. And, an 8-bit scheme includes codes for additional characters as well. In other words, the 8-bit scheme does not involve different notations for arrangements that were established in the 7-bit scheme. The 7-bit representations of characters have been expanded to 8-bits simply by adding a 0 as the eighth bit. Additional characters are represented by using all of the same character combinations that have been used for the 7-bit bytes and then adding a 1 instead of 0 as the last bit. The expanded coding schemes are referred to as "8-bit ASCII" (or EBCDIC) or "extended ASCII" (or EBCDIC). Although there is one standardized 8-bit ASCII scheme, there are at least two widely used variations of 8-bit EBCDIC.

The 8-bit ASCII includes the 7-bit code established as ANSI standard X3.4 (titled "Code for Information Interchange") and the extensions defined in ANSI standard Z39.47 (titled "Extended Latin Alphabet Coded Character Set for Bibliographic Use"). Z39.47 is also referred to as ANSEL. The predecessor of ANSI Z39.47 was a standardized definition called the "ALA Character Set" or "ALA Extended ASCII." (Yes, "ALA" stands for "American Library Association.") The ALA Character Set, devised more than a decade before the ANSI standard, is also intended for use in MARC records as well as other bibliographic information interchange. The two standards are in some ways considered to be synonymous, although some theoretical and mechanical differences exist. The Library of Congress and many other MARC record distributors now stipulate their adherence to the ANSI standard, although the phrase *ALA Character Set* may be used as an informal and more traditional way of communicating the same idea.

MARC RECORDS ON TAPE

Introduction

Magnetic tape has been used as a computer storage medium since the 1950s and has retained many of its original properties. Computer tape looks and feels a lot like audiocassette tape, which makes sense, since video, audio, and computer tapes are all magnetic tapes. Computer tape is usually brown and measures one-half-inch wide. Common tape lengths are 2,400, 1,200, and 600 feet. The tape is stored on reels.

Although the use of tape does have its disadvantages (for example, records on tape are not as readily accessible as those on disk), most transporting of records from one place to another is done by placing the records on tape and shipping the tape. When a library obtains its MARC database from a MARC vendor, the records are usually sent to the library on tape, especially if large numbers of records are involved. When a library wants to have its records processed for authority control or other database preparation purposes, records will generally be sent to the processing vendor on tape. When processing is completed, the original records from the library, the input tapes, will be sent back to the library by the vendor, along with the processed records on another set of tapes, the output tapes. When the library loads the processed (output) tapes into an in-house system, they are considered in that case to be *input* tapes! In addition to being a preferred method for transporting records, computer tape is also the method of choice for storing archival or backup copies of machine-readable databases.

How Computer Tapes Work

The computer reads records from or writes records to a magnetic tape through the use of a tape drive. A tape drive holds two tape reels, the source reel and the take-up reel. (In this manner, the tape drive works somewhat like a film projector.) The tape drive moves the tape across the read/write head, which uses electricity to "read" a previously magnetized pattern of bits or to "write" information to the tape by magnetizing the tracks in a predetermined pattern. Data is processed in blocks, instead of all at once, because only a limited amount of computer memory, called the "buffer," is used as a holding area for data that is being input or output. The computer does not process the tape at a uniform speed. There are gaps between the blocks of data that allow the computer to complete processing on each block before moving on to the next.

MARC Tape Characteristics

The discussion below focuses on terms and concepts that are used regarding records on computer tape. Some of the characteristics involve alternatives that libraries will be required to specify when ordering MARC records on tape or having tapes processed by a vendor. In most cases, these specifications are not a matter of choice but a matter of how the tapes will be used by the library. For example, if the library is having its tapes processed prior to loading them into an online system, then the online system vendor should be consulted to determine which characteristics are appropriate to the online system.

Nine-track Tape

There are nine tracks that run the length of the tape, and bits on the tape are arranged in rows that run the width of the tape. The first eight tracks hold the 8-bit ASCII (or EBCDIC) code. The last track holds an extra bit, known as the parity bit, which is used as an error check but is not interpreted as part of the code itself.

BPI (Bytes Per Inch)

Tape density is measured in bytes per inch, also called CPI (characters per inch). This is a measure of how many characters are stored within an inch of tape. The most commonly used densities are 1600 bpi (the most-used density), 800 bpi (the lowest density), and 6250 bpi.

Parity

A parity check is a type of error detection used to determine whether tapes are still readable. Tapes are either *even* parity or *odd* parity. *Even parity* means that the sum of the bits in each row will be an even number. Parity is set by using the parity bit, the bit in the ninth track of the tape. This track is used only for error-checking purposes, not as part of the binary code. When the tape is being written, the parity bit is set to 0 or 1, according to the total of the other characters in a given row. In a parity check, the computer adds together the bits from all nine tracks. For example, the sum of the characters in the binary number 01000001 is 2; for 01110001, the sum is 4. For each of these binary numbers, the parity bit would be set to 0 to achieve even parity and to 1 for odd parity. Parity errors indicate that not all bits on the tape can be read. Usually they occur either because the tape needs cleaning or because it has sustained damage. The more parity errors there are, the less usable the tape is.

To determine whether a tape should be replaced because of parity errors, one should consider the cost of replacing a tape as compared to the cost of replacing the individual records that cannot be read. If only a few records are affected, then it may be much more practical to lose those few records (and try to replace them some other way) than to spend the time and money on acquiring a replacement tape of all of the records. In fact, if the library has a high rate of duplication because of multiple uses of a record, then replacing the records may be uncalled for. On the other hand, if hundreds of records are involved, it may be necessary, for practical as well as economic reasons, to simply replace the tape. In any case, if parity errors are found on a tape that is still under warranty, then the tape should be replaced under the warranty.

Blocked, Unblocked Records

Because there is not enough room in a computer's buffer to process all input or output data at one time, a computer tape is not completely filled with rows of bits from beginning to end. Instead, a certain number of rows of bits are grouped together, in groupings small enough to be held in the buffer at one time. These grouped rows, or data blocks, are separated by blank spaces, or gaps, known as "interrecord gaps," or "interblock gaps." The two primary ways of grouping data are *blocked* and *unblocked*.

Blocked data on a computer tape is arranged in groupings of a consistent size. USMARC records follow the standard of 2,048 characters per block. Each block may contain a portion of a record, a complete record, or more than one record. At the beginning of each MARC record (or portion of a record within a block), a special code indicates one of four conditions:

1. a complete record that begins and ends within the 2,048-character data block

2. the beginning of a record that is continued within the next block

3. the end of a record that has been continued from the previous block

4. the intermediate portion of a record that began in the previous block and is continued in the next block

In situation number 1, the MARC record obviously has fewer than 2,048 characters; situation number 4 obviously involves a MARC record that has more than 2,048 characters. Because the average MARC record contains fewer than 1,000 characters, most blocks will include two or more complete MARC records.

Unblocked data on a computer tape involves groupings of data that differ in size. Usually data is grouped according to the size of the particular record on the tape. For example, a MARC record that is 1,500 characters in size will be separated from other records by a blank gap. OCLC and many other MARC record distributors adhere to a standard maximum of 2,048 characters per data grouping; the minimum is 24 characters. MARC records that include more than 2,048 characters are carried in as many groupings of 2,048 characters (or less) as are necessary. (Maximum record size is 6,144 characters.) For example, a record that is 3,000 characters long would be held within two groupings: one, with the maximum 2,048 characters; the other, in a grouping of 52 characters. Rather than using special codes to indicate the length of a record, as with blocked records, the computer recognizes the length of the record through evaluation of the record length information that is carried as part of all MARC records on tape.

There are advantages and disadvantages to each method of grouping data. Because blocked records require fewer interrecord gaps, it is possible to fit more data on a tape by blocking records. On the other hand, not all computers are equipped to process the more complex arrangement of blocking; they can only deal with records that are explicitly separated from each other. This latter reason is one explanation why OCLC and some other MARC tape distributors still use the simpler method of unblocked records.

Physical Records, Logical Records

There are two different ways of grouping records; there are also two different ways of counting them. Basically, a *physical record* is the unit of data that is read or written to the computer's buffer at one time. In other words, a physical record is the data block on the tape, which may contain more or less than one MARC record. A *logical record* is an actual record, in this case, a MARC record, that will not necessarily be the same entity as a data block. Usually, there is a difference in the number of physical records and logical records on a tape.

Blocked records of 2,048 characters usually involve fewer physical records (data blocks) than logical records (MARC records), because each physical record usually contains more than one MARC record (MARC records average approximately 800 characters). On the other hand, unblocked records usually involve a greater number of physical records than logical records because each data block contains only one MARC record or part of a MARC record.

Headers and Trailers

Headers and trailers are spare amounts of blank tape at the beginning and end of tape reels that are used to thread the tapes onto the tape drive. The header is sometimes referred to as the "leader," but it should not be confused with the MARC record leader, the identifying information included at the beginning of each MARC tape record. Internal tape labels, which are explained below, are also sometimes called headers and trailers.

Tape Labels

There are two types of tape labels: external labels and internal labels. *External labels* are adhesive labels that are placed on the outside of a tape reel. These include eye-readable information that identifies the tape.

Internal labels are readable by the computer, not by humans. They include information that identifies the tape and its contents. Internal labels also signify the boundaries of files or volumes of information: header labels are placed at the beginning, and trailer labels are placed at the end.

ANSI standard X3.27 provides specifications for the type of information to be included in internal tape labels and how the information is to be arranged. Label information includes codes or full text that identifies the producer of the tape, the organization for whom the tapes were produced, the date the tapes were produced, a unique identifying code for the specific tape, and the type of system that produced the tapes. Because a library's file may require more than one tape, the "volume sequence number" contains 0001 for the first volume (tape) of that file and increases by one for each successive volume (tape). For the same reason, the code *EOF* is included in the label information to indicate the end of a one-volume file or multivolume file. When a file fills more than one volume (tape), the code *EOV* is used to indicate the end of a volume of a multivolume (multitape) file. The last volume of the file will include the code *EOF* to indicate the end of the file.

Because computer tapes are very "anonymous-looking" to the human eye, and because external labels may be removed or obliterated, internal tape labels are vital. Internal tape labels provide for a valuable double-check for tape processing, too, because the computer will compare the internal tape label information to the identifying information that has been provided by the programmer or computer operator. Significant problems can arise from inadvertently processing the same tape twice, from processing the wrong tape, or from processing tapes in the wrong order. Internal tape labels can help to prevent such problems in tape use.

ANSI Z39.2-1985 (American National Standard for Bibliographic Information Interchange)

Originally set in 1971, ANSI Z39.2 stipulates a structure that is followed for MARC records; however, it is not the same thing as MARC format. USMARC and other MARC formats actually supply specific meaning to various parts of the "shell" provided by Z39.2. For example, Z39.2 establishes the structure of tags, indicators, and subfield codes, but the MARC formats actually specify which particular tags and so forth will be used and what their meaning will be (i.e., content designation). In addition to the codes and conventions used by a person who is coding a catalog record using MARC, Z39.2 specifies an additional framework to be used when MARC records are placed on computer tape or other magnetic media. This additional framework includes information that facilitates processing of the records by a computer. Specifically, the additional information includes a record leader and a record directory.

Care and Storage of Tapes

Checking the Tapes

Upon receiving a MARC tape, the library should check the tape to verify both the physical condition and the contents of the tape. A tape that is physically defective or includes an incorrect or incomplete file can have an effect on library services that is, at best, annoying and, at worst, an expensive disaster. Because most tape vendors or processors have a limited warranty period, tapes should be checked as soon as possible after their receipt. Replacing an out-of-warranty tape can be expensive and time-consuming.

Methods for checking the physical condition and file contents range from cursory to thorough routines. The simplest routines are inexpensive, take very little time, and can be performed manually, but they provide a limited amount of protection. The more sophisticated methods require more time and expense and involve the use of special computer programs. Although the latter method usually involves contracting out the service for a fee, it provides a more thorough method of error checking and a greater measure of protection for the library. Considering the time and expense the library has already invested in compiling a bibliographic file, making a comparatively small investment in thoroughly checking the tapes is a prudent move.

If errors are detected or questions arise in regard to condition of the tapes or the files, libraries should contact the tape provider immediately. The tape provider will probably initially suggest that the library complete some routine diagnostics. Such activities may be as simple as double-checking the library's own computations in determining record counts, or they may be more complex, such as investigating the specific operating system or applications software used by the library (or other agency) to check the tapes. If initial diagnostic routines do not result in a resolution, then the vendor may ask the library to return the tape. In this case, the library will need to return the vendor's tape, not a copy of the tape. The vendor should reply to the library's complaint and/or send a replacement tape within a reasonable amount of time.

Methods for checking tapes can be considered at three levels of complexity and thoroughness: (1) minimal, (2) intermediate, and (3) maximum. These levels are described below. It should be noted that there are limitations to even the maximum level of a computerized tape checking routine. Such a routine will determine only whether the structure or framework of the records is correct and whether they can be manipulated successfully as MARC records. There are no computer programs that will determine the accuracy or correctness of the information contained in the records, their conformity to cataloging rules, or even whether information has been placed in the correct MARC fields. Such error detection can only be done through the use of human judgment.

At the minimal level, the library should visually check the tape and read the labels applied to the tape reel and any other documentation that accompanies the tape. A visual check of the tape should be done to detect irregularities in the tape reel, such as whether it is broken, cracked, or bent. The tape itself should be wound uniformly on the reel, appearing to be consistently wound from the inside of the reel outward.

Labels on the tape reel should be checked for information regarding the library name or code, dates or date ranges, and number of records included, either logical or physical, or both. Accompanying documentation should also be checked for similar types of information. Any questions the library has in regard to the physical condition of the tape or its contents should be referred to the tape producer immediately. In some cases, the library may need to learn to interpret codes or other information on the labels or documentation. In these situations, the library should be responsible for maintaining written instructions to use for this purpose.

At the intermediate level, a more complete level of tape checking involves all the steps taken at the minimal level plus a relatively simple computer check that can help to determine a great deal about the physical condition of the tape, as well as the records contained on the tape.

Having a tape "read" by a computer is a fairly generic routine used for all types of computer files, not just MARC files. Although it cannot detect problems in the structure of MARC records, it will help to detect some problems regarding the physical condition of the tapes and their contents. By reading the tapes, some of the following problems may be discovered: blank tape, tape that has been partially or completely demagnetized, parity errors in the tape, and read errors or data checks, which indicate problems in reading parts of the file. Also by reading the tapes, a record count can be provided. This number should match the record counts given on the label applied to the reel and record counts provided in any accompanying documentation, such as a tape log.

Any questions the library has in regard to the physical condition of the tape or its contents should be referred to the tape producer immediately.

At the maximum level, the most complete level of tape and record checking involves a computer check of the structure of each individual record to determine the correctness of the format and structure of the record. Computer software to provide such error detection is not generally available; many libraries contract out this service to a tape processing vendor.

The AMIGOS Bibliographic Council, a regional library network based in Dallas that provides many MARC tape services, provides the following information in regard to its procedures for tape verification:

AMIGOS' verification procedures are designed to determine that library tapes conform to OCLC/MARC specifications for record structure and that the records contain valid data elements. The process cannot determine that a valid data element has been correctly applied. Verification may be undertaken for bibliographic, holdings, and authority records.

Three levels of verification are available, of which Level Three represents the highest degree of conformance to OCLC/MARC standards. Depending upon project specifications, AMIGOS may, at its option, accept records that verify at lower levels, discontinue further processing of exceptional records, or programmatically modify the records to bring them into conformance with the appropriate verification level. Additional programming and/or processing fees may be incurred for these procedures. Level One represents a base level of acceptability as a prerequisite to further tape processing by AMIGOS.

Verification Level One

Records must conform to the following characteristics:

Each field must contain a field terminator in the last character position.

There must be no imbedded nulls or record terminators within the record.

The last character of the records must be a record terminator.

Each byte of the directory must contain only numeric data.

Leader bytes 0-4 (logical record length). All elements must contain numeric values. The length must be less than 6144 bytes and greater than 24 bytes for bibliographic records and greater than 112 bytes for holdings records.

Leader bytes 10-11 (indicator count, subfield code count). Only the value "2" is valid for these positions.

Leader bytes 12-16 (base address of data). Must contain numeric values. The base address must be less than the record length and greater than 24 bytes.

Leader bytes 20-21 (length of field, length of starting character position). Only the values "4" and "5" are valid for these positions.

Verification Level Two

Level Two includes all of the items defined for Level One. In addition, data appearing in each of the following Leader byte positions is compared to tables containing valid data elements* for that position:

Leader byte 6 (record type).

Leader byte 7 (bibliographic level).

Leader byte 17 (encoding level).

Leader byte 18 (description).

Verification Level Three

Level Three includes all the items defined for Levels One and Two. In addition, data appearing in each of the following Leader byte positions is compared to tables containing valid data elements* for that position:

Leader byte 19 (linked record code).

Leader byte 8-9 (blanks).

Leader byte 22 (transaction type code in hexadecimal).

Leader byte 23 (undefined). This element must always contain the value of "0."

*As defined in *OCLC-MARC tape format*, 1984 September and subsequent revisions.[1]

Backup Copies of Tapes

Having backup copies of MARC tapes is a good idea, particularly when large numbers of records are involved, when the tapes will be stored for lengths of time, or when it is certain that the tapes will be used again. Backup copies should be stored in a remote area, under the same storage conditions as those recommended for MARC tapes in general.

One precaution is offered to libraries making their own backup tapes of MARC records: some computers automatically translate ASCII characters into EBCDIC characters as part of the copying process. Because MARC records include an extended character set that has not been fully standardized in EBCDIC, such copies may not be usable. Libraries should check before making copies.

Tape Storage

Storage of MARC tapes involves the same conditions that apply to any other computer tapes. Some general guidelines are provided below, but libraries should request information from tape producers about the most desirable conditions for tape storage.

Temperature

The recommended storage temperature is 70 degrees Fahrenheit, but generally speaking, a temperature ranging a few degrees either way can be considered safe.

Humidity

Generally speaking, a range from 40 to 60 percent humidity can be considered a safe condition for storing tapes.

Position of Tapes

Tapes should not be stacked on top of one another for lengths of time. The ideal method for storing tapes is to use a tape cabinet in which each tape can be hung vertically on a tape rack. Tape cabinets and racks are available from office furniture suppliers.

Other Considerations

Avoid exposing tapes to direct sunlight, sources of extreme heat, such as heat vents, or any magnetic field. A controlled environment which includes protection from such environmental factors as dust, cigarette smoke, and static electricity is desirable.

Tape Shipment

When shipping tapes, several precautions should be used.

Containers

A sturdy cardboard box is the best container, particularly when two or more tapes are being shipped together. A well-padded mailing envelope is the second choice.

Internal Packing

Placing plastic bubble wrap around the tape reel is recommended. Additional cushioning or packing, such as styrofoam or even newspaper, will increase protection.

Enclosures

Enclose copies of original tape documentation (e.g., tape log), any additional library documentation, and an appropriate note of explanation, including the name of a contact person at the library and at the receiving address. This will help to ensure that the tape is delivered to the appropriate party when it is received and that time will not be wasted in determining why the tape has been sent.

Tape Format vs. Screen Display vs. Printed Cards

Most people who are familiar with MARC records have seen the records in a screen display format, which is not the same record arrangement as the records are found on tape. For example, although MARC-formatted screen displays include the appropriate tags at the beginning of each field display, the record on tape does not include the tag with each field; the tags are included in the Directory, which gives the "address" for each field. (Further information in regard to the record directory is included in chapter 2, MARC Format Structure and Content Designation.) As compared to a screen display format, the MARC tape format (or transmission format) is an extremely simple arrangement, without any of the special formatting (such as separate lines for each field) that records receive when they are displayed on a system. The transmission format basically consists of all the elements of the record strung together. This is a sparse arrangement designed for a computer to use and to provide for a more compact tape record. Figure 5.2 includes an example of a record in MARC transmission format. Figure 5.3 includes an example of the same record in a screen display format.

```
00727namƀƀ2200241ƀiƀ45ƀ0001001300000008004100013005001700005401000
1700710400018000880190012001060200015001180350018001330490009001
5105000220016108200110018210000230019324500820021626005500298300
004100353504003000394650002500424650003600449¶ocm03585754ƀ¶780713
s1977ƀƀƀƀcauaƀƀƀƀƀƀƀƀƀƀ00010cengƀƀ¶19841126093626.0ƀ¶ƀƀ‡aƀƀƀƀ760245
94ƀ¶ƀƀ‡aDLC‡cDLC‡dTRN¶ƀƀ‡a3942833¶ƀƀ‡a0520033280¶ƀƀ‡aB641736‡bTRN
M¶ƀƀ‡aTRNM¶0ƀ‡aND190‡b.N57ƀ1977b¶ƀƀ‡a759.05¶10‡aNorman,ƀGeraldine
.¶10‡aNineteenth-centuryƀpaintersƀandƀpaintingƀ:‡baƀdictionaryƀ/‡
cGeraldineƀNorman.¶0ƀ‡aBerkeleyƀ:‡bUniversityƀofƀCaliforniaƀPress
,‡c1977.¶ƀƀ‡a240ƀp.ƀ:‡bill.ƀ(someƀcol.)ƀ;‡c28ƀcm.¶ƀƀ‡aBibliograph
y:ƀp.ƀ223-229.¶ƀ0‡aPainters‡xBiography.¶ƀ0‡aPainting,ƀModern‡y19t
hƀcentury.¶+
```

Fig. 5.2. Example of a MARC record in transmission format.[2]

```
LDR        00727nam   2200241 i 45 0
001        358574 ¶
008        780713s1977      caua      b      00010ceng      ¶
010        76-24594 ¶
019        3942833 ¶
020        0520033280 ¶
035        B641736 ‡b TRNM ¶
040        DLC ‡c DLC ¶
049        TRNM ¶
050        ND190 ‡b .N57 1977b ¶
082        759.05 ¶
100  10    Norman, Geraldine. ¶
245  10    Nineteenth-century painters and painting : ‡b a
           dictionary / ‡c by Geraldine Norman. ¶
260  0     Berkeley : ‡b University of California Press, ‡c
           1977. ¶
300        240 p. : ‡b ill. (some col.) ; ‡c 28 cm. ¶
504        Bibliography: p. 223-229. ¶
650  0     Painters ‡x Biography. ¶
650  0     Painting, Modern ‡y 19th century. ¶
```

Fig. 5.3. Sample screen display format of the MARC record shown in figure 5.2.

Aside from being arranged differently, MARC records on tape do not always contain the same information as is found in screen displays or printed cards. Some of the contents of screen displays or printed cards are system-generated, that is, they are provided by special computer programs developed according to the library's, or the system's, needs. Examples of these types of information (punctuation, special formatting, etc.) are included in figure 5.4, which is part of the documentation OCLC provides for its users in regard to the OCLC-MARC tape format.

Item	Included on Tape	Not Included on Tape
Subject Headings	All subject headings present in the bibliographic record when PRODUCE and SEND, or UPDATE and SEND, are pressed	Brackets specified in the institution's Profile to be placed around non-LC subject headings on cards
Stamps	Input stamps entered by the terminal operator	Automatic stamps specified in the institution's Profile
Oversize	Oversize designations entered by the terminal operator as input stamps	Oversize designations added automatically on catalog cards
Uniform Title	Uniform titles present in the bibliographic record when PRODUCE and SEND, or UPDATE and SEND, are pressed	Brackets placed around uniform titles on cards
User Option Data	User option data input at the terminal in the 910 field	User option data specified in the institution's Profile
Call Numbers	All call numbers present in the bibliographic record when PRODUCE and SEND, or UPDATE and SEND, are pressed	For Replace ("rep" UPDATE, SEND) transactions: 090 (if record contains 050), 092 (if record contains 082), 096 (if record contains 060) 098, and 099
Dates	Date record was created and date institution performed a PRODUCE and SEND, or UPDATE and SEND, on the record	Date of last use of record, prior to the institution's use of record, and the date of the revision on the record
Print Constants		Print constants supplied by card print programs
Local Fields	For PRODUCE and SEND, or UPDATE and SEND, transactions other than Replace ("rep" UPDATE, SEND): Local fields present in the bibliographic record when PRODUCE and SEND, or UPDATE and SEND, are pressed. For Replace ("rep" UPDATE, SEND) transactions: local default 049 field	For Replace ("rep" UPDATE, SEND) transactions: any field not present in master record (009, 049, 059, 098, 099, 590, 599, 69x, 910, and 949). The edited field 049 will be replaced by the default 049 for the institution
ISBD Punctuation		Space-dash-space (or period-space-dash-space if the field preceding the space-dash-space has no terminal punctuation)
Cataloging Source		For Replace ("rep" UPDATE, SEND) transactions: any Source 040 field containing only subfields \a & \c
Location Information		Custodial location (050 \u and 051 \u) and holdings recorded in field 850

Fig. 5.4. Data on tape and data not on tape.[3] (Courtesy of OCLC Online Computer Library Center, Inc.)

In some cases, information included in the tape record does not appear on printed cards. Figure 5.5 includes a list of fields that do not print on cards but are present on OCLC-MARC tapes if they were present in the OCLC screen display when the cards were produced. Other vendors should have their own documentation regarding differences between tape, screen, and card representations of MARC records.

1.5.4 Data Not on Cards

The following fields (which do NOT print on catalog cards) will be present in records on tapes if they were present in the bibliographic records when the PRODUCE or UPDATE key was pressed.

001	043	210	527	776
005	044	211	535	777
007	045	212	540	787
008	046	214	541	870
011	047	241	543	871
015	048	242	544	872
016	049 (input stamp	243	562	873
017	may appear	263	565	886
018	on cards)	265	567	890
019	051	302s	583	900
024	052	306	584	901
025	055	308	585	911
027	059	315	652	920
030	061	340	653	921
032	066	350	681	930
033	069	351	683	936
034	070	359	760	940
035	071	362	762	949
037	072	512	765	980
039	074	516	767	981
040	080	517	770	982
041	082	520	772	983
042	088	524	775	990

Fig. 5.5. Data not on cards.[4]

RECORDS ON FLOPPY DISK

Introduction

Common sizes of floppy disk are 5¼ inches and 3½ inches. These flexible disks are enclosed in a protective case made of stiff paper or plastic. This housing is not removed when the disk is used. There are openings in the protective case which allow the disk to be accessed by the computer for reading or writing data.

Among many other uses, floppy disks are used for downloading MARC records from a microcomputer, when smaller numbers of records are involved. They are also used for such purposes as uploading smaller numbers of records to an in-house system, offline editing of MARC records, and transporting sample or problem records to system vendors for diagnostic purposes.

How Floppy Disks Work

Records are read from or written to floppy disks by using a floppy disk drive. The drive spins the disk at a very high rate of speed. A floppy disk drive includes a read/write head that senses or places the magnetized bits on the disk surface.

Floppy disks provide the advantage of direct access to data, which is not available with data on tape. There are three separate activities involved in the direct access operation. In the first step, the read/write head locates the track that includes the desired data. The time involved in this activity is called "seek time." Once the read/write head has reached the correct track, the second step involves waiting until the desired record is beneath it, as the disk rotates. The time it takes for this part of the operation is referred to as "rotational delay." In the third step, the data is actually transferred from the disk. The speed at which it is transferred is called the "data transfer rate." All these steps take place within a few seconds or less, depending upon the speed of the computer and the amount of data involved.

Floppy Disk Characteristics

Size

Floppy disks are a comparatively new magnetic storage device, and technological advances are constantly changing the "standards" against which floppy disks are measured. For example, the 5¼-inch floppy was introduced just a few years ago as a "minifloppy" because it was so much smaller than the then-standard 8-inch floppy. Now, the 5¼-inch floppy is the larger of the most commonly used diskettes.

Tracks and Sectors

Magnetic bits are recorded on a floppy disk in concentric circles called "tracks." (The analogy of a bull's eye is more appropriate than that of a phonograph disc, because the tracks on a floppy disk do not spiral inward.) Double-sided disks include tracks on both sides. Disks are divided into pie-shaped sections called "sectors." Sectors cannot be seen by the human eye, but they are recognized by the computer because of special magnetic marks that indicate the sector boundaries. The use of tracks and sectors provides the capability of direct access to files on a disk. By being directed to a specific track and sector at which a desired file begins, the computer can move directly to that file, rather than having to move through all the previous files, as is the case with sequential access for magnetic tapes.

Care and Storage of Floppy Disks

Checking the Disks

Often, records transported on floppy disk do not include the same amount or level of documentation (internal or external) that accompanies records on tape. In many cases, the only external documentation will be a disk label, which may or may not contain a list of files included on the disk. The contents of the disk can be checked by performing a "directory" command, which will provide a list of the files contained on the disk, the size of the file (in bytes), and the date that it was entered to the disk. Individual records can be retrieved and examined, but not all the codes required by the computer for processing will be displayed for a visual review of the record contents.

Backup and Recovery of Data on Floppy Disk

It is a good idea for libraries to have backup copies of disks, particularly if the disks are to be transported to another site and may be lost or damaged in transport. Libraries should follow the directions supplied by their microcomputer hardware or software vendor to create additional copies of disks. When a library finds that desired data cannot be accessed on a floppy disk, it may be because of damage to the disk or simply because the desired file is not on the disk. If the library receives an "error message" when trying to access data on a disk, the instructions provided by the hardware or software vendor should be followed to try to alleviate problems caused by the "error." If no error message appears, but the desired file cannot be retrieved, then the directory command should be used to access the list of files contained on the disk. It may be that the file is not contained on the disk. Libraries may find that lists or files that are retrieved include "garbage" characters, an indication that the disk has sustained damage. There are two primary methods for trying to recover data on damaged disks. The first method is to simply make a copy of the disk onto a new, formatted disk, through the use of either a copy command that copies all files (such as "copy a:*.* b:") or a "diskcopy" command. If this method does not provide accessible, clean data on the new disk, then the second method, which is to utilize utilities software designed for recovery purposes (such as the Norton Utilities), should be used. In some cases, data may still be unrecoverable, in which case the library will hopefully be able to acquire a backup copy of the data from the vendor that supplied the data disks. If the data disks were created by the library and no backup disks were made, then usually the library's only alternative is to replace the records manually, one at a time.

Disk Storage

The floppy disk is a fragile medium and is not as reliable for long-range storage as is computer tape. Generally speaking, the same storage considerations are required for floppy disk as those given for magnetic tape (discussed above). Because floppy disks usually receive more hands-on and day-to-day use, particular care must be taken to avoid magnetic fields (for instance, telephones involve a magnetic charge) and static electricity (data can be damaged if disks are accidentally "zapped" with static electricity). For larger numbers of records or for long-term storage, it is recommended that records be stored on tape rather than floppy disk.

Shipping Disks

Disks that are to be transported should be well-protected with padded mailing envelopes or any of a variety of specially designed mailing containers that are available from office supply stores and other sources. The outside of the mailing container should note that computer disks are enclosed and that necessary precautions should be taken to protect the disks from damage. Particularly when disks are sent to another site on a regular basis, libraries would do well to keep a log of disks shipped, including such information as a disk identification number (devised by the library), the number of records included, and the date the disks were sent.

NOTES

1.   AMIGOS tape verification procedures [3/1/88, F1234] (Dallas, Tex.: AMIGOS Bibliographic Council, 1988).

2.   *OCLC-MARC tape format* (Dublin, Ohio: OCLC, 1989), A:2.

3.   Ibid., 1:4.

4.   Ibid., 1:5.

RELATED READINGS

Byrne, Deborah. "Your library's MARC tapes [column]." *Action for libraries* 11-13 (December 1985-January 1987).

Schenck, Thomas. "Magnetic tape care, storage, and error recovery." *Library hi tech* 2 (4): 51-59 (1984).

6

MARC Database Processing

INTRODUCTION

Libraries are using their MARC catalog records for a variety of purposes beyond the production of cards. Probably the single most popular use of MARC records is as a database for in-house systems, particularly online public access catalogs. Regardless of the use or the particular end-product involved, a library's MARC records are generally not loaded directly into a system, or used for any other product, without one or more types of pre-processing. Generically known as "database clean-up" or "database preparation," this type of processing is also called "MARC tape processing," since usually both the input and the output are MARC records on tape. In this procedure, a library's MARC records are loaded into a computer and the records are then manipulated by specially designed computer programs. The end result is a computer tape containing the processed records, which can be loaded into an in-house system or submitted for processing for other end-products, such as a CD-ROM catalog.

Another name for this type of computer activity is *batch processing*, since it involves processing batches of data or transactions at one time, as opposed to performing the same activity manually, one transaction at a time. Of course, the computer programs actually perform just one transaction at a time, but the advantages of being able to process massive amounts of data within a short time make the computer the most efficient and effective tool for repetitive tasks. (The fact that the computer does not become bored, distracted, or demoralized while performing monotonous routines is also a plus.)

In addition to being fast, computers are extremely consistent, a characteristic that is an advantage in most uses, but it can have unexpected and undesirable results in the processing of MARC databases. Library MARC databases are large, complex collections of data that differ in very significant ways from one library to the next or even from one time period to the next within the same library. For example, the location and formatting of call number information, including call number fields, automatic stamps and/or input stamps, is just one of the characteristics that may be quite different from one MARC record to the next. Batch programs are designed to manipulate MARC records in a given manner; however, if the computer programs do not accurately reflect the library's practices, the results may not fulfill the library's expectations. Because a library's MARC database represents a substantial investment of time and money, and because the success of the library's automation is largely dependent upon database quality, it is very important for libraries to understand both their MARC databases and the computer programs that are used to manipulate the databases.

The six major MARC batch processes are discussed in this chapter. Each discussion of MARC tape processing is divided into three sections. The first section is a general introduction, including a description of the process and guidelines as to what the process can and cannot achieve. Also included is information that can help libraries to decide whether the process is appropriate for their own situation.

The second section is about computer programs and other vendor responsibilities. It is a specific, technical description of standard or desirable features of the process. Although the information in this section is useful for programmers, systems analysts, and others who are involved in the provision of tape processing services, it is also important for libraries to understand the computer programs and to know that the programs can differ from one vendor to the next. Libraries need to recognize these aspects of database processing because there is no standardization of computer programs for MARC database processing. Each program is developed independently by each tape processing vendor. Programming languages, hardware, the number and type of routines, and other features of the process may be quite different from one vendor to the next. Given this situation, it is not surprising that the results of similarly named processes may differ in significant ways. Although computer programs are, to a degree, proprietary information, libraries need to have and should obtain at least basic information from the vendor in regard to the ways in which their records will be manipulated.

The third section is about library specifications and other considerations, and it deals with information libraries will need to supply to vendors, decisions they will need to make, and options they will need to consider. The discussion provides guidance to libraries for preparing specifications and instructions for processing of their records. Also included are suggestions for ways in which libraries can maximize the usefulness of a given process, beyond the benefits that can be expected from a vendor's standard batch process.

The first process discussed in this chapter is deduping or duplicate resolution which is generally required as an initial preparation of OCLC tapes. This process may or may not be necessary for records produced by other vendors. All the other processes discussed are applicable to all MARC databases, regardless of the source. This chapter includes sections on six batch processes, in the following order:

Deduping

Holdings consolidation

Special select

Filing indicator correction

Smart barcode processing

Authority control

The chapter is concluded by a discussion of pricing.

In this chapter, the terms *batch processing* and *tape processing* are used to describe offline computer processing that does not involve human intervention and that is usually contracted out by a library to a tape processing vendor. The terms *online system* or *in-house system* refer to an interactive computer system used by the library as an online catalog, circulation system, or for other purposes.

DEDUPING

Deduping (also known as "duplicate resolution" or "duplicate removal") is often one of the first steps in the processing and use of a library's OCLC-MARC database. It may also be required for databases provided by other vendors, depending upon how the database was created. The deduping procedure removes all but one occurrence of any given bibliographic record from a MARC file.

To understand deduping, it is first necessary to understand what is meant by "duplicate records" and why duplicates occur in library files. In the case of OCLC users, duplicate records occur because of multiple uses of the same record (i.e., one OCLC record number) during OCLC cataloging procedures. Each time a library uses a specific OCLC record for any "update" or "produce" function, that particular version of the record is placed on tape at OCLC. Each use of a record is an isolated incident and does not affect any previous or future use. Figure 6.1 illustrates multiple uses of an OCLC record and their effect on the library's OCLC tapes.

Activity performed on OCLC	Total number of occurrences of this record on tape
Record #53421 first used to produce card set	1
Record #53421 used again to produce a corrected card set	2
Record #53421 used again to update holdings for a second copy (no cards produced)	3
Record #53421 used to cancel holdings when item is withdrawn from collection	4

Fig. 6.1. Example of multiple uses of an OCLC record and their effect on a library's OCLC tapes.

It may be surprising to learn that a "cancel holdings" command on OCLC does not actually delete the record from a library's OCLC tapes. The cancel holdings command simply adds a delete record to the file, that is, a copy of the record with a special code. Further processing, such as deduping, is required to delete the record (in other words, all copies of the record) from a library's tapes.

For records that have not been cancelled, deduping will remove all but one copy of a record from a library's file. This is necessary for most uses of a library's OCLC tapes because multiple copies of the same record in a file can cause technical and practical problems. For example, loading an OCLC file into an online catalog without deduping will waste computer storage space and cause a confusing situation for users of the system. Similarly, using such a file for generation of statistics or collection analysis will give unreliable, probably unusable, results.

A rare few OCLC users will have no duplication within their OCLC tapes because their procedures do not involve using an OCLC record more than once, but most libraries will have a significant amount of duplication (10 percent or more). Some libraries, such as processing centers, may have a duplication rate of well over 100 percent.

Libraries may find out more about the duplication rate within their own OCLC tapes by contacting their OCLC network for statistics generated by OCLC. Another way to find out about recent duplication rates is to check the *Marketing and User Trends Report* (*MUTRS*), a quarterly statistical report published by OCLC and sent to OCLC networks for distribution to member libraries. By looking at the totals found in the "Subsequent Uses" section, which includes all but the first use of OCLC records by a library, libraries can get an idea of the subsequent uses during a given time period. By comparing subsequent uses to the combined totals for first-time uses, first-time updates and original cataloging, libraries can determine the approximate ratio of initial uses to subsequent uses. Two caveats apply to such a method for determining OCLC duplication rates. One is that this provides information only for a given time period, which may not be representative of the library's entire file. Another caution is that the *MUTRS* statistics, though reliable, are not always 100 percent accurate.

Computer Programs and Other Vendor Responsibilities

Although programs for deduping may differ from one tape processing vendor or system to the next, a few basic rules apply for successful deduping of OCLC tapes.

1. Since deduping usually involves retaining either the first or last use of a record, deduping programs should include a means for determining the sequence of the records within a library's tapes. Since OCLC produces MARC tapes in chronological order, a simple way to determine the sequence of records is simply to number records consecutively as they are being loaded for deduping. The highest-numbered use of an OCLC record will, of course, be the latest use; the converse will be true for the earliest use. This consecutive numbering will generally not be maintained as part of the record once it has been used for deduping purposes.

    Sometimes records are not arranged in strictly chronological order when they are received on tape for deduping. There are several situations in which a library's records would not be in sequential order on tape.

    a. The library's records have received some type of prior processing, and the output tape from that process was not arranged in chronological order.

    b. The library has one set of tapes from its online OCLC cataloging procedures and a separate set of tapes from MICROCON, the OCLC batch retrospective conversion process.

c. The library has cataloged under two different three-letter symbols and has acquired tapes for those symbols separately. For example, a library may have originally shared a symbol with another library, then later switched to cataloging using its own separate institution code. Or, perhaps cataloging for a campus main library and a campus law library have been done using two different three-letter codes.

In the cases noted above, and in any other situations where records may be out of sequence, deduping programs must be able to check the date and time of use of each record. For OCLC records, the location of date information depends upon when the record was used. The date and time of use may appear in one of two fields in the record, or not at all, as noted below.

Records used prior to June 30, 1980 do not include the date or time of use.

For records used between June 30, 1980, and June 26, 1983, the date of use is recorded in the 001 field after the OCLC number, using the pattern YYMMDD.

For records used after June 26, 1983, the date and time of use are recorded in the 005 field. The pattern used is YYYYMMDD, hour (using a 24-hour clock), minute, second, decimal point, and decimal second. The last character will always be zero on OCLC tapes. (By the way, the time recorded is the time at OCLC (Eastern time) not at the site at which the record was used.)

For records used prior to June 30, 1980, the sequence of use will not be important in the following situations:

- The record has only been used once.

- The latest use of the record is being retained and at least one of the uses of the record is after June 30, 1980.

- The earliest use of the record is being retained and only one of the uses of the record is prior to June 30, 1980.

When determining the sequence of use for multiple records used prior to June 30, 1980, it may be necessary to use information from other parts of the records to indicate a sequence. For example, Record status code c (for "corrected") in the Leader indicates a later use of the record than code n (for "new"). Also, each additional subfield d within the 040 field generally indicates a later use of the record (assuming that the subfields ‡a and ‡c remain the same). There is another way to determine sequence for some items. When an OCLC record includes an 019 field (which includes the OCLC number for a duplicate record deleted from the OCLC database), any records containing that OCLC number within the 001 field will have predated the record with the 019 field. There are other ways in which the sequence of undated records can be determined, and, of course, there is the alternative of making printouts of the duplicates and having the library determine which should be retained.

2. Deduping programs should include a way to identify the status of the record in the library's file. At the very least, they should provide a way to determine whether the record is a cancel (or delete) record so that the cancel record and all previous occurrences of the record can be removed from the file. For some purposes, the programs may need to identify other types of local transactions, such

as whether the use of a record was a produce function (for cards) or an update function (record added to tape, no cards produced).

Within OCLC records on tape, the individual transactions of a library are indicated by a code (for update, produce, cancel, etc.) within the record Leader. This code is included as part of the OCLC tape record, but it is not part of the OCLC display and is not automatically placed within records that are downloaded from an OCLC terminal by a library.

The transaction code for individual libraries should not be confused with the Record status code in the Leader, which indicates the status of the record (new, corrected, etc.) within the OCLC master database. The Record status code does display as on the OCLC screen; however, it does not change according to each use of the record by a user library.

3. Deduping programs generally look only at the OCLC number in determining which records are duplicates. Bibliographic information in the records is not compared.[1] This may not provide satisfactory results when a library has used a single OCLC record to produce cards for various editions, titles, and so forth by changing the bibliographic information in the record rather than inputting a new record. Only one of those editions or titles will remain in the deduped file. This is one of several reasons why libraries have discarded the practice of using an OCLC record in this way.

If a library's procedures have included using a single OCLC record for varying editions, then the library may want to request printouts of records that have been removed as duplicates in the deduping process. This is a standard feature of some deduping programs (generally done at cost to the library), and it assists libraries in determining which and how many records for unique titles (rather than additional records for the same title) have been removed from their files and may need to be reentered. The safest method, of course, is for libraries to do their cataloging using OCLC records only for the titles that they actually represent and inputting new OCLC records for titles that are not in the OCLC database.

4. Deduping programs should take into consideration the differing prefixes and locations for OCLC control numbers. Duplicate OCLC control numbers may appear different because differing prefixes have been used with OCLC numbers depending on when the records were added to tape. OCLC numbers may appear in one of two locations: the 001 field or the 019 field.

For records added to tape prior to June 28, 1981, OCLC record numbers include the prefix *ocl7* (three alpha characters followed by one numeric). Records added to a library's archival tape after that date include the prefix *ocm*. Matching record numbers should be considered as duplicates, regardless of the prefix.

The deduping process should refer to both the 001 field (OCLC control number) and the 019 field (OCLC control number cross-reference) for OCLC record numbers. The 019 field contains record numbers for matching OCLC records that have been deleted from the OCLC master database. When OCLC deletes duplicates from the OCLC master database, the OCLC record numbers for the deleted records are placed in the 019 field of the record that has been retained. For example, if two libraries input records for the same item, one of the records will be deleted as a duplicate by OCLC. The OCLC number of the deleted record will be placed within a 019 field within the retained record. (The holdings symbols from the deleted record will also be moved to the retained record within the OCLC master database.)

When a library has used both the retained record as well as a corresponding record that was later removed, then record numbers from the 001 and the 019 should be considered as OCLC numbers for the same record during the deduping process. This is especially important when the last use of the record is a cancellation, since not all uses of the record will be removed if only the 001 field is checked.

Library Specifications and Other Considerations

Libraries should be aware of the following decisions and considerations that need to be kept in mind for proper deduping of their files.

1. The primary decision that needs to be made in regard to duplicate removal is "Which one of the duplicate records should be retained?" Unfortunately, the answer is not as simple as saying, "The best one." Since computers need more specific guidance than that in making decisions, the specification needs to be something that can be judged easily by looking at one or more explicit elements of the record. As often as not, the record that is retained is either the first or last use of the record, which a computer can determine by comparing the dates and times found within the tape record.

    The decision on whether to retain the first or last use of a record usually depends upon the library's cataloging practices during the time that the records have been added to tape. Have cataloging practices changed considerably since beginning on OCLC, so that more recent uses of records would be more representative of what the library wants to have in an online catalog? Are early cataloging practices undocumented or such an unknown variable that the library feels safer working with the latest use? Have subsequent produce or update uses of records been performed to provide for more correct or complete information within the record?

2. Sometimes a library will decide upon alternate or additional specifications to that of simply "first or last use." One example would be to retain the latest use within more than one holding library (for example, reference and circulating collection or special collections and circulating collection) if the bibliographic information is distinctive enough for each collection to warrant retaining both of them.

3. Because of the way a vendor's computer programs or pricing are set up, it may be possible to have other types of tape processing (such as holdings consolidation) performed at the same time or at the same cost as the deduping. The library should request information from the tape processing vendor in regard to this possibility.

4. A library will need to provide specifications for the output tapes that contain the deduped file. (See discussion of "MARC tape characteristics" in chapter 5, MARC Records on Magnetic Tape and Floppy Disk.)

HOLDINGS CONSOLIDATION

Holdings consolidation (also called 049 field consolidation) merges 049 field information from all uses of an OCLC record into the one record that is retained in deduping. Basically the contents of the 049 fields from all uses of the record are strung together into one long 049 field.

This procedure is particularly useful for libraries that have maintained holdings information for added copies and volumes. It is also of value to libraries that have duplication among many different holding libraries (regardless of whether they have maintained copy and volume information), since the retained record will then include a listing of all holding codes under which the item has been cataloged.

For libraries that have manually updated all holdings information with each use of a record, holdings consolidation is probably not useful or even recommended. Libraries that are investing a significant amount of time and effort into updating holdings manually may want to reconsider their practices in light of the availability of this type of automated procedure.

Computer Programs and Other Vendor Responsibilities

Computer programs for holdings consolidation generally include some of the features or limitations that follow.

1. Most holdings consolidation programs deal only with the 049 field and not with other fields in which a library may have included holdings information, such as the 590 or 949 fields. The more the field contents and formatting vary from OCLC specifications for the 049 field, the less likely it is that a library will be able to take advantage of standard programs. Nonstandard holdings fields generally require custom programming (usually at extra cost to the library).

2. Many holdings consolidation programs simply move the contents of the 049 field from one record to another. They do not otherwise manipulate the information or combine holdings statements. Figure 6.2 illustrates this point.

Fields in individual records	Consolidated 049 field
049 XXXA ‡c 1	049 XXXA ‡c 1 ‡a XXXA ‡c 2-3
049 XXXA ‡c 2-3	NOT 049 XXXA ‡c 1-3

Fig. 6.2. Results of one type of holdings consolidation program.

3. Holdings consolidation programs should normalize four-letter holding codes so that they can be identified in either uppercase or lowercase.

4. Generally, other types of information, such as call numbers or local notes, are not checked or manipulated by holdings consolidation programs.

Library Specifications and Other Considerations

Libraries will need to provide explicit information and instructions for proper holdings consolidation. Primary considerations are as follows.

1. Libraries should provide a complete listing of all four-letter holding codes. This is particularly important if the library uses extension codes (i.e., codes in which the first three letters are not the same in all cases).

2. Libraries should specify whether different holding library codes in the same 049 field are separated by a comma or a subfield code *a*.

3. Libraries should provide examples of all 049 field contents including the use of input stamps in the 049 subfield ‡*a*, as well as uses of all other subfields.

SPECIAL SELECT

The purpose of performing a special select (also known as a "custom select" or a "tailored select") is to divide out or separate some records from others, generally for some use or treatment that is not required or desired for all records within a file.

A not-uncommon situation in which a special select is used involves two or more libraries that have been sharing a single three-letter OCLC holding code for cataloging. The OCLC tapes include the records for all the libraries. When one of the libraries wants to have only its own records selected from the OCLC tapes, perhaps to load into an online catalog, then the special select would seek out the records with the four-letter code(s) for that library. The records for only that library could then be put onto tape for further processing or loading into a system.

Virtually any piece of information found within a record can be the basis for a special select, including elements of the fixed fields or the variable fields. Several criteria may be used in combination when the selection needs to be very precise.

Computer Programs and Other Vendor Responsibilities

Computer programs for the special select process are relatively simple; the success of the process depends mostly upon specifications provided by the library. The program simply looks for whatever the library has specified and separates those records into a file.

Library Specifications and Other Considerations

Specifications for the special select are not as easy to design as they might appear to be. Some basic rules for determining the specific identifiers, or parameters, for a special select are listed below.

1. Parameters should be designed to include everything that the library wants to have included, but nothing more.

2. Parameters should take into account cataloging practices throughout the library's automated cataloging history, as well as any profile changes that may have taken place.

3. Parameters should take into account the card production programs that have been used (for example, those discussed in the OCLC *Cataloging user manual*, format documents, profiling guide, and OCLC-MARC tape format materials), particularly if the library has previously only dealt with cards and not at all with tapes.

One good illustration of these rules is the case of a library that is setting parameters to select out records for inclusion in a periodicals list that will be used to direct users to materials in their periodicals room. The library knows exactly what is in the periodicals room and has to identify the records in a way that a computer can understand.

One parameter that suggests itself immediately is the fixed field Bibliographical level code *s* for "serials," which would include everything in the periodicals room. It also includes many materials housed in other parts of the library, including yearbooks shelved with encyclopedias and other reference items, among other types of materials. The parameter of Bibliographic level code *s* is too broad and needs to be replaced or used with another parameter that can define the subset of code *s* material that is desired.

Another method of identifying records for materials in the periodicals room is through the use of the four-letter holding code *XXXP*, which is used in the 049 field for cataloging of all materials in the periodicals room. This parameter would work perfectly for all materials cataloged recently, but earlier cataloging for materials was done using *XXXA* and the input stamp *PER RM* in the 049 field (to print above the call number on the cards).

Although all cards for these materials have the prefix *PER RM* printed above the call number, the prefix stamp for the more recent XXXP cards has been printed automatically by OCLC card production programs and is not actually included in the tape record. Taking all the above factors into account, the library's final specifications are to select all records that include either of the following:

1. holding code *XXXP* in the 049 field

2.   any of these input stamps preceding the holding code *XXXA* in the 049 field

   [PER RM]   [Per Rm]

   [PER ROOM]   [Per Room]

   [PER. RM.]   [Per. Rm.]

   [PER. ROOM]   [Per. Room]

The variations on the prefix *PER RM* were included to cover cases in which such variations may have been input accidentally. This is a particularly likely possibility if there has not been documentation of procedures, or if a number of people have worked on the inputting of records. Some vendors' programs do not differentiate between upper-case and lowercase, so it may not be necessary to include case-specific variations. Also, some programs do not include punctuation (such as final periods) as a criterion because such punctuation is so often erroneously included or excluded.

FILING INDICATOR CORRECTION

MARC fields that include titles as the first part of the field (subfield ≠a) contain a filing indicator in either the first or second position. The purpose of the filing indicator (more formally known as the "nonfiling character indicator") is to instruct the computer to skip initial articles in the titles for filing and searching purposes. The indicator is set to a number from *0* to *9*, according to how many characters should be skipped at the beginning of the title. For example, the title "An apple a day" would require a filing indicator set to *3* because there are two letters and a space before the first character to be used for filing purposes.

Many older MARC records, and a fewer number of newer ones, contain blank or incorrectly set filing indicators. There are several reasons for this situation, including the following:

- Some incorrect indicators are the result of human error.

- Since cards produced from MARC records can be filed correctly regardless of the indicator, many libraries have not seen the usefulness of filing indicators and have not taken the time to correct them when producing card sets.

- Indicators for several of the title fields were not defined until 1981, so MARC records created before that time are more likely to have missing filing indicators.

- In its earliest years, the OCLC system did not provide for inputting of filing indicators.

- Generally, no full-scale cleanup of filing indicators has taken place within major databases of vendors. Even if this had occurred, a comprehensive cleanup of, say, the OCLC database would not affect records that were already on the archival tapes of OCLC users.

In an online catalog or other automated system, the filing indicator makes the difference between finding a title and not finding it. Some filing indicator errors are easily found (by searching under initial article) and can be manually corrected through a library's online system; however, other such errors are not as easily detected. Correcting the indicators through a batch process is usually quicker, cheaper, and easier than correcting them manually through a special project. And, most libraries have more than enough "special projects" when implementing an online system.

Filing indicator correction is accomplished by comparing the first word of a title field to a list or table of initial articles. If the first word in the title field matches one of the words in the table, the computer checks the filing indicator and changes it, if necessary. In a few instances, of course, the indicators are changed from correct to incorrect values, but many more indicators are corrected than changed to incorrect characters. Libraries should receive a report of all indicators changed as part of the process, which they can easily check for indicators that may have been incorrectly reset.

Computer Programs and Other
Vendor Responsibilities

The following features are most valuable to programs for filing indicator correction:

1. Both the fixed field Language code and the 041 field (for multilanguage works and translations) should be checked to determine which languages may be found within the record.

2. Articles for the language represented in the fixed field Language code (which should be the same as the first code in the 041 field) should be checked first. Then, articles in the other languages should be checked, in the same order as the codes found in field 041, which are arranged in order of predominance. Once an indicator has been validated or corrected for a given language, it should not be part of any further checking for other languages.

3. Articles in as many languages as possible should be part of the program. It should be noted that some languages (for example, Serbocroatian, Language codes *scr* and *scc*) do not include initial articles. A list of languages and the corresponding articles is included as appendix 2 of the *ALA filing rules* (1980). A list of articles is also included in the Library of Congress *Cataloging service bulletin*, no. 41 (Summer 1988) and in appendix F of the *USMARC format for bibliographic data*.

4. All filing indicators should be checked. MARC tags and filing indicator positions are listed in figure 6.3 (see next page).

5. Since a few filing indicators will probably be set incorrectly by the program, reports listing all of the reset indicators should be produced and made available to the library.

MARC tag	Filing indicator position
130	1st indicator
211	2nd indicator
214	2nd indicator
222	2nd indicator
240	2nd indicator
241	2nd indicator
242	2nd indicator
243	2nd indicator
245	2nd indicator
440	2nd indicator
630	1st indicator
730	1st indicator
740	1st indicator
830	2nd indicator
840	2nd indicator

Fig. 6.3. MARC tags and indicator positions for fields containing filing indicators.

Library Specifications and Other Considerations

Libraries should be certain that all the program features listed above are part of the program with which their records are being processed. It is in the library's best interest to request all reports that are produced, then review them and make any corrections on a case-by-case basis, as necessary. The number of records requiring manual correction after the batch process will be a fraction of the number that would have been needed otherwise.

SMART BARCODE PROCESSING

There are two major phases of library barcoding projects. One phase, called "labeling," involves physically attaching the barcode labels to library materials. The other phase, called "linking," involves placing the barcode numbers within the appropriate bibliographic records in the library's database. This phase creates a link between the physical item and the bibliographic record in a system.

The predominant method of completing these two phases is to label the materials using "dumb" barcodes, search manually for the matching records in the online database, and input the barcode number to the record to create a link. This type of procedure presents a number of difficulties, all of which are related to the complexity and timing of the manual linking procedure. The major issues are the following:

- Manual linking processes are too often left for circulation clerks to complete within high-pressure situations, such as while patrons wait to check out books.

- Successful manual linking requires an understanding of how to search the online system and how to match materials with their bibliographic records, both of which can be surprisingly complex operations. When these operations are handled inadequately, the results are an error-ridden database and public relations disasters.

- The implementation and initial use of an online system is a very critical and very busy time. Manual linking is one of many major operations that must take place while the system is being implemented.

The use of "smart," or "prelinked," barcodes has arisen as a way to resolve such difficulties. With the use of smart barcodes, the linking process is accomplished by a batch computer process prior to the labeling of materials. The smart barcoding process requires that a library have a machine-readable database. The usefulness of smart barcodes is related to the completeness of the library's database: the more materials that are represented in the database, the better.

In the first part of this procedure, the library's bibliographic database receives special batch processing. Usually, a computer program sorts the records into shelflist order or other desired order and places consecutive barcode numbers within the bibliographic records. The resultant computer tape, which will be the library's system database, is used to produce smart barcode labels.

Smart barcode labels include the call number of the bibliographic item with which they have been linked during batch processing. The library may also choose to have brief author and title information and other identifying information (such as LC card number or ISBN) included on the label if call numbers would be either insufficient or inaccurate identifiers. The barcode labels are produced in shelf order, according to library specifications. Then, in a special labeling project, each barcode label must be carefully matched to the proper bibliographic item.

Insofar as the linking process is concerned, the use of smart barcodes compares favorably to the manual linking processes used with dumb barcodes. When smart barcodes are used, the item is automatically linked, and the labor-intensive activity of manual linking has been eliminated. Of course, the labeling phase of a barcoding project is more complex using smart barcodes than "dumb" barcodes, which can be placed on materials at random. The advantages of smart barcodes are still significant and include the following:

- Because barcodes and books are both arranged in the same order, the searching and matching procedures are markedly simplified compared with those of randomly searching database records online and manually inputting a barcode number to each record.

- Through the use of smart barcode labels, linking and labeling can both be completed prior to implementing a system, which removes one major project from the busy time following system implementation.

- The matching and labeling phase of the project can be completed without the pressures that accompany manual linking of dumb barcodes, thereby allowing for a much lower error rate.

Computer Programs and Other Vendor Responsibilities

Features of smart barcode production programs vary greatly from one vendor to the next. Often the production of the smart barcode computer tape will be carried out by one vendor who then sends the tape to a barcode producer for production of the labels.

Some smart barcode computer programs incorporate more options than others. The following features are important aspects of computer programs for smart barcodes:

1. Since smart barcode tape production and smart barcode label production may be carried out by two separate agencies, the programs of the tape producer should be compatible with the programs of the label producer.

2. The programs should be able to produce tape records and barcode labels with or without check digits, as required by the library's system and needs.

3. Programs for label production may produce only one label per bibliographic record, or they may produce labels for multiple copies or volumes according to holdings statements in the bibliographic records provided by the library. In some cases, programs that produce labels for multiple copies or volumes simply note the highest number within the holdings statement and produce that many labels for the item. When multiple copies or volumes are involved, the copy or volume numbers should be printed on the barcode labels.

4. Sorting of the barcode labels into the proper call number order is of the utmost importance, since the speed and accuracy of the matching and application of the labels depends on the labels being in the same order as books on the shelf. Among many other features, computer programs for sorting call numbers must include alphabetical (sometimes case-specific), numerical, and decimal sorts in ascending order, as well as subsorts on various elements.

5. Because most libraries are divided into separate sections (such as reference and fiction) with materials shelved in a linear fashion within each section, programs for label production should be able to sort subsets according to the "section" of the collection, as indicated by holding code, input stamp, or other criterion.

Library Specifications and Other Considerations

To successfully use smart barcodes, libraries will need to consider the system that they will be using, implementation methods, and the condition of their database in regard to holdings information.

1. The library will need to determine, through discussion with the system vendor and/or others, what types of barcode labels they need (e.g., Codabar, Code 39) and how they should be organized (e.g., sheets, rolls). The library should specify

beginning and ending barcode numbers for production. Another important specification is the location of the barcode number within the library's bibliographic records on tape (049 field, 949 field, or other location) and any special punctuation or formatting for the barcode number. The system vendor should provide information on all such matters, including system requirements as well as options that are open to the library.

2. The library must provide thorough and precise instructions as to where the call number information can be found within their bibliographic records and how the information should be formatted on barcode labels. Specifications should include such information as: MARC call number tags used and which holding library they are used with; 049 field input stamps or other information used as call number prefixes or suffixes; and which, if any, automatic prefix or suffix stamps or other such system-generated designations (e.g., for oversize) are called for. If the library has complete, up-to-date card profile information (from OCLC or other card supplier used), they should refer to that when devising call number specifications for label production.

    If the library's call numbers are not title-specific, then the library should also specify additional identifying information to be printed on the barcode label. Brief author, title, and publication date information are possible options; other information (such as LC card number, ISBN, or accession number) may also be included.

3. If holdings statements within the library's database are to be used for production of labels for multiple copies or volumes of an item, then the library should specify where the holdings information can be found (e.g., MARC tags and subfield codes), what the information will look like, and how it should be interpreted.

4. Although the filing order of call numbers would seem to be fairly standardized, a surprising number of variations can be found among libraries. For example, some libraries sort Cutter numbers in decimal order, while others sort them in numerical order. For this reason, the library should be absolutely certain that the vendor's programs will sort their call numbers (and thus barcode labels) in the correct order. The library should submit to the vendor a sizable sample listing of call numbers in correct order and should request a sample listing from the vendor, as sorted by the vendor's programs.

    If barcode labels are to be sorted into sections according to collection as well as call number (e.g., materials in reference are separate from materials in the general collection), then the library should provide a list of collections that require separate sorts. Instructions should be provided for determining which collection each item is in (e.g., by checking holding codes or input stamps in the 049 field).

5. An important consideration regarding the use of smart barcodes has to do with how accurately and completely the library's holdings are reflected in the machine-readable database. The barcoding project will proceed much more quickly and smoothly if the library's database has been kept up-to-date with

regard to holdings information, specifically with (1) withdrawn items and (2) added copies, added volumes, and multivolume titles.

If the database contains many records for items that have actually been removed from the collection, but not deleted from the library's database, then this will of course complicate the smart barcoding process. In the case of items that are actually part of the library's collection, but for which copy and volume information has not been included or kept up-to-date, the library may want to plan on the basis of one smart barcode per title. Additional copies and volumes would receive dumb, unlinked barcodes.

If complete, detailed holdings information has been kept within bibliographic records, the library should specify thoroughly and carefully how to interpret holdings information for tape processing purposes and how information such as copy and volume numbers should be printed on the barcode labels. The barcode vendor or system vendor should apprise the library of other situations that require custom specifications. One example of such a situation is that of a library with numerous branches. Other custom specifications might involve portions of the collection for which the library may not want to receive smart barcodes, such as serials or special collections.

AUTHORITY CONTROL PROCESSING

Authority control is even more important in an automated environment than in a card catalog. Within a card catalog, even radically different forms of a heading (such as "Twain" and "Clemens") can be manually interfiled. However, within an automated file, forms of a heading with major or minor differences will file separately; they cannot be manually interfiled. Patrons will have to search under every variation of a heading to find all the works that should be filed under a single heading. An even more likely — and less satisfactory — scenario is that patrons will check only one form of a heading. Works entered under other forms of the heading will not be found, giving the impression that they are not held by the library.

There are two primary goals of authority control: uniformity (so that patrons will have to search only one form of a heading) and cross-referencing (so that patrons searching under related forms of a heading will be guided to the established form). In-house library systems vary greatly in accommodating these two goals. Although all major systems include at least minimal operational authority control features, in-house library systems will not automatically clean up a library's database or provide cross-references. Library systems make this type of process easier and faster (cards do not have to be pulled, corrected one by one, and refiled, for example), but each heading will still need to be treated on a case-by-case basis, and typos and other errors will still need to be corrected. When a library's cataloging procedures have not included authority control, batch authority processing is a fast, convenient method for resolving some types of inconsistencies before loading the database into an in-house system or using it for some other type of end product.

Unlike most other MARC tape processing, batch authority control does not simply make desired changes according to instructions specified within the computer programs. In other words, headings within a library's database are not changed from old to new forms simply by manipulating or rearranging the information within the library's records. Batch authority control relies upon the use of an additional database, a database of authority records that will be compared to bibliographic records in the library's database. The authority records contain established forms of headings and variant forms of headings, which are coded as such. For example, a typical name authority record would include the following types of fields:

Established Heading: Twain, Mark.

"See from" reference: Clemens, Samuel.

Batch authority processing compares each heading (the established form and the "see from" reference) in the authority file to each heading within the library's bibliographic records. When every heading in the library's bibliographic file has been compared to each heading and "see from" reference in the authority file, each of the headings in the bibliographic file will fall into one of three categories: (1) validated headings, which matched the established form of heading in the authority file; (2) flipped headings, which matched the "see from" form heading and thus were "flipped" to the established form of heading; and (3) exceptions, which match neither the established form of heading nor the "see from" cross reference.

The headings that fall into the exceptions category are generally one of two types: (1) headings that were not included in the authority file or (2) headings that were included in the authority file but were not recognized in the library's bibliographic records because they included some type of "error," such as a misspelling or a missing middle initial.

Batch authority control is especially useful when a library's bibliographic database contains MARC records created prior to 1981 (when *AACR2* was introduced), since there will very likely be old, pre-*AACR2* name headings that need to be changed to the new *AACR2* forms. Regardless of how recently a library has acquired its MARC records, the database records may have been created as long ago as 1968. Records for items published prior to 1981 may or may not include new forms of headings, depending upon when the records were created and what type of processing the records have received since they were created. Some vendor cataloging databases have received authority control processing, such as the "*AACR2* flip" that was performed on the OCLC database in December, 1980.

There are some guidelines for determining whether a library's database has received prior authority control processing:

- OCLC performed a batch name authority flip of the OCLC master database in December, 1980. OCLC also provides ongoing manual name authority control for the master database. None of the above activities affects records that are already on library archive tapes. Records used by a library prior to a change to the OCLC master database remain unchanged. Only records used after the change will reflect the authority work.

- Other commercial vendor databases may not have received any authority control or may not have received batch processing such as the OCLC *AACR2* flip for records created prior to 1981. Information on authority processing should be requested from each vendor from which a library receives MARC records.

- For other commercial vendor databases that have received batch processing such as the OCLC flip, the same limitations may apply as for the OCLC database (as noted above). Libraries should check with their MARC database vendors to determine which limitations apply and to what extent they apply to the library's own records.

Regardless of the vendor, batch authority control involves these basic limitations:

- Since a library's bibliographic file will contain some headings that are not represented in the Library of Congress authority file, not all headings will be updated.

- The success of the batch authority control is dependent upon finding a cross-reference form of heading within a library's bibliographic file to replace with the "new" form. The batch authority process is designed to update headings in the library's database, not to correct headings that are incorrect.

- Because new headings are being added to the Library of Congress authority file all the time, and because headings are sometimes corrected or changed, a library database that has received batch authority control is outdated by the time the batch processing is completed. To minimize the negative effects of time lags, the batch authority control should be completed as nearly as possible to the time that the library's database is going to be loaded into a system. Authority control will need to be maintained after the database is put online, for the above-mentioned reasons and also because new headings will be added to the database through current cataloging.

- Because batch authority processing is often referred to as an "*AACR2* upgrade," libraries may mistakenly assume that their bibliographic records will be recataloged into *AACR2* form through this process. This is not the case. The only aspects of a record that are changed to *AACR2* form are the forms of the access points (main and added entries and subject headings). The descriptive cataloging is not affected (for example, ISBD punctuation is not entered), and the choice of entry is not changed to conform to *AACR2* (for example, records are not changed from entry under editor to title main entry, as called for under *AACR2*).

There are three levels of batch authority control available to libraries, which range from a simple, limited procedure to a complex, comprehensive one. The most limited process would be of interest only to libraries that have OCLC records that were added to tape prior to the database flip in December, 1980. The other two more comprehensive procedures should be considered by all libraries that have MARC bibliographic records, regardless of the source. The three levels of batch authority control are described below.

One limited approach to batch authority control is available to libraries that have OCLC records that were added to tape prior to the December 1980 authority flip of the OCLC database. This process places all pre-December 1980 records into a separate file, then performs the changes that were made to the OCLC database at that time. The result is to provide some internal consistency within the library's file; however, this does not bring the library's database up-to-date. This process affects only name authority headings (personal, corporate, and conference headings, uniform titles, and series titles), not topical subject headings.

A more comprehensive approach to authority control, an authority flip or *AACR2* flip, is available for all MARC tapes, regardless of their date or source. The authority flip utilizes the current Library of Congress authority files (name and/or subject), which are compared to the library's bibliographic database. Old headings in the library's database are flipped to new headings according to information found in the LCAF. This authority control process generally affects only name and subject headings, but does not affect most subject subdivisions (subfields *x*, *y*, and *z* in subject fields) or the title portions of author-title added entries. Series and uniform titles generally are included in this processing. Depending on the vendor, this level of batch authority control may include an output tape of the MARC authority records for headings in the library's file. This tape can be loaded into the library's online system for authority control purposes, including cross-referencing and database maintenance.

The most comprehensive approach to batch authority control is actually a combination of three major processes: (1) batch processing to correct portions of headings and subject heading subdivisions; (2) an authority flip; and (3) manual review and correction. These three steps are discussed below.

The batch correction process, which is often completed prior to the authority flip to provide for more potential matches, is a procedure that spells out words that were formerly abbreviated as a practice in name and subject headings. Examples of those types of abbreviations include "U.S." for "United States" and "Desc. & trav." for the general subject subdivision "Description and travel." Even if a library is not considering having any other batch authority processing performed upon its database, this spelling out process can save the library from having to complete a lot of manual correction. Since computer filing will separate the full forms and abbreviated forms of words into separate files (thus creating two different files to search for the same term), these corrections will need to be made at some point.

The authority flip is basically the same as discussed above, but it may also include more name and subject headings than the LC file (supplied by the authority control vendor), subject heading subdivisions, and title portions of some author-title headings.

The manual review and correction are performed after the batch correction and the authority flip phases have been completed. The purpose of this phase of the process is to correct errors within the library's MARC bibliographic tapes that may have prevented a match against the authority database. Errors that can prevent otherwise identical headings from being matched include the following:

- incorrect MARC tags (for example, corporate headings mistagged as personal name headings)

- incorrect indicators (such as a forename coded as a single surname)

- typographical errors (the computer cannot tell that "Twian, Mark" is supposed to be "Twain, Mark")

- transposed numbers in birth and death dates

The manual review process may also serve to change nonstandard forms of headings into standard forms, something that is not accomplished through batch authority control. This particular type of decision involves judgments that cannot be made by the computer. For example, personnel completing the manual review may need to refer to another bibliographic database to determine if titles under the standard form of the name are the same as titles found under the nonstandard form in the library's file. Once the manual review has been completed, the affected records are submitted for batch processing again.

An additional end product of this level of authority control processing is a tape containing Library of Congress authority records for headings found in the library's database. Depending upon the vendor, libraries may also be able to acquire a tape including brief authority records for non-LC headings that were found in their database. Both of these types of authority records are useful for database maintenance. Only the Library of Congress authority records will include cross-references. The records for non-LC, or local, headings will include only the heading and MARC coding that was included in the library's bibliographic record.

Once batch authority control is completed, it must be kept up-to-date by the library. At least one vendor offers an update service that notifies libraries of changes to the headings that were in their database when it was processed by the vendor.

Computer Programs and Other Vendor Responsibilities

The features listed below are necessary or desirable for successful authority batch processing.

1. Computer programs for batch authority processing should make the most conservative comparisons possible while still allowing for insignificant differences in headings.

    Conservative matches are those that require all or most elements of two headings to match before they are considered to be the same heading. This strictness is necessary so that mismatches do not occur, with headings being switched incorrectly to other forms of names. Safe comparisons usually include the following elements:

    -   last two characters of the tag
    -   first indicator for name headings; second indicator for subject headings
    -   all alphabetical characters
    -   all numerical characters, with the possible exception of death dates for personal name headings
    -   all text of all subfields in the name or subject heading (the match may or may not include the subfield codes themselves)

    Insignificant differences, in the case of batch authority processing, are those differences that would not denote two discrete headings within an authority file. Generally, initial normalization of headings in both files is performed to prevent insignificant differences from precluding a match. The normalization process usually includes the following changes to headings:

- All alphabetical characters are shifted to uppercase.

- All special characters, such as diacritics and punctuation, are deleted.

- Extra blank spaces are deleted.

Subfield codes may or may not be deleted as part of the normalization process.

Normalization is used only for the purpose of computer matching, and the normalized headings do not become part of a library's file. A matching procedure that includes more than minimal normalization and involves, for example, ignoring entire subfields of text as part of the matching process is called a "fuzzy match." The "fuzzier" the match, the more likely that inaccurate matches will be made.

2. When a normalized heading in a bibliographic record matches a normalized heading in an authority record, the authority heading should replace the heading that is in the library's bibliographic record. Replacement is necessary because the heading in the bibliographic record may have included errors that were obscured by the normalization process, such as missing punctuation or lowercase letters that should be uppercase. Such differences could affect searching and filing of the heading or, at the very least, be confusing to users of the records. It is especially important to replace the validated heading in the bibliographic record with the authority form if subfield codes have been deleted as part of the normalization process.

3. All subject heading fields except 650 fields (topical term subject added entries) should be compared to the name authority file because name (and title) headings are included in the name authority file even when they have only been used as subject headings. The form of name is generally the same, regardless of their use. A few names and titles are included in the subject authority file, either because they are used as examples for all similar subject headings or because they have been assigned subject heading subdivisions that apply only to that particular heading (e.g., chronological subdivisions for United States history). The LC name authority file includes headings for personal, corporate and conference names, geographic names, uniform titles, and series titles. The subject authority file includes topical subject headings.

4. In addition to established forms of headings and "see from" references, authority records include "see also from" headings. These three types of terms are tagged as 1XX, 4XX, and 5XX fields, respectively. The 5XX fields are established headings that are related to the 1XX term and are included as cross-references to guide users to other related names or subjects. (For more information on the structure of authority records, see chapter 9, MARC Authority Format.)

The 5XX fields should not be used as a basis of comparison for a batch authority flip. There are separate records for the headings found in 5XX fields that include the heading as a 1XX field, with appropriate 4XX references. Headings that match 5XX fields should not be flipped to the 1XX heading.

5. There are a number of reports that provide useful information about batch authority processing. Libraries may find it useful to have statistical reports on the total number of name and subject headings in their database, as well as the total number of validated headings, flipped headings, and exception headings. A list of validated headings may be desirable, as well as a list of headings that were flipped, including the pre-flip and post-flip headings.

    For many libraries, the most useful report will be the exceptions report, which includes a listing of all headings in the library's file that did not match against the authority file in any way (i.e., did not match an established or variant form of a heading). Some of the headings will appear on this report simply because they are headings for which LC has not provided authority records. Most of the headings on the exceptions report, however, will be headings that include some type of error. This report will be the basis for any clean up activities to be performed upon the library's database.

Library Specifications and Other Considerations

The library will need to take a good look at its past practices and future plans in order to maximize the usefulness of batch authority processing. The advantages and the limitations of authority control should be understood, so that the library can understand the value of the process without operating under unrealistic expectations. The library should consider the four points below and be ready to include appropriate specifications within its plans. For libraries that plan to use authority control products in an in-house system, the capabilities and limitations of that system will also need to be considered.

1. Because the Library of Congress authority files are the only files used by all vendors for batch authority processing, libraries should evaluate the appropriateness of using LC files to process their databases. When libraries have departed from LC practice, they will need to include a consideration of those differences in their plans for batch authority control.

    A common example of a library's departure from LC authority practice is the use of title-page forms of pseudonyms. In this case, whereas the Library of Congress has used one predominantly found name instead of the pseudonym found on the title page, many libraries have used the various pseudonyms, when those pseudonyms apply. Probably the most prominent example of LC's practice is the use of the name *Jean Plaidy* for all of Eleanor Hibbert's works, which include books written under the names Victoria Holt and Philippa Carr, among other pseudonyms. Although LC practice has changed, authority records will not be changed en masse, and the practice will still affect batch authority control for some time to come.

    Other, more radical departures from LC practice may be found within a library's subject heading practice. If a library does not use LC subject headings, for example, but uses Sears or MeSH headings instead, then subject authority control will not be as readily available, if it is available at all. This is because MeSH, Sears, and other non-LC subject headings are not produced on MARC tape by their creators, as LC subject headings are. Libraries that use a significant number of local subject headings may also need to consider alternatives to the usual batch process.

When a library's name or subject authority practices have differed from LC practice, the library has several options, including the following:

a. The library can specify that affected portions of the bibliographic file be excluded from batch authority processing. The library may need to provide parameters for selecting out the affected headings or records. For example, local subject headings might be specified as "690 and 691 fields." In some cases, such as the use of pseudonyms, parameters cannot be identified as specifically as a tag or indicator value or other MARC code, so broader parameters may have to suffice. For example, since pseudonyms are used mainly in works of fiction, libraries may specify that MARC records with the fixed field code for fiction (or with certain call numbers) be excluded from authority control processing. Using this broad categorization, many more headings will be exempted than necessary; however, there is no way a computer can determine specifically which records include pseudonyms. (See the "Special select" section of this chapter for further information on devising parameters for identifying specific types of MARC records.)

The library may want to provide its own manual processing for categories of headings that have not received batch authority processing.

b. The library can specify that the affected portions of the bibliographic file receive batch authority processing against an alternative authority file. This is an option only if an appropriate authority file is available. The vendor may be able to accommodate this option by using a printed list of headings (either with or without MARC coding) or by using a machine-readable tape supplied by the library. For example, a library that relies heavily upon local subject headings may be able to provide a list of those subject headings for the vendor to use in batch authority control.

A limited number of vendors have specialized non-LC authority files available. The alternative files have usually been prepared by the vendor or by a library that has agreed to have its files used for such a purpose.

c. The library can have the batch authority process performed upon its entire database and then clean up undesirable changes after the batch process is completed. For example, a library that does not want to have all pseudonyms changed to one name can identify through its own research (in the LC authority file) the headings that will need to be switched to their desired forms after the batch authority process. Then the changes will need to be effected, through an in-house system, or by having the vendor change them manually, or by some other means.

d. The library may decide to start following LC practice or using the LC authority headings instead of others. A batch authority flip against the LC file may serve to retrospectively change many headings to LC form.

For example, a library switching from Sears to LC subject headings will find that a significant number of Sears headings are the same as LC headings. And, a substantial number of those Sears headings that do not match headings in the LC file are actually the terms that LC uses as "see" references. Because of this, many of the non-LC headings in the library's bibliographic database will be successfully flipped to LC form through batch authority processing. There will, of course, still be a percentage of the records that will need to be manually corrected after the batch processing is completed.

2. When name headings in a library's database are changed through batch processing, the library will need to consider all the ramifications of such changes. For example, when the main entry of a catalog record changes significantly (i.e., the author's last name is different), then this may also affect cuttering in the call number. If call numbers are to be changed, then spine labels will also need to be changed and materials reshelved. The library should specify that the vendor provide a listing of all headings changed (i.e., flipped) in the batch authority process, so that these types of differences can be researched and appropriate measures taken.

3. The library should determine in advance what types of statistics and lists it will require as a result of the batch authority process. These types of output are discussed in the previous section under number 5. For purposes of completing the authority work begun by the batch process, the library should request a list of exception headings.

4. Libraries that are interested in receiving authority records on tape should make certain that such a tape can be loaded into their online system. They should also provide output tape specifications to the authority control vendor, particularly if the specifications differ from those for their bibliographic database.

PRICING OF MARC DATABASE PROCESSING SERVICES

The pricing of batch processing services is, of course, based on the costs the vendor must cover. Libraries may better understand what they are being charged for if they know what the costs are to the vendor.

- salaries and benefits for professional, technical, and managerial personnel (including programmers, systems analysts, computer operators, team leaders, account managers, computer technicians, documentalists, and others)

- salaries and benefits for support personnel (including secretaries, clerks, word processing specialists, assistants, shipping clerks, maintenance personnel, and others)

- costs of computer equipment, peripherals, and other hardware (including the purchase or lease price of computers and other hardware, such as printers, disk drives, tape drives, and monitors, as well as maintenance contracts, costs of repair and upgrades, surge protectors and emergency backup generators, among other costs)

- costs of environmental control (including costs for heat and air conditioning, dust and humidity control, among other costs)

- overhead costs (including costs of buying or leasing a building, cost of utilities, insurance, building maintenance services, security, furniture, telephone (usually including an 800 number), postage, photocopying, and related costs)

- costs of materials and supplies (including costs of paper, printer paper, envelopes, forms, computer tapes, printer ribbons, ink cartridges, and many other related items)

The amount that a library pays for batch processing is based on the type and number of processes being performed, the number of records, the amount of customization involved, the type of output desired, and the vendor providing the service, among other variables. Different types of charges and the major variables that can affect them are discussed below.

Setup Fees

A setup fee may be charged to cover the costs of such activities as the following: setting up a library's account; consulting with the library about specifications; performing initial computer programming to set all the library's parameters; running preliminary tests to determine appropriateness of specifications and parameters; and communicating with the library throughout the process.

Processing Charges (Per Record or Unit Charges)

For any given process, the cost to the vendor is related to the volume of work involved, and generally the volume is measured by the number of records processed. Computer time and staff time (e.g., computer operators) increase as the number of records increases, and wear and tear on equipment such as tape drives, disk drives, and printers also is related to the number of records processed. Processing charges are charged for the processing of a certain number of records; they are usually a set amount multiplied by the number of records (or units) processed.

Generally speaking, per record charges are based on the number of records on the input tapes, not the number of records output. For example, if a tape of 15,000 records is submitted for a special select process to create a separate output tape for 2,000 government documents records, then the library will be charged for processing of 15,000 records even though they are receiving only 2,000. This is because all 15,000 records have to be inspected, or processed, by the computer to select out the desired records.

If two or more processes can be performed simultaneously (such as deduping and holdings resolution), vendors may charge only the per record cost for one of the processes. In some cases, vendors may offer volume discounts for large numbers of records.

Customization
(Custom Programming)

When a vendor's standard programs cannot be used to process a library's database, customization will be required. Customization may be necessary because the library's records differ in some way from those that are usually processed by the vendor. Customization may also be requested by the library for output products that are different from those generally produced by the vendor, such as the way in which records are displayed or arranged on a printout. Often the major cost to the vendor for customization is the programming that is involved, which includes a programmer's salary, computer time (for programming and testing programs), and the cost of output, such as sample printouts or sample tapes. Vendors usually charge an hourly programming rate for such activities. Even minor changes to programs can take one to two hours, or more.

Charges for Output

Output includes the tangible end products of batch processing, such as computer tapes and printouts. Sometimes the costs of such products are included in the processing charge, but they are often charged separately. For computer tapes, there is generally a set price for each tape, regardless of how many records the tape contains. A standard-sized reel of computer tape will hold approximately 20,000 records, but the price charged for the tape will be the same whether there are 100 or 20,000 records on the tape.

Prices of printouts may be charged at a certain price per page or per record, or both. Often, if the printouts include standard reports from the process (e.g., statistics, exceptions lists), the cost is included in the processing cost.

Charges for Shipping, Insurance,
and So Forth

Libraries should ascertain whether the costs of shipping tapes or other output products will be paid by the vendor or the library. Libraries should try to negotiate an agreement that holds the vendor responsible for costs of overnight shipping for products that are produced after agreed-upon deadlines. All shipped items should be insured, but it should be noted that insurance from the U.S. postal service or any other shipper usually covers only the cost of the computer tapes, paper, or other physical items being shipped. The cost of the data on the tapes (printouts, etc.) or cost of processing of the data is generally not covered by shipping insurance.

Product Support

There are various types of product support that may take place before, during, or after tape processing. For example, support in the form of technical assistance is generally available to the library during the specifications phase of the process. The charge for this is generally included as part of the standard setup fee. If it becomes apparent, during the testing or the processing phase, that the library's specifications were in error or were incomplete, then the vendor may interrupt the process and contact the library for more information. The library may or may not be charged for the amount of time the vendor spends working on the library's specifications at this point and, of course, a change in specifications at any point may affect the cost to the library.

For product support after output tapes have been produced, vendors' prices may include a limited warranty, for example, a 90-day warranty for computer tapes that contain a library's processed database. The cost of the warranty may be included in the cost of processing or the cost of the tapes. The meaning of such a warranty may be nebulous, however, when it is unclear whether the warranty covers simply the physical condition of the tapes or whether it also includes the work performed on the tapes. For example, if a library finds that it cannot load tapes provided by a vendor and the problem is not a result of the physical condition of the tapes, then the library may find itself having to perform diagnostics on the tape or to otherwise prove that the fault lies with the vendor's work. If the library's specifications were incorrect, or even unclear, or if the inability to load or work with the tapes is a result of the library's ineptness, then the vendor's warranty probably will not apply. Vendors differ in the extent of technical support that they will supply to a library without charging an additional fee.

Extras

In general, libraries should expect to be charged extra for anything that is not part of a vendor's standard package or was not included as part of the initial agreement or contract with the vendor. Examples of extras are: additional copies of printouts or reports, additional programming, extra copies of tapes, and costs of overnight shipping (if tapes are produced on schedule).

NOTES

1. Duplicate resolution through the use of some other means of comparison besides OCLC record number is a complex, error-prone process. Discussions of this process can be found in the following articles:

Coyle, Karen. "Record matching: A discussion." *Information technology and libraries* 4 (1): 57-59 (March 1985).

Hickey, Thomas B., and David J. Rypka. "Automatic detection of duplicate monographic records." *Journal of library automation* 12 (2): 125-42 (June 1979)

MacLaury, Keith D. "Automatic merging of monographic data bases—Use of fixed-length keys derived from title strings." *Journal of library automation* 12 (2): 143-55 (June 1979).

Williams, Martha E., and Keith D. MacLaury. "Automatic merging of monographic data bases—Identification of duplicate records in multiple files." *Journal of library automation* 12 (2): 156-68 (June 1979).

RELATED READINGS

Baker, Barry, and Lynn Lysiak. *From tape to product: Some practical considerations on the use of OCLC-MARC tapes.* Ann Arbor, Mich.: Pierian Press, 1985.

Renaud, Robert. "Resolving conflicts in MARC exchange: The structure and impact of local options." *Information technology and libraries* 3 (3): 255-61 (September 1984).

7

MARC Database
Products

INTRODUCTION

The three types of MARC database products examined in this chapter are catalogs, bibliographies, and collection analysis. The characteristics of each product and considerations for library specifications are discussed. Computer-generated products offer many opportunities for variation that their manual counterparts do not. For this reason, some of the manifestations of the products discussed in this chapter may not correspond directly to the traditional definition of the product. For example, the discussion of bibliographies in this chapter also includes information regarding new accessions lists. The lack of distinct boundaries and precise definitions often places additional decision-making responsibilities upon librarians, who may consider it a burden to try to make informed decisions in such a volatile environment. On the other hand, the additional responsibilities are accompanied by vastly increased opportunities for fulfilling library goals. Librarians can consider the discussions in this chapter as a starting point for satisfying as-yet-undefined needs and providing services in ways that have never before been possible.

The discussion of each product in this chapter includes three sections. The first section is a description and background, including the definition of the product and background information on the characteristics of the product.

The second section includes input considerations, information that the library will need to consider and/or communicate to the product vendor(s) regarding the library's MARC records and database(s), which will be the basis for the product.

The third section includes output considerations, information that the library will need to consider and/or communicate to the product vendor(s) regarding the end product, such as the specific form the product should take, how it should look, and the goals it is intended to fulfill. Such features as record display, record arrangement, and filing are topics of discussion.

A number of considerations that are common to all MARC database products are discussed in the section entitled "Preliminary considerations." Catalogs, bibliographies, and collection analysis are discussed separately, and the final section of this chapter is devoted to "Contracting for MARC database products."

When devising specifications for MARC database products or preliminary processing, libraries will find it useful to refer to chapter 4, Major MARC Bibliographic Codes and chapter 6, MARC Database Processing for examples and suggestions relating to particular MARC fields or processes.

PRELIMINARY CONSIDERATIONS

Database Characteristics

Libraries will need to provide information to vendors regarding the makeup of their MARC database. The most basic piece of information that will need to be supplied is the number of MARC records in the database. Costs and time schedules will be based in part on the number of records to be processed.

The source(s) of the MARC records in the database will also be an important piece of information to relay to a product vendor. The three primary sources for MARC records are bibliographic utilities and networks (e.g., OCLC, WLN, RLIN, Amigos), commercial vendors (e.g., Brodart, Blackwell North America, MARCIVE), and original input (i.e., records created and input to an in-house system by the library).

A third important piece of information a product vendor will need to know is the location of local data, such as call numbers, within database records. For example, if the 092 field has been used for Dewey call numbers and the 590 field has been used for copy and volume information, then the vendor should be informed of this arrangement. No two libraries use exactly the same configuration of local information and the vendor should not have to guess as to the location and arrangement of such vital information.

Preprocessing of the Database

A number of services have been designed to ensure the usability and integrity of MARC databases. Such processes as duplicate resolution, filing indicator correction, and authority control are discussed in chapter 6, MARC Database Processing. Libraries should determine which of these processes is necessary or desirable for their database and the product they are considering. In almost all cases, such database processing will need to be completed before the database is used to produce a catalog or other product. In some cases, the special processing can be accomplished concurrently. Libraries should always ascertain, through discussion with the vendor, whether such special processes will be completed as part of the product creation.

Time Frames and Scheduling

Time frames and production scheduling need to be negotiated to both the library's and the vendor's satisfaction. In most cases, agreements that deal with time frames usually obligate both parties, not just one. In other words, if the vendor does not receive delivery of the library's database at the agreed-upon time, then the vendor is not necessarily bound to deliver the product according to the agreed-upon schedule.

A separate consideration in regard to time frames has to do with products that will be produced over a period of time, such as a catalog with quarterly supplements. Such arrangements will need to be negotiated well in advance with the vendor. Libraries should determine whether each new "version" of a product will be a cumulation or a supplement and how often a completely new cumulation will be produced. If supplements are to be produced, then libraries must decide whether each supplement will be cumulative. If, in processing the database, the vendor finds that the condition of the library's database is not what has been described by the library, then the vendor may not be able to perform the desired processing within the negotiated time frames.

Computer Filing

One of the least-standardized aspects of MARC database products is the filing of entries. Although both the current *ALA filing rules* and *Library of Congress filing rules* were devised on the "file-as-is" principles that accommodate computer filing, these rules are not adhered to as an industry standard. The standardization of computer filing for bibliographic files would provide many advantages to libraries and their patrons. Libraries should include filing rules as part of the technical specifications submitted to the vendor. Once the product is received, the library should evaluate the vendor's performance and work with the vendor to rectify errors. It does not make sense to invest time and money in a MARC product if filing problems cause user frustration or prevent users from finding the items they need.

The filing of each individual entry is a primary matter for consideration. Although it would seem that vendors should simply follow the ALA or LC filing rules, this is often not the case. Often, filing of entries has been programmed according to the best guess of a programmer or systems analyst who is not well-acquainted with library filing rules. Sometimes, the library is requested to provide specifications for filing. One decision that may be left up to the library is a determination as to which MARC subfields should be considered for filing purposes. It might seem that all portions of an entry should be filed upon; however, this is definitely not the case. For example, MARC 100 and 700 fields (personal name main and added entries) may include a subfield ǂe, which contains a relator term such as "editor" or "defendant" which is, in most libraries, ignored for filing purposes. When the relator term is used for filing purposes by computer filing routines, the person's name may be filed out of alphabetical order. And, if the person's name is entered in the catalog both with and without the relator term (e.g., for different works), then two separate subfiles for the person's name will automatically be created — one for the person's name with the relator term and the other for the name without the relator term.

An example of this type of filing problem is illustrated in the examples below, which are listings of items by two authors: Evan Woodward, a children's author and illustrator, and Evan George Woodward, an environmental scientist. In the first group of entries, the ǂe subfield relator term has been included as part of the filing routine and thus functions, in effect, as part of the author's name, which places entries for Evan Woodward on either side of that of Evan G. Woodward.

Woodward, Evan. Sand in my shoes.

Woodward, Evan. Who said so?

Woodward, Evan G. Topics in atmospheric research.

Woodward, Evan, illus. Fun stuff for kids.

In the second group of entries, the relator term has been ignored for purposes of filing; however, it does display. By disregarding the ǂe subfield for filing purposes, the entries are filed in the correct order.

Woodward, Evan, illus. Fun stuff for kids.

Woodward, Evan. Sand in my shoes.

Woodward, Evan. Who said so?

Woodward, Evan G. Topics in atmospheric research.

Another aspect of computer filing routines has to do with the number of characters within a field that are considered for filing purposes. Even when all characters of a field are printed or displayed, the number of characters considered for filing purposes may be far fewer than the total number. When computer filing routines refer to less than the total number of characters, then fields that differ only in the last portion of text may be filed out of order. For example, if computer filing routines file only upon the first 20 characters of the title field, then all titles that begin with the words *Introduction to the* (which includes a total of 20 characters, including blanks) will be arranged in random order in relation to each other. It is preferable that computer filing routines refer to all appropriate characters within the subfields being filed upon, as there are many lengthy fields (such as series titles, conference headings, and corporate names) that differ only in the latter part of the field.

Subsorts are an aspect of computer filing that require much more attention than they usually receive. When there are multiple records within a file with the same access point, the subarrangement of these records should be stipulated through the identification of other fields or subfields that are to be referred to for filing purposes. For example, when a number of items by the same author are filed within a catalog, the primary sort is on the author's name and the first subsort should refer to the title. When the text within the title field is identical for two or more items, then a second subsort should be specified. For example, if a library holds five different editions of an author's work that all share the identical title, these items will be arranged in random order in relation to each other if only a primary sort (author) and a first subsort (title) are used. By using the date of publication as a second subsort, the editions of the work will file in chronological order.

In some cases, problems with filing arise because subsorts have not been specified. In other cases, filing problems arise because subsorts are being performed upon the wrong fields or subfields. Both the ALA and LC filing rules stipulate the fields and subfields to be considered for filing in catalogs, and libraries may refer to these rules for filing within catalogs, bibliographies, and other products.

In some cases, correct computer filing may be quite different from what users have been accustomed to within their own manual catalog. For example, all numbers are filed using their numeric values, rather than being filed as if they were spelled out alphabetically. This is correct filing according to the ALA and LC filing rules. In such cases, a title added entry, which includes the number spelled out, is required to have the entry file alphabetically as a word rather than in numerical order.

One aberration libraries may find regarding the filing of numbers is that they may be sorted in decimal order rather than in their correct order as whole numbers. This affects titles that begin with numerical values more than it affects titles with numerals elsewhere within the field. This also affects filing of series titles that include volume numbering. A sample list is given below of entries incorrectly filed as if they were decimal numbers.

101 hints for gardeners

13 is my lucky number

2 books for Sarah

236 days as a hostage

25 ways to improve your cholesterol level

7th heaven

The list below includes the same entries filed correctly—in numerical order.

2 books for Sarah

7th heaven

13 is my lucky number

25 ways to improve your cholesterol level

101 hints for gardeners

236 days as a hostage

Incorrect filing obviously can cause confusion and frustration on the part of library patrons and may even prevent them from finding desired items. If questions arise about the correctness of computer filing, the library can (and should) check the computer filing of catalog entries against the ALA or LC filing rules. And the vendor should be contacted about rectifying filing problems.

CATALOGS

The three types of catalog products discussed in this chapter are COM (computer output microform), CD-ROM (compact disc-read only memory), and printed catalogs (also known as "book catalogs"). Generally speaking, a product is defined as a catalog if it provides at least the same types of access as a traditional card catalog (e.g., name, title, subject). For all such computer-generated products, libraries do have the option of specifying a more limited access (e.g., by subject headings only) or additional access points (e.g., material type, language). Such options will be discussed in this chapter even though the products may not be considered as catalogs in the strictest sense of the word.

Computer Output Microform Catalogs (Comcatalogs)

Description and Background

Comcatalogs are microfiche or microfilm catalogs that have been produced from a machine-readable (e.g., MARC) database. Microfiche or microfilm readers are used to display the records and some of the readers also produce hardcopy prints of the catalog entries. Comcatalogs have the advantage of being much more compact than card catalogs; however, they are not as compact as CD-ROM catalogs. A microfiche comcatalog can consist of hundreds of microfiche. A user must locate the appropriate fiche through the use of eye-readable headings that are usually printed at the top of the fiche; the heading notes the range of the entries on that particular fiche. For a time, comcatalogs were the medium of choice for union catalogs, including regional, state, and consortium databases; however, the size of the catalogs (i.e., the large number of fiche), questions about cost-effectiveness, and the rise of other technologies have resulted in the abandonment of COM in many such cases. COM still holds a number of advantages for smaller libraries and for other uses, and it is not unreasonable to predict that comcatalogs will see a future resurgence of popularity, as has occurred with printed catalogs.

Input Considerations

A major consideration for a library that is producing a comcatalog from its MARC database is that of record selection. A library will need to determine which records of its MARC database to include in a comcatalog. The proper decision may well be to include all records for all materials in a comcatalog, or the library may have some reason to omit some types of records or records for specific types of materials. For example, if records added to the database during a given time period are incomplete or substandard, the library may decide to omit those and add newer, more complete records. Or, the library may decide to omit serials from the comcatalog because they will be handled in another manner.

Generally speaking, the decisions surrounding record selection are relatively easy when a single institution is involved. In the case of a multi-institutional catalog, using the combined databases of two or more libraries, however, the question of record selection involves an added dimension. In order to minimize the number of fiche or frames within the catalog (and the number of entries a user will need to look through), union comcatalogs usually include only one bibliographic record per given item, regardless of the number of copies held or the number of institutions that hold the item. To indicate which libraries hold a particular item, the names of the libraries (or a representative abbreviation or symbol) are listed with the bibliographic record.

When multiple databases are merged to produce a union comcatalog, a decision will need to be made as to which of several duplicate bibliographic records should be selected as the comcatalog entry. One method of selection that is often used involves prioritizing the contributing institutions on the basis of the quality and completeness of their MARC records. When more than one institution has contributed a record for an item, then the prioritized institution listing will determine which of the duplicate records will be selected for inclusion in the catalog. Other possible criteria for prioritizing bibliographic records are record currency (e.g., the record with the most recent date in the MARC 005 field) and completeness of the record (e.g., the record containing the most characters or the largest number of MARC fields).

Output Specifications

A comcatalog is similar to a card catalog in the ways that bibliographic records are arranged and displayed. A separate bibliographic record is entered for each access point within the record, just as a separate catalog card is filed for each access point. And, a library has the choice of specifying whether the individual entries will be full or partial entries. Partial entries (i.e., less than a full catalog record) are used to minimize the size of comcatalogs for two reasons. One reason is to make the comcatalog easier for library patrons to use; the other is to minimize the cost of the comcatalog, when costs are based on the number of frames, fiches, and so on, rather than the number of bibliographic records included.

Specifications for record display will usually center on two points: (1) which fields are to be displayed for full and partial records and (2) under which access points will each type of record (full or partial) be displayed. Often, a comcatalog vendor will have a set of standard specifications from which libraries may choose. For example, a common arrangement is to include a full bibliographic entry (1XX-8XX MARC fields) for each main entry (1XX field, or 245 field when there is no 1XX field); a partial entry (e.g., 1XX-3XX MARC fields) is included for all other access points.

Another significant issue for bibliographic display is that of call number formatting. Placing the call number vertically in the upper left corner of the record display will provide for a more easily recognizable arrangement that matches the call number arrangement on the spine labels of library materials. On the other hand, arranging the call number horizontally at the top or bottom of the record display is a less error-prone method (insofar as computer programs are concerned). Using one line per call number also makes for a smaller record display overall, using less space than the vertical arrangement (always an important consideration).

One valuable COM product that is not a traditional catalog feature is that of a MARC display of the library's bibliographic records, as they appear in the library's database. The MARC display includes all the MARC tags, subfield codes, and all other MARC coding. Because the successful use of the records is largely dependent upon the proper MARC coding, a MARC display can serve as a useful resource for cataloging and bibliographic maintenance purposes.

The filing of records is also a major consideration for comcatalog production. A primary decision to be made in regard to filing of records is whether the comcatalog will be a dictionary or divided catalog. A dictionary catalog will include all entries filed in sequence, regardless of the type of access point. A divided catalog includes separate subfiles for different types of access points. Usually, a divided catalog will include a combined author-title and separate subject file or three separate files (author, title, and subject). For comcatalog filing specifications, the library may be required to designate, by MARC tag, the particular access points to be included in each file. Generally speaking, this selection will involve the same criteria as for a card catalog.

A separate file arranged in shelflist (call number) order can be a particularly valuable COM product that expands the value of catalog services to library users. The shelf order arrangement can facilitate browsing and some types of subject searching. In devising their specifications for shelflist order, libraries will need to provide complete and specific instructions for call number filing. Examples of the types of information the library will need to supply are: whether to ignore or file on call number prefixes, such as "Ref," and whether to file specific numbers in the call number as decimals or whole numbers.

More comprehensive information is provided in the discussion on computer filing in the previous section, "Preliminary considerations."

CD-ROM Catalogs

Description and Background

CD-ROM (compact disc-read only memory) utilizes laser technology to store large amounts of data on a small, durable plastic disc. A CD-ROM drive, a computer, and appropriate software are required to use CD-ROM catalogs. The compactness of the CD-ROM disc is one of the major advantages of this technology, and the record display (online or hard copy) is arguably more user-friendly and more readable than that of a comcatalog. On the other hand, the CD-ROM technology has been—and apparently will continue to be—a somewhat unreliable and unpredictable medium. When dealing with CD-ROM catalogs, librarians will face unresolved questions regarding both hardware (e.g., standards and multi-user configurations) and software (e.g., search and retrieval problems).

Input Considerations

Alternatives for record selection are a primary consideration for CD-ROM catalogs. For single institution CD-ROM catalogs, the record selection considerations are essentially the same as those for single institution comcatalogs, as discussed above. For multi-institutional catalogs, libraries have two primary options: a single union catalog or a group of individual catalogs, one for each library. The union catalog would include a record for each title held by the group, with an indication of the owning libraries. The union catalog alternative holds the advantages of a smaller file (which may lower costs) and the ability to search all collections at the same time. However, the merging of individual files into a union catalog can be a very expensive process and is a complex undertaking, involving many of the considerations discussed above for comcatalogs.

Output Considerations

CD-ROM catalogs do not include multiple iterations of a record, one filed under each access point. Instead, each record is included within the CD-ROM database just once, and, through the use of microcomputer applications software, the record is retrieved when search keys input by the user match one of the access points in the record. So, instead of determining which files (e.g., author, title, subject) the access points should be filed in, the library will need to consider which fields and subfields should be indexed (i.e., should be searchable). If keyword searching is to be included as a feature of the catalog, then the library will also need to consider which fields (e.g., which types of notes and subject headings) should be indexed for keyword searches. In these matters, vendors may simply have a standard set of selections the library will be expected to accept, or there may be a few different options from which the library may choose.

Printed Catalogs

Description and Background

Printed catalogs are also called "book catalogs" because they are in book format. They are more compact than card catalogs and they offer an advantage over other computer-generated catalogs (e.g., COM and CD-ROM) in that their use does not require any special equipment. Printed catalogs are enjoying a resurgence of popularity, particularly among smaller libraries, but also for specialized uses by larger libraries.

For smaller libraries, it may be feasible and desirable to include all materials within a printed catalog. For larger libraries, the preferred option may be to include only specified materials within printed catalogs. Such limited catalogs are often produced with a specialized use and/or specific audience in mind. For example, a library may issue a new accessions catalog of materials that have been acquired within the last six months, or other specified time period. Another focus of printed catalogs is selected material types, such as serials. A third option is to include materials within a given subject area or special collection, with the intent of distributing the catalogs to researchers and other interested parties.

Input Considerations

Printed catalogs often involve the use of only a specific subset of a library's database, such as a particular collection or a particular type of material. It is necessary to carefully define and describe the parameters to be used in selecting out the desired records. Instructions and examples for setting parameters are given in the discussion on library specifications and other considerations in the "Special select" section of chapter 6, MARC Database Processing.

Output Considerations

Output considerations for printed catalogs are generally the same as those discussed above for comcatalogs: full vs. partial entries, access points, call number arrangement, and filing of records. Usually, as many space-saving methods as possible are used to keep the catalog a manageable size.

BIBLIOGRAPHIES

Description and Background

For the purposes of this discussion, a *bibliography* is a list of resources that are related to each other in some way or that share a common characteristic. The primary distinguishing difference between bibliographies and catalogs is that bibliographies use fewer access points (usually only one). Bibliographies also generally provide a less complete record display than is used within a catalog.

Manually compiled bibliographies have long played an important role in library reference services, and the use of MARC databases can enhance that role. As with other types of sophisticated intellectual activities, the computer will not replace a well-trained professional, but it will allow some activities to be carried out more easily and more quickly, and it will expand the capabilities of library staff.

There are two primary methods for obtaining computer-generated bibliographies through the use of a MARC database. Users may request that such lists be displayed online or printed offline through the use of an in-house system, generally as a service provided through an online catalog. For more extensive or complex requests, or for libraries that do not have an in-house system, the library's MARC database can be manipulated by a vendor (or other data processing facility) to provide the desired output. Generally speaking, the options provided through an in-house system are more limited than those of a MARC processing vendor.

MARC databases provide a widely expanded set of options for bibliography compilation. In addition to the more traditional subject and author bibliographies, record selection criteria can include virtually any part of the traditional catalog record (such as publisher), as well as a number of identifiers that have not traditionally been explicitly included within descriptive cataloging. The latter type of option consists mostly of fixed field elements, such as language, intellectual level, and other such characteristics. The major fixed field codes for books are discussed in chapter 4, Major MARC Bibliographic Codes, which serves as an introduction to the potential uses of specific MARC fields. Libraries should refer to appropriate MARC documentation, such as the *USMARC format for bibliographic data*, for comprehensive information on MARC fields for all types of materials.

Because of the capabilities of computers and the versatility of the MARC record, virtually any element of a MARC database can be considered as an access point. A few examples follow:

- A bibliography of foreign language dictionaries can be compiled through the use of the fixed field Language code, the 041 Language field, and the fixed field Nature of contents code.

- A bibliography of conference publications published during the last five years (or other time period) can be compiled through the use of the fixed field Conference publication code and the fixed field Date 1 and Date 2 codes.

- When different collections within a library are classified and shelved according to two different classification systems (e.g., Dewey and LC), records for materials classed according to one system can be selected and listed within a bibliography in order by the other classification system. For libraries that have, for example, residual Dewey collections that have not been reclassified to LC, this type of bibliography can help to provide access to and enhance the use of such materials. The success of such an operation is dependent upon being able to identify the desired records (e.g., by holding library code or by location prefix) and assumes that both types of call numbers are included in the record (e.g., that unused call numbers have not been deleted).

Libraries may also be able to arrange for production of new accessions lists from their tapes or as a feature of an in-house system.

Input Considerations

Record selection—selecting records from a database for inclusion in a bibliography—is a particularly crucial step for computer-generated bibliographies. Selection criteria are not always easily defined. For example, the most commonly found orientation of bibliographies is that of subject. Selecting MARC database records by subject is in some ways similar to performing a search in an online reference database. When searching by subject, libraries will need to determine the following: (1) the terms to be searched; (2) the fields in which the terms should be searched; and (3) any exceptions to those selection criteria. For example, the term to be searched could be a Library of Congress subject heading and the field to be searched could be the MARC 650 field (topical subject heading). An exception to the search criteria could be to ignore any fiction items, which could be identified by the appearance of the term *fiction* in a subfield $\neq x$ of the 650 field or by checking the value of the fixed field Fiction code.

A more complex search, which more fully utilizes the capabilities of library automation, could involve a search using a combination of several subject heading terms, or a term not found in a subject heading list. The fields to be searched might include subject fields, as well as notes fields (e.g., the MARC 505 Contents note and 520 Summary note fields), and title fields (e.g., MARC X30, 24X, and 740 fields). And the exceptions might be fiction items and items with publication dates prior to 1965 (which could be detected by checking the fixed field Date 1 and Date 2 values).

Bibliographies compiled on the basis of other criteria, such as author, language, or publisher, are among the many other possibilities for creation of bibliographies from MARC databases. Selection criteria must always be designed with extreme care. Specific instructions and examples for setting parameters are given in the discussion on library specifications and other considerations in the "Special select" section of chapter 6, MARC Database Processing.

Output Considerations

Decisions regarding record display for bibliographies involve some of the same considerations as for catalogs (discussed above). But, there are not as many factors to consider, since bibliographies generally contain only one entry (access) point and thus, only one type of entry. The major decisions to be made focus on: (1) the record elements to be displayed and (2) the arrangement of the displayed elements.

In choosing the record elements to be displayed, libraries may select to have a complete catalog entry or simply an author, short title, date, and call number. (By the way, the local call number is a vital piece of information, not just a nicety.) There are many options in between the two extremes, and of course, the library may choose to include information that may not traditionally have been a part of the catalog entry, taken perhaps from the MARC fixed field or MARC 007 field (for example, information about whether a film is live action or animated). The library's decision regarding display options will depend upon the audience and the uses for which the bibliography is intended, the limitations imposed by physical size of the end product, and financial considerations.

The order of the elements within each entry should also be specified according to the intended audience and uses of the bibliography. In many cases, the traditional arrangement of elements (e.g., as they are found on a catalog card) is most reasonable if for no other reason than that it is familiar to users. In other cases, the arrangement of elements within an entry may be considered in light of the element that is being used to file (sort) the entries. For example, if the name of the publisher is the element by which entries are filed, then the publisher's name can be used as the first element in the entry, with the other elements being displayed in traditional order. In this case, the publisher's name would probably not be displayed a second time, in its traditional location. Another option would be to have the publisher's name used once, as a heading, with all appropriate records filed beneath the heading. This would save more space than the repetitive use of the publisher's name with each individual entry.

Information within the MARC record can be used to file the bibliography records into one or more arrangements. For example, it is possible to provide lists in one call number order (e.g., LC call number) for items classed and shelved in another call number order (e.g., Superintendent of Documents numbers), as long as both types of call numbers are included in the MARC record. (This is one of many arguments for leaving all types of call numbers in the record when cataloging.) Subarrangement, or subsorting, of entries filed under the same access point can also be accomplished in one or more of a variety of ways. For example, a bibliography of works by selected authors can include each author's works subsorted alphabetically by title, chronologically by date, by type of material, or even in ascending or descending order by the total number of pages in each book.

COLLECTION ANALYSIS

Description and Background

For the purposes of this discussion, *collection analysis* is defined as the statistical examination of any of a number of attributes of a library's collection. The end product is usually a printed report that presents the desired information in a specified format. Traditional collection analysis techniques have often focused on evaluating the strengths of the collection by determining the numbers and proportions of materials within a particular call number range. Other characteristics of an individual library's collection have also been examined through collection analysis. As cooperative library endeavors have increased, collection analysis has served to compare the collections of two or more libraries as the basis of cooperative collection development efforts and for other such purposes. MARC databases offer a dramatically increased potential for statistical analysis of collections, with focuses that previously could not have realistically been considered or that would have required an excessive amount of time or financial support.

Any of the MARC fixed field elements, such as material type, language, intellectual level, fiction/nonfiction, biographical material, place of publication, and many other codes, can be considered as a basis for statistical analysis. Theoretically, any element of the MARC record can be used as a focus; however, the fixed field codes were more specifically designed for such analysis, as they are concise and easily identifiable within a MARC record.

When devising specifications for collection analysis or preliminary processing, libraries will find it useful to refer to chapter 4, Major MARC Bibliographic Codes and chapter 6, MARC Database Processing for examples and suggestions relating to particular MARC fields or processes.

There are two characteristics of MARC databases that can significantly affect the reliability of collection analysis. One is that, for older records in particular, the MARC fixed field codes (and other data that was not used within card catalogs) may be incorrect. Libraries will need to evaluate the impact of this condition by considering the cataloging procedures that have taken place (e.g., were fixed field codes checked and corrected?). If no cataloging documentation exists, the most reasonable method for evaluating MARC fixed field integrity is to actually examine a sample of MARC records from the library's database. The discussions of MARC fixed field codes in chapter 4, Major MARC Bibliographic Codes, include information on commonly found inconsistencies in the use of MARC fixed field codes.

The completeness of the database in relation to the library's collection is the second database condition that can significantly impact upon the success of collection analysis. If all the library's materials are not represented in the database, then the statistical analysis may be skewed. Although using a partial database for catalog production does not present significant problems, using an incomplete database for collection analysis leaves the reliability of the resultant data open to question. Libraries should consider all of the ramifications of this situation and should, at the very least, develop a clear understanding of the inherent biases. A reasonable and viable interpretation of the statistical analysis can be made only in light of the biases that are involved.

Input Considerations

The two main input considerations for collection analysis are: (1) selecting the records in the database that are to be analyzed and (2) specifying the portion(s) of the records that are to be analyzed. Libraries may decide to have the entire database analyzed or just a few collections. If only a subset of the collection is to be analyzed, the library will need to specify exactly how the subset will be identified. For example, the collection(s) to be analyzed may be selected by the computer on the basis of holding library codes, call number prefixes (such as "Ref"), or by call number groups (such as all LC call numbers beginning with *P* or all Dewey call numbers in the 800 range).

In specifying which portions of the record are to be analyzed, libraries are communicating two sets of instructions. First, the library is stating explicitly *what* is being analyzed, such as call numbers, language, or country of publication. Secondly, the library is stating, also very explicitly, *how* the features to be analyzed will be recognized by computer programs. Examples are given below of some of the questions that will need to be answered regarding analysis by call number.

- Is the same type of call number included in all records?

- Is the call number always located in the same field, or could it be in one of several fields (e.g., for LC call numbers, 050, 090, or 099 fields)?

- Is there a hierarchy of call number fields to be analyzed when more than one valid field is found in a record (e.g., 099 first, followed by 090, then by 050)?

- How specific should call number analysis be? How much of the call number should be considered? For example, for Dewey numbers, should only the major divisions be considered (the first character of the Dewey number); should all numbers before the decimal point be considered; should all numbers before and after the decimal point be considered?

Databases can be analyzed on the basis of any of a number of aspects besides call number. Libraries must consider their specifications carefully to evaluate the biases introduced by the specifications. For example, the library may specify an analysis of fiction vs. nonfiction items with selection based on the Fiction code in the 008 field. In this case, the library should understand that poetry and drama, although both classified and considered as literary works, are coded as nonfiction in the 008 field.

Output Considerations

Libraries need to be very specific about the output they expect from the analysis and the ways in which the results should be presented. The questions below indicate the types of information the library will need to provide to the vendor.

- Does the library need to have a record count or percentages or both?

- Will subtotals of categories and totals need to be shown on the output report?

- Should the analysis be done in relation to volumes or titles or both?

- If volumes, rather than titles, are to be counted, how will computer programs be able to determine the number of physical volumes?

CONTRACTING FOR MARC DATABASE PRODUCTS

Researching Vendors

The first step in selecting a vendor is to build a list of prospective vendors. There are a number of resources that can provide information about potential vendors; professional journals, other libraries, conference exhibits, and professional meetings and programs all can provide leads regarding vendors.

Libraries should consider and treat potential vendors in much the same way that potential staff members are treated. Request information about qualifications and background, including relevant experience with other libraries. Ask for a list of references and then check with those references. When requesting information from the references, compare the needs of that library to those of your own library.

RFIs, RFPs, RFQs

An RFI (Request for Information) is a request for the vendor's literature or marketing information regarding products or services in which the library is interested. The library will also want to request a price list or pricing information. An RFP (Request for Proposals) is usually not done until after the library has determined at least general specifications for the product or process desired. An RFP, or an RFQ (Request for Quotes), is often done as part of the formalized competitive bidding process of the organization, and it may or may not be legally binding to both the library and the vendors. In comparison to an RFQ, the RFP provides more general information about what the library desires, to which the vendor is expected to respond with a proposed method or product. The RFQ includes much more specific information about what the library desires, and it requires the vendor to respond in relation to the library's specifications. The RFQ does not usually involve as much room for the vendor to suggest alternatives or vary an approach. When the library is open to suggestions for products or methods, an RFP is usually preferable to an RFQ. The RFP (or RFQ) process can be a valuable process for the library to go through, even when it is not required for a competitive bidding situation. Preparation of the RFP is a good exercise in communication between various library departments and helps in determining and explicitly stating library wants and needs.

Libraries should be aware that preparing a proposal or bid involves a substantial commitment of a vendor's organizational resources, particularly the salaries of the employees preparing the proposal. Because a proposal or bid is usually legally binding, the vendor must be very careful in communicating qualifications, timetables, costs, and other important aspects of the proposal. The bidding process is also usually competitive, which places additional pressures on the vendor. If the RFP does not represent a reasonable return on the vendor's investment, either financially or in terms of additional business, the vendor may choose not to respond.

Technical and Other Specifications

Technical specifications focus on the input, processing, and output for a product. Timetables and performance standards are among the other types of specifications that also need to be considered.

There are four main sources for information on specifications: professional publications, vendors, other libraries, and organizational purchasing agencies. The category of professional publications includes books, journal articles, and databases (such as the ERIC database, which provides access to valuable unpublished documents). Vendors usually have specification sheets or forms that include questions that need to be answered and options from which libraries will need to choose. (A vendor that does not have such forms may not have had significant experience with that particular product or process.)

Specifications prepared by other libraries can be extremely valuable. When using other libraries' specifications, however, keep in mind that the specifications may have been devised within a different environment or situation. It is also useful to know how the other library, in hindsight, would have prepared their specifications differently.

Purchasing agencies or contracts and grants departments related to the library should be able to provide information as to legal or organizational guidelines for preparation of specifications.

One important factor to keep in mind in regard to technical specifications, timetables, performance standards, and other such features of a contract is that the library has the responsibility to uphold its end of the deal. For example, if database processing specifications prepared by the library do not accurately reflect the condition of the library's database, the cost of additional processing (to rectify the library's errors) and the delays in the timetable caused by such additional processing, will be considered to be the library's responsibility, not the vendor's.

Costs

Setup costs, unit costs for processing, and output costs (for extra copies, etc.) are a few of the different types of costs involved with MARC database products. A detailed discussion of costs is included at the end of chapter 6, MARC Database Processing.

Product Evaluation

Too often, product evaluation consists only of monitoring timetables and superficially checking the product. Libraries should thoroughly evaluate the product as soon as it is received. The first step is to compare the product to the library's specifications. If the vendor has not followed the specifications or has not adhered to other portions of the contract, the library should contact the vendor as soon as possible.

Libraries should check a sample of the entries in the product to determine whether records have been processed properly. For example, within a catalog, the main and added entries for a given record should be checked to determine whether each entry is formatted and filed properly. The library should check examples of as many different types of records as possible (e.g., records for all materials types) and as many different fields and subfields as possible (e.g., MARC 100, 110, 111, and 130 fields with various combinations of subfields).

RELATED READINGS

Chwe, Steven Seokho. "A study of data elements for the COM catalog." *Journal of library automation* 12 (1): 94-97 (March 1979).

Kim, David U. "OCLC-MARC tapes and collection management." *Information technology and libraries* 1 (1): 22-27 (March 1982).

Payson, Evelyn, and Barbara Moore. "Statistical collection management analysis of OCLC-MARC tape records." *Information technology and libraries* 4 (3): 220-32 (September 1985).

8

MARC-based Online Systems

INTRODUCTION

For many librarians, the first experience with MARC-based online systems is also a first introduction to MARC format. In some cases, smaller libraries have never been involved with MARC prior to system installation. For larger libraries, usually only the cataloging staff have been acquainted with MARC. With the introduction of an online system, many more librarians will need to become acquainted with MARC format in order to devise appropriate system specifications, optimize their use of the system, and help patrons in their use of the system. Noncataloging library staff may have had "close calls" with learning MARC before, but now that they will have to work closely with the providers and the users of their MARC-based system, they will definitely need to know more.

In many cases, MARC format is seen as something that a librarian has to put up with to use the online system. But MARC format is not just a way to get records into a system; MARC format allows librarians and users to get the most out of a system. In the most literal and direct manner, MARC format has made online library systems possible. Without MARC, none of the systems that we know would exist. MARC is a standard that system developers can follow when creating the extremely complex programs for circulation, online catalogs, and other library applications. Even with a standard format, the development of library systems is expensive and systems are expensive for libraries to buy. If each library's system had to be developed according to a different record format, major system development would not be feasible in terms of time or money.

Historically speaking, the first online systems (implemented before microcomputers were in use) were used for circulation purposes, basically for tracking materials, sending out overdue notices, and other such functions. These systems included short-entry records with enough information to identify the item for circulation purposes, but they did not include such information as series statements, notes, subject headings, or added entries.

As computers became more powerful and could handle larger amounts of data, libraries saw the opportunity to use the computer for many of the routine functions involved in library catalogs, such as filing. It soon became clear that the computer could enable libraries to expand greatly the number and types of services that they had fulfilled prior to the introduction of the computer, as opposed to simply providing the same services more efficiently through the computer. The enhancement of service that the computer provides is not simply a frill; it is a significant and essential step toward the library goal of access to information.

The card catalogs and manual systems that have been libraries' best attempts at fulfilling information needs have included severe restrictions and limitations. Unfortunately, in many cases, libraries have allowed these restrictions—rather than patrons' needs—to define library goals and services. For example, card catalogs have traditionally been limited to just a few access points *not* because patrons only know those particular access points, but because libraries could not afford the costs/time/staff/floor space/furniture to buy/file/house/maintain more cards.

One definitive difference between manual library systems and computerized library systems can be illustrated through a comparison of searching by title within a card catalog and within an online catalog that provides keyword access. A patron who is looking for a specific title within a card catalog must know the first word of the title and may even need to know several (or all) words of the title in their correct order to find that particular title in the card catalog. For example, a patron looking in the card catalog for the *Wallace-Homestead price guide to American country antiques* will probably not find that item in the catalog if he only remembers the title as being the *Price guide to American country antiques* or the *Price guide for American country antiques* or the *Price guide to country antiques* or the *Price guide to American antiques*. An online catalog with keyword search capabilities, on the other hand, which can provide access by any word or words in the title, would allow the patron to search by combining the key terms of the title, including *price*, *guide*, and *antiques*, to successfully retrieve the desired title. In addition, the online catalog would also retrieve a "bibliography" of other titles with the same words, some of which would likely be of interest to the patron.

Many of the system features discussed in this chapter are generally available only as capabilities of mainframe or minicomputer-based systems. A few of the operations, such as public access catalogs and circulation systems, are also available as microcomputer-based systems.

COMPUTER CAPABILITIES

The three basic capabilities of the computer are: (1) the ability to store massive amounts of data (i.e., storage); (2) the ability to follow instructions (i.e., routines); and (3) the ability to process information or instructions rapidly (i.e., speed). The value of the computer for any application can be assessed as one or a combination of these three capabilities. Storage, routines, and speed can be the weaknesses, as well as the strengths, of a computer system; their successful use is dependent upon the knowledge of the people who design and use the system. A brief introduction to the three basic computer capabilities is given below to provide a better understanding of how computers work and what their limitations are, particularly in regard to library applications.

Storage

The ability to store massive amounts of data is a significant strength of the computer as it relates to library uses. For instance: the same amount of floor space that was previously required to house a single card catalog can accommodate several computer terminals; a remote corner of the library that could not have accommodated a card catalog can house a computer terminal, which can offer much more information than the card catalog provided.

The data that is stored for library systems can be categorized into three types: (1) databases, (2) computer programs, and (3) auxiliary data. The databases are generally created or provided by the library and may include bibliographic databases, patron databases, and authority databases, among others. The computer programs are usually created or provided by the system vendor, with the library being involved to a greater or lesser degree in program design through the provision of specifications. Auxiliary data includes other types of information or instructions required to accomplish the system functions, such as index tables (for search and retrieval purposes). The term *overhead* is sometimes used to refer to the auxiliary data and/or computer programs.

The amount of storage required for a given library's system is dependent upon a number of factors, including the size of the bibliographic database, the number of user stations, and the number and types of functions the library expects to use. For example, an online catalog with keyword access will require much more storage than an online catalog without keyword access because of the additional computer routines that are required and because of the additional auxiliary data that is required for search and retrieval functions. Similarly, a system that includes automated authority control will require more storage, for the programs, the authority database, and the auxiliary data, than will the same system without authority control functions.

One reason for system "failure" of earlier installations of library systems was the failure of vendors and librarians to accurately project the amount of computer storage that was required. Too often, storage needs for library systems were assessed with an eye toward more commonly known business-oriented applications. Because library records are much larger than those used for business or commercial applications (an average of more than 700 characters per record as compared to 100 characters) and because the computer routines are more complex (and thus lengthier), storage estimates were often woefully inadequate. Inadequate storage can negatively impact upon many aspects of system functions, including system response time, and, unfortunately, because of the financial, practical, and technical considerations involved, revising storage capacity upwards is not easily accomplished. Fortunately, methods for projecting required memory are now much more accurate than they have been in the past.

Routines

The ability of the computer to follow instructions allows humans to delegate to the computer many tasks that are either too simple and monotonous to be rewarding or too complex and sophisticated to be remembered by a human being. The computer will faithfully execute the routines, communicated as computer programs, without boredom or fatigue, regardless of how simple or complex those routines are. Because the computer "knows" absolutely nothing, the development of computer programs is an extremely labor-intensive, precise, detailed, error-prone, exacting task. Instructions that human beings take for granted as being "understood" have to be explained in exhaustive detail to a computer. For example, a computer cannot simply be told to file something in alphabetical order, as a human being can. The computer must be told, explicitly and comprehensively, what each letter of the alphabet is and the order in which it should be arranged in relation to other letters.

Computer programs for library systems are unusually complex and require an extremely high level of computer expertise. Because it is still quite rare to find expert programmers who also have a high level of library/cataloging expertise, the creation of computer programs for library systems is, of necessity, a team effort and an ongoing task. Often initial system development includes librarians, systems analysts and programmers, and others. The complexity of the system is further impacted by the unpredictability of the data (e.g., catalog records) and uses that the system will need to accommodate. All this means that libraries can often plan on "debugging" the vendor's programs as they use the system. Careful communication is of the utmost importance where computer routines are involved. Because library communications are usually filtered through a user representative to a systems analyst and then to the programmer, the library should provide specific, comprehensive, and explicit instructions regarding correction or enhancement of computer routines. Examples should always be included.

Development of computer programs is the largest single item in a system vendor's budget, and libraries should not take development of routines for granted. The expensive and time-consuming task of program development is always subject to prioritization by the vendor. There are three ways libraries can optimize their efforts toward having system changes and enhancements made: (1) prove that the current program is incorrect or inaccurate, according to contract specifications or standards the vendor has agreed to follow (e.g., the *ALA filing rules*); (2) prove that the requested change or development is one that many libraries are interested in having done; and (3) communicate the specifications for changes to computer routines.

The more reasonable the request and the less time that the vendor needs to spend on researching and debugging a program change or enhancement, the more likely it is that the vendor will be agreeable to making the requested change.

Speed

The ability of the computer to process information or instructions rapidly is, for some processes, the only difference between a manual system and a computerized system. This deceptively simple distinguishing characteristic is the dynamic that makes the difference between the "possible" and the "impossible," where many library services are concerned. Imagine, for instance, that a patron is looking for a particular fiction item that includes the word *run* as the last word of the title. Although it would be technically possible for the library staff to check each card in the card catalog for items that include the word *run* as the last word of the title, this task would not be possible in financial or practical terms. The patron's need would probably go unfulfilled. On the other hand, through the use of an online catalog with keyword search capability, the patron could conduct his own search, using the word *run* and qualifying for fiction items only, which provides a much greater probability that the patron will find what he is seeking. In this instance, the distinguishing difference between the manual catalog and the automated catalog is the speed with which each title entry can be checked for the word *run*. Because it takes considerably less time for the computer to check each title than it would for library staff to perform the same task, the task that was formerly "impossible" in financial and practical terms now becomes "possible"—and even "taken for granted."

The speed of system operation can be measured in both absolute and relative terms. Contract specifications for library systems may include stipulations that a particular response time be maintained or that a particular number of items can be circulated within a given time frame. In this case, system speed is expressed in specific, absolute terms; however, patron satisfaction sometimes focuses on less exacting measurements that are more a matter of perception or comparison with other (usually simpler) computerized systems.

System speed is a function of both the computer hardware and the software. The speed with which the central processing unit (CPU) can process data is one variable upon which the speed of a particular system is dependent. The manner in which the software or programs instruct the CPU to perform routines can also affect system speed greatly. If the instructions are not efficiently stated, the speed of the CPU will not be used effectively. In some cases, inefficient programs used with a quick, powerful CPU will actually function more slowly than well-designed programs used with a slower, less powerful processor.

SYSTEM SPECIFICATIONS

For the purposes of this discussion, *system specifications* are considered either as "initial specifications" or "ongoing specifications." Generally speaking, the initial specifications are those that the library should determine prior to selecting a system. Ongoing specifications are those that the library will need to determine once a system has been selected, as it is being implemented, and each time a new release of the system or a system enhancement is implemented. All of these types of specifications should be kept in mind in both the pre- and post-contract phases of system use.

Initial Specifications

Initial specifications often focus on the major capabilities and functions of a system and a vendor, such as the types of functions a system can carry out, the system response time, and the ability of the vendor to fulfill the library's needs in a timely manner. Some of the major initial specifications issues include system modules, system capacities, and input and output capabilities.

Modules

The term *modules* refers to major system functions that the library requires or desires. These functions include such operations as ordering and acquisitions, circulation, online catalog, keyword searching, boolean searching, serials control, authority control, bibliographic maintenance, media booking, interlibrary loan, and statistical reporting. Libraries need to be aware that two systems with similar-sounding functions may handle the functions in quite different ways. For example, two systems that provide "statistical reporting" may differ in that one system provides only current statistics (e.g., the number of items that are currently checked out), while the other system also provides "aging" of statistics (e.g., how many times a specific item has been checked out during a specified time period). Because the aging of statistics provides valuable information for inventory control, weeding, and other purposes, the two systems cannot be considered as offering the same service, although the same generic term, *statistical reporting*, is used to describe the functions of both.

System Capacities

System capacities refers to the upper limits of a system in regard to a number of system variables, such as the number of items that can be circulated within a given time period, the number of records that can be accommodated by the system, or the number of public access or circulation terminals that can reasonably be operated on the system at one time. There are two primary options a library has for evaluating this type of system capacity: (1) carefully and thoroughly examine system operation in similar libraries or (2) perform a test of the system in a simulated environment. In either case, any of a number of variables may impact upon system operations in a way that cannot be properly monitored. The second option, performing a test, can be an expensive and complicated endeavor. Unless the library's situation presents untested limits, a vendor may not be open to carrying out a full-scale test of the system. If a library can fully evaluate system operation at one or more existing sites with similar specifications, this can help provide the information the library needs regarding system capacity.

Input and Output Capabilities

The ability of a system to accept, maintain, and output data will have a major impact on the system's value, both in the long and short term. For example, a system may accept full MARC records but then strip out or delete portions of the record as part of the loading process. When, in future versions of the system software, the system is enhanced to use more of the MARC information (such as fixed field codes), the data that was previously deleted by the system may have to be added to the records again. In many cases, this would have to be done manually by the library on a record-by-record basis, an expensive and time-consuming process. Some of the questions that libraries should ask in regard to system input and output capabilities are:

- Does the system accept and maintain full MARC bibliographic records? As illustrated in the preceding paragraph, a system that does not maintain the full MARC information may eventually prove to be a much costlier system than was anticipated by the library.

- Does the system accept and maintain full MARC authority records? If the library plans on using authority control functions of the system, the capability for loading MARC authority records can save the library the expense of creating and/or manually entering authority information. Although more and more systems provide the capability for automatically creating an authority file from the library's bibliographic database, the authority records generated from this procedure generally include only a heading and not cross-references. Because cross-reference capabilities are a significant part of authority control services to library patrons, libraries may want to be able to load full MARC authority records (such as those created by the Library of Congress or by authority control vendors) when they are available, rather than unnecessarily performing the initial authority work.

- Does the system accept, maintain, and use the full ALA character set? The ALA (American Library Association) character set includes the full range of characters found in MARC bibliographic and authority records, including special punctuation, diacritical marks, and symbols used in the sciences. The ways in which a system deals with such characters can impact significantly upon the quality of the system and its usefulness to library patrons. For example, a system that does not recognize the ALA character set may simply substitute spaces for the characters it does not recognize. Unfortunately, because of the way systems retrieve and file information, this kind of substitution will mean that the information will not be retrieved or filed correctly when a patron requests the information and the patron will probably not find the information.

- Does the system output full MARC records? Libraries are increasingly finding that they need to supply a copy of their system database to another library or vendor, for such purposes as cooperative automation or collection development, statistical analysis, or other services not available through the online system, or to switch from one system to another. Most systems, however, do not retain or use the records exactly as they have been input. Information is often either deleted or rearranged in some way for system use. If the records cannot be output by the system in the full MARC format — basically in their original format — it may not be possible to use them for other such purposes.

Ongoing Specifications

To a greater or lesser extent, the library will continuously be involved in providing specifications for various aspects of system operation. The computer programs of the library's system will often include a number of options from which the library will need to choose. In some cases, the vendor may recommend default options, which the system will use if the library does not decide to have the system operate differently. For example, the vendor may set a default value of 5 for the maximum number of items circulated to a patron at one time. The library can opt to either reset this value to a higher or lower number or use an override function for exceptions and leave the maximum number at 5. Libraries should evaluate all options thoroughly, and they should reevaluate options at some point after the system has been in use, when terminology and functions have become more familiar.

A library will have many separate collections for which specifications may differ. The collections may simply be separate reference, fiction, and nonfiction titles within a single building, or they may involve a number of branches at widely dispersed sites, all with differing types of materials and policies. In some cases, system options will allow for differing specifications for different collections and sites. In other cases, the computer system may not include the flexibility of differing options for sites or collections, and it will be necessary to decide on uniform specifications for all situations.

System vendors generally release at least one new version of the system software per year that includes revisions and enhancements. In between these new releases, vendors may also issue software changes to correct bugs in the software or to make minor changes in the way the system works. In many of these cases, the library will need to evaluate the options involved in the release/change and decide on specifications accordingly. Obviously, the specifications process is a cyclical, ongoing process that will require constant reevaluation.

The next three paragraphs address specifications for three major system functions: circulation, public access catalog, and statistical reporting.

For circulation purposes, libraries will need to categorize patrons and materials into different types to enable the computer system to treat each type of patron and material appropriately. For example, within a school library, types of patrons may include students, teaching faculty, other staff, and parents. These categories of borrowers will probably be treated differently from one another in such ways as types of materials that can be checked out or the number of items that can be checked out at one time. Likewise, library materials might be categorized by type of material (such as books, computer software, periodicals), by collection type (such as reference, reserve, special collections), and by some additional categorization (such as noncirculating items or in-library use only). Categorizations of materials will allow the library's system to treat materials according to type, for example, automatically stipulating the correct (library-specified) loan period for reference and circulating items or flagging a noncirculating item if a patron tries to check one out. The various categorizations of patrons and materials specified by the library are noted within the patron's or item's database record through the use of a predesignated code. When a particular code is noted by the computer, the computer refers to the instructions that have been specified for that code.

The major areas for specifications for public access catalogs will include indexing, filing, and display of records. Libraries may also need to (or want to) provide specifications for help screens, the screen displays within the online catalog that provide instructions to users. Indexing of records is the process by which portions of the record become searchable by users. For example, the titles of books in a database can be searched by users only if the computer has indexed the title fields. Libraries will usually be asked to provide, to some extent, specifications for the fields and subfields to be indexed.

Specifications regarding statistics may relate to such aspects as aging of statistics, reporting of statistics, and printed output. For example, aging of statistics refers primarily to cumulation of statistics over time, such as the number of times an item has circulated or the number of items a patron has checked out during a given time period. Libraries may be required to specify time periods during which the statistics will be cumulated (e.g., a library's reporting year, a school year for school libraries) and the total amount of time for which statistics will be maintained within the system (e.g., three years). For reporting of statistics, libraries may be required to specify which types of categorization will be required for statistical reports (e.g., fiction items vs. nonfiction items, reserve items, reference materials, or categorization by call number or area). In some cases, libraries may only have access to electronic displays of the statistics (on computer terminals) or they may have the capability of structuring detailed, well-formatted printed reports. Libraries should also be aware that some systems will require the purchase of additional commercial software packages (such as SAS "Statistical Analysis System") to produce sophisticated statistical reports.

PREPROCESSING THE MARC DATABASE

A wide range of services are available that provide necessary or desirable changes to a library's database. Such processes include deduping, holdings consolidation, special select, smart barcode production, filing indicator correction, and authority control. A discussion of these processes and the cost factors involved is included as chapter 6, MARC Database Processing.

LOADING AND MAINTAINING MARC RECORDS

Even the highest quality and most sophisticated hardware and software will not provide successful results if the library's database is of poor quality. In fact, a good automated system with a problem-ridden database can be much more damaging to library services and alienating to patrons than a good, well-maintained manual system. However, libraries often focus exclusively on the hardware and software vendors' performance and adherence to standards, without considering the very significant impact that their own database will have on system usefulness and performance. In reality, the quality of the database can make or break a system. The two discussions in this section focus on loading the library's database and maintaining that database once it is in use.

Loading Records to an Online System

There are several ways to load MARC records to an online system. The method(s) a library uses will depend upon the capabilities of the system the library uses and the vendor's recommendations. The four commonly used ways of loading records to a system — tapeloading, loading from floppy disk, electronic interface, and manual entry — are discussed below. (More specific information in regard to magnetic media can be found in chapter 5, MARC Records on Magnetic Tape and Floppy Disk.) Several questions about system loading capabilities and procedures are the focus of the concluding paragraphs of this discussion.

Magnetic tape is usually the method of choice when large numbers of records are involved. This is because many thousands of records can be loaded from one tape, as opposed to only 200 or so per floppy disk, or one at a time using other methods. In some cases, an initial tapeload is performed for a library's accumulated MARC records, while current cataloging — consisting of smaller batches — is loaded in some other way. When a library receives records on MARC tape through a subscription service, the records are usually loaded from tape regardless of the number on the tape. A library may be able to acquire a tape drive for temporary use to load unusually large numbers of records, rather than trying to use more time-consuming methods.

The portable and ubiquitous floppy disk is often used to load smaller numbers of records. A library may download records from a bibliographic utility or receive records from an outside source via floppy disk. Floppy disk can be a very fragile medium. Making backups of all disks can save much time and many headaches, but floppy disk should not be considered as a long-range storage medium.

Records may also be electronically transmitted from a workstation (e.g., OCLC terminal) to an online system via the use of an interface or "black box" (which is often another color). For loading of current cataloging, this method often has advantages over all other methods. Usually, the record is sent to the system simply by entering a print command at the cataloging terminal. Downloading (from the cataloging source) and uploading (to the system) are thus accomplished within the same transaction, instead of the two separate activities required by tape or disk.

Manual entry of records via keyboard is another method used by libraries to enter records to an online system. Generally, this is the most time-consuming and expensive method of entering records, particularly if full MARC records (rather than abbreviated records) are being entered. Given that MARC records are readily available at a low cost (and that well-trained personnel often are not), manual entry is not recommended for entry of anything but original cataloging (i.e., items for which a MARC record is not available elsewhere).

One significant question regarding the loading of records to a system involves the matter of duplicate records. If the system has a "duplicate detection" routine, what does that routine examine to determine whether the record is a duplicate? What happens when a duplicate record is entered to the system? Does it bump (replace) the previous record? Is it added in addition to the previous record? Does the system reject it? Another question involving the loading of records has to do with the manipulation of the records so that they can be used by the system. In particular, it is important to know whether fields or codes are deleted from the records and whether the library has any control over what is maintained within the records. Ideally, the system should delete information that the library definitely does not want and will never use (the OCLC subfield $\neq w$ within name fields is a good candidate for removal) and should retain all information that the library may want to use with current or future systems (including all fixed field codes and different types of call numbers that may be included in the record).

Database Maintenance

When a library moves from a card catalog to an online catalog, "catalog maintenance" is replaced by "database maintenance." Contrary to what may have been predicted, there is more work involved in maintaining an online catalog than a card catalog. The fact that card sets no longer have to be removed, corrected, and refiled in the card catalog has led some to believe that most of the work of catalog maintenance has thus been eliminated. However, the pulling and refiling of card sets has been replaced by problem resolution involving any one or all of a number of system elements.

A good illustration of the differences between the manual (or card) environment and the automated environment is the case of a misfiled catalog entry. Within a card catalog, if a particular card is misfiled, then it simply needs to be removed and refiled—a comparatively quick and simple operation. If an entry misfiles within an online catalog, however, rectification can be a much more complex and time-consuming matter. The person who encounters the misfiled entry will not be able to move the entry from one place to another on the screen display. When an entry is misfiled by a computer, there is always a reason that it has been misfiled and that reason must be determined before the entry can be refiled correctly. In those simple cases in which the reason for the misfiling is obvious (e.g., a typographical error), the record must still be corrected before it will file correctly. In many cases, the cause of the misfiling is not apparent from the online catalog display of the record. In most such cases, either the applications software or the MARC coding within the bibliographic record is causing the record to misfile. In either of these cases, the errant computer program or MARC code will need to be detected and corrected. Correcting the MARC coding may be a relatively simple task, but having changes made to the computer programs will probably take a good bit more time and some explicit communication with the system vendor.

To ensure proper and timely database maintenance, a reporting system should be implemented so that library staff and patrons know how to report a problem and who to report it to. It is a good idea to have different types of problems prioritized, so that the more crucial changes are made first (e.g., errors that affect retrieval are more important than those that do not). Unfortunately, database maintenance is one of the least-developed aspects of library automation. This is due in part to the fact that patron-oriented functions (such as circulation and keyword searching) are more visible to system users in general and thus receive more attention from system developers.

TROUBLESHOOTING AND PROBLEM SOLVING

Diagnosing System Problems

Before a problem can be solved, the cause of the problem must be determined. Because library systems involve so many interdependent factors, determining the cause of a problem is often the most difficult and time-consuming part. In many ways, problem solving within the automation environment is similar to diagnosing an illness. Often, all that one has to go on are the symptoms, and the symptoms alone do not necessarily indicate either the cause or the cure. A primary exercise in troubleshooting and problem solving involves the detection of patterns related to the problem. In many cases, a pattern will suggest a possible cause and method of resolution. To detect patterns, libraries will need to determine a common thread among occurrences of a problem. For example, occurrences may involve only one terminal or one type of printer. Or, they may involve bibliographic records that were created or loaded during a specific time period. Or, perhaps only specific fields or records of a particular type (such as records for video-cassettes) or records from a particular vendor (if the library has received records from more than one vendor) are involved. When investigating system problems, libraries should not rely on memory. Written documentation (including printouts of complete records when database problems are involved), should be made to serve as documentation, to allow for full and logical evaluation, and to assist with resolution once the cause has been determined.

A knowledge of the various elements of the system is a valuable asset when diagnosing system problems. There are three basic elements of library systems: the hardware, the software, and the database. (A fourth basic element, the human element, is responsible for the other three elements and for the success of the system itself, of course.) When troubleshooting system problems, librarians will first need to isolate the source of the problem to one of the elements. For each of the three basic elements, there are a number of factors that may contribute to system problems. The major elements and some of the major factors are as follows:

Hardware

> Machinery
>
> Operating software

Applications software

> Vendor computer programs
>
> Library specifications and changes

Database

> Medium by which records are entered (e.g., tape, floppy disk, electronic transfer)
>
> Profile and computer programs of cataloging vendor (e.g., OCLC, BiblioFile, Brodart)
>
> Local cataloging practice and procedure
>
> MARC coding
>
> Text of MARC record (including errors, etc.)

An explanation of each of the factors and examples of their effect upon system use is given below.

Hardware: Machinery

System hardware machinery includes the computer, terminals, and peripherals, such as printers and barcode readers. In addition to their mechanical and electrical systems, all these pieces of machinery function through the use of operating software and applications software, which are discussed below. Some system problems are the result of a malfunction or misuse of the machinery. Some of the most common hardware problems are also the easiest to resolve. For example, a lack of response from a computer terminal is often resolved by turning on the power switch, making certain the terminal is connected to a power source, or resetting the surge protector. When the terminal is obviously on, but there is no screen display, often the cause is either that the monitor is not connected correctly or that screen adjustments (such as brightness control) need to be made. Another common problem is that the data being input through the keyboard (or barcode reader) does not display at all or is displaying incorrectly. In this case, the first step is to check the cable that connects the keyboard (or reader) to the computer at both ends to ensure proper connection. Also, the keyboard may accidently have been set to Caps Lock (for uppercase) or to Num Lock (for the number keypad).

Hardware: Operating Software

The operating software of a system is somewhat analogous to the involuntary functions of the human body (such as breathing), while applications software, which is discussed in the next section, is analagous to voluntary functions of the body (such as walking or talking). Operating software is essential to the use of the system and enables the machinery to perform specific tasks (via the applications software). Libraries generally do not have much control over the type of operating software that is used; it is usually related to the hardware. Nevertheless, libraries may designate a type of hardware or operating software in their contract specifications; this is often done when the library wants to acquire hardware or software that will correspond to that already owned by the library or the larger organization. Operating software may affect or impose limits on the use of the system, including such factors as response time and the size and configuration of the database, among other factors. When negative impacts are caused by the operating software, the library may have little control over the problem, because adjustments to operating software involve technical and practical complexities, as well as legal and licensing restrictions. Two options for dealing with operating system problems are (1) adjust the applications software to minimize impacts or (2) wait for (and campaign for) improvements in a new version of the operating software.

Applications Software: Vendor Computer Programs

The computer programs that control the specific library automation functions of the system (such as circulation, online catalog, serials control, etc.) are developed by the vendor or by another party under contract to the vendor. The programs include such activities as search and retrieval routines, filing routines, manipulation of the records for display purposes, and other such functions. The user-friendliness of a system depends greatly on the power and flexibility of the application programs. The vendor's programs represent the single most significant expenditure of the vendor's resources. Most vendors release updated, enhanced versions of the applications software every 6 to 18 months. Two of the more common types of problems caused by inappropriate applications programs are those involving inaccurate statistics or calculations (within circulation and statistical applications) and incorrect filing routines. Incorrect filing routines often either file on portions of the field that they should not (such as subfields or punctuation that should not be considered for filing purposes) or file specific characters with incorrect values (i.e., file whole numbers in decimal order or file uppercase and lowercase letters as different values). If libraries believe that filing is incorrect, they should check the appropriate filing rules (ALA, LC, etc.); rules for computerized filing do not always correspond to rules for manual filing in a card catalog. See the Preliminary Considerations section of chapter 7, MARC Database Products, for a more comprehensive discussion of computer filing.

Applications Software: Library Specifications and Changes

The library may be asked by the vendor to provide specifications for many system functions, including searching, filing, display, and manipulation of the records. Often the vendor indicates a number of standard options and asks the library to choose from among them. This gives the library a more customized product, but also places more responsibility on the library. It is difficult to foresee all the implications of any given decision, so libraries should research decisions carefully before making them, then evaluate the results thoroughly after the decisions have been put into effect. For example, suppose a library decides to make all series statements in its database accessible through a title search capability, including all fields tagged 490 (series untraced or traced differently), that were previously not used as access points. The library's reasoning is that series that were previously untraced were untraced simply because the library could not support the filing of the additional entries in the card catalog; automatic computer filing can eliminate this problem. Once the library's decision has been implemented within the online catalog, however, the result is a proliferation of conflicting series entries, with many items being entered twice under series titles that are only marginally different. This presents a confusing situation for catalog users and an undesirable duplication of access points in many cases. After further evaluation of the decision, the library decides to limit the indexing of 490 fields to those with a first indicator 0 (series untraced), and to discontinue indexing those with a first indicator 1 (series traced differently). This decision will alleviate the problem of duplication of access points for many series (those that were traced from the 490 field and from the 830 field); however, there will still be many nonstandardized series entries that have been created from 490 fields (first indicator 0), that are not subject to authority control. The library will want to further monitor this decision and its impacts.

Database: Medium by Which Records Are Entered

The medium used to enter database records into a system can have an impact on the condition of the records and whether they are loaded correctly (or loaded at all). Where magnetic media, such as tape or floppy disk, are involved, the condition of the tape or disk, as well as the tape or disk specifications, will affect the usefulness of the database records and the success in loading the records. For example, tapes or disks that are in poor physical condition may contain records that have been rendered unreadable and therefore will not be loaded into the system. Inappropriate tape or disk specifications may also impact upon whether the records can be loaded into a system. For example, if a system is configured to accept unblocked records and the tape being loaded contains blocked records, the records will not be entered into the system successfully. Or, the tape may be the wrong density (or BPI). Further information on the care of tapes and disks and on specifications is included in chapter 5, MARC Records on Magnetic Tape and Floppy Disk.

Records that are transferred electronically (such as directly from the cataloging terminal to the online system through the use of the print function) usually undergo some type of manipulation or modification as part of the transfer. This type of modification is usually made so that the online system will be able to use the record more efficiently or effectively. In some cases, however, some aspect of the transfer may work inappropriately, due to hardware or software problems, or due to human error in the transfer process. One example of an error caused by software programs would be the deletion of fields or codes that the library expects to be included as part of its record within the system. In this case, the library would need to discuss the problem and a possible resolution with the system vendor.

Manual keying of records into an online system is another means of entering records into the system. The success of this method is largely dependent upon the qualifications of the staff creating and entering the records. Another highly significant factor in the success of this method is the quality of the computer validation and editing routines that check the data entered. The system into which the data is being entered will check the data for errors and either correct the information or warn the inputter that a problem has been detected. Editing routines vary greatly from one system to the next.

Database: Profile and Computer Programs of Cataloging Vendor

Many libraries receive their cataloging (either on catalog cards or in machine-readable form) from an outside source, such as a commercial vendor or a bibliographic utility, or from an intermediary, such as a processing center. These catalog records have usually received at least minimal modification or manipulation, according to the library's or the vendor's needs or requirements. Often, cataloging suppliers use a *profile*, which is basically a list of the library preferences for options available, such as printing special prefixes above call numbers (e.g., "Ref" for reference materials) or printing subject heading entries in uppercase. When implementing an online system, or using their machine-readable records for other purposes, libraries will need to understand that such customization of records is not necessarily provided by the online system or other service. It may be that the new system does not provide the same modifications or that such modification is not necessary within the new environment.

When troubleshooting a situation that may involve a cataloging vendor's profile and customization, the library will need to determine whether the customized data was actually part of the catalog record or whether it was simply generated through a computer program without being a part of the library's machine-readable record. For example, subject entries that are printed in uppercase letters at the top of subject entry cards are not actually included in the machine-readable record in uppercase. In fact, they remain in conventional uppercase and lowercase form in the record. A special computer program includes instructions to print the letters in uppercase only when a subject entry card is produced; otherwise, the letters remain in their conventional form. The subject entries may or may not display in uppercase in an online catalog. This function is dependent upon the online system software and the library's system profile.

Database: Local Cataloging Practice and Procedure

Local cataloging practices and procedures can have a negative impact upon system usefulness. There are two major characteristics of local cataloging practice that will predictably have a negative impact. The first characteristic is local practices that have varied significantly over time. The second characteristic is local library practices that vary significantly from prevailing cataloging standards. In either of these cases, a lack of internal documentation about past and current procedures can complicate the trouble-shooting and problem-solving process.

Inconsistent cataloging practices can involve such aspects as completeness of the catalog record or whether or not possible access points have been traced. For example, a library may have at one point followed a policy of excluding illustration statements and bibliography notes from a catalog record. Then, the library may have rescinded that policy, and included illustration statements and bibliography notes within a catalog record, when applicable. In this case, the absence of such information within a catalog record may mean that illustrations and a bibliography are not included in the item that has been cataloged. It may also mean that, even though illustrations and a bibliography are included in the item that has been cataloged, this information has been excluded from the catalog record for the item, based on past policy. In any case, users of the catalog (whether it be card or online) will receive mixed messages from the library's catalog.

Another example of inconsistent cataloging practice involves the tracing of access points. In one instance, a library may decide to begin making series added entries for a series after receiving numerous volumes of the series, without taking the step of making added entries for the volumes previously received. Catalog users searching under the series title will be led to believe that the library does not hold the volumes for which there are no added entries, even though the lack of an entry for earlier volumes is based upon an earlier policy, not the lack of the materials themselves. A similar case involves libraries that have maintained dictionary (rather than divided) catalogs and have not traced titles for books for which the title matched a subject heading. Within a dictionary card catalog, this practice has helped to avoid unnecessary duplication—a title and subject entry for the same item filed together. An online catalog will function as a divided catalog. Generally, users are required to specify their search by author, title, or subject. If the title added entry has been omitted due to past dictionary cataloging practice, a title search within an online catalog will not retrieve that item. This result may well lead the user to believe that the desired item is not in the library's collection, even though it actually is.

Libraries that have varied significantly from prevailing standards may find that online system programs do not manipulate or process their records appropriately. The cause of this problem often is that system vendors refer to the prevailing standards when developing their software, and, because the library has not followed such standards, the software design is not appropriate for the library's local practice.

Database: MARC Coding

Incorrect MARC coding, including fixed and variable field codes (tags, indicators, subfield codes) can impact negatively upon system use. There are three main ways incorrect coding may occur. One is the library's misuse or misapplication (either purposeful or accidental) of any of the MARC codes. The second way relates to the evolution of the MARC format, particularly in regard to varying dates of implementation of specific codes. The third way involves codes that have been defined and/or used in an ambiguous manner.

A library's purposeful misapplication of the MARC format may seem advantageous within one situation; however, such misuse will often have significantly negative effects within other environments. An example of such misuse might be the case of a library that has previously used a comcatalog but is currently using an online catalog. Within the comcatalog environment, the library had requested that the vendor file all title entries (e.g., MARC field 245) on both the title proper (subfield ≠a) and the subtitle (subfield ≠b); however, the vendor did not offer this option and the vendor programs looked at only the title proper (subfield ≠a) for filing purposes. So, in order to achieve the results they wanted, the library decided to "fool" the vendor's computer programs into filing on both the title proper and the subtitle. Because the computer programs recognized the title proper by the subfield code a and simply filed on all characters within that subfield, the library "fooled" the computer into filing through the subfield ≠b by deleting the subfield code *b* (not the text of the field) from each MARC record. Because of this deletion, the computer programs recognized both the title proper and subtitle fields as being the "title proper" and therefore filed on the text of both the title proper and subtitle.

Although this misuse of the MARC format allowed the library their desired results in the instance of the comcatalog, it has effectively ruled out proper use of the records for most other purposes, including use within an online catalog. Both the *ALA filing rules* and the *Library of Congress filing rules* stipulate that filing of titles include only the title proper (subfield ≠*a*) and not the subtitle (subfield ≠*b*). The deletion of the MARC sub-field code *b* by the library will affect many search, retrieval, filing, and display functions and will produce results that will make use of the records confusing to library users. For example, because the computer will consider subtitles as part of the title proper in all cases, the library is effectively precluded from specifying a "truncated title" display (e.g., a "short record" display that includes only the main part of the title). And, in an online system that requires the user to search by the entire title proper (subfield ≠*a*) to retrieve an item, users will need to know both the title proper and the subtitle to retrieve the item. For example, to find a book entitled *Pulling the plug: Unanswered questions about life support systems*, the user would have to know and input the entire title and subtitle to retrieve the desired item, rather than knowing and inputting the short title *Pulling the plug*. Because in most instances users do not have complete information on both the title proper and subtitle, many items may go unused because of the library's aberration in the use of the MARC format coding.

In short, trying to "fool" the computer through unprescribed use of the MARC format coding will eventually backfire on the library and have impacts that will negatively affect use of the library's records by library users. In some cases, it may produce results that create an automated system that is less reliable, less useful, and more alienating than a similar manual, card-based system. This of course generates bad public relations for the library in particular and library automation in general.

Inappropriate MARC coding that has been supplied inadvertently (rather than as part of a library procedure or policy) will always occur to some extent within MARC data-bases. The cause of this misapplication is usually human error; however, in some cases, incorrectly set or missing codes are the result of evolutionary changes within the MARC formats themselves. For example, within some older MARC records, filing indicators may be incorrectly set as blank indicators because the filing indicator had not yet been made a part of the MARC format for that particular field. Regardless of the cause of the error, the results of such miscoding will vary according to the way in which the record is being used.

There are three methods for minimizing the negative effects of this type of error. One method is to use quality control procedures for the creation of records, including both manual review of records by personnel and automated review of the records through editing and validation routines available in cataloging or bibliographic maintenance systems. Such automated checking routines will, for example, give an error message when an invalid MARC tag or indicator has been used. The system into which the data is being entered will check the data for errors and either correct the information or warn the inputter that a problem has been detected. Generally speaking, systems designed primarily as cataloging utilities, such as OCLC, provide more extensive editing than other types of systems. And generally mainframe-based cataloging systems provide more extensive editing than micro-based systems, such as CD-ROM cataloging systems.

The other two methods for minimizing MARC coding errors are "after the fact" methods. One involves the reporting of errors found by system users and library staff. A specific, documented procedure for filling out error reports must be instituted by the library for this type of error detection and correction to be effective. The other "after the fact" method involves routinely searching and correcting, within the library's database, the most predictable and/or commonly found types of MARC coding errors. Two examples of such errors are (1) incorrect filing indicators and (2) corporate names (MARC X10 fields) incorrectly tagged as personal names (MARC X00 fields). By regularly "going fishing" for these types of errors (e.g., by searching on initial articles *a*, *an*, and *the*, which will retrieve titles for which filing indicators have been erroneously set to *0* or *b̸*), library bibliographic maintenance staff can rectify errors before they cause further problems in use of the library's database.

A third example of "miscoding" within MARC databases results from the structure and use of the MARC format itself. For example, in some cases, the same code has been used to signify two different meanings, such as when the MARC fixed field Index code *0* may mean either "no index" or "not evaluated." Other instances include fixed field codes for which several values may apply, but the fixed field provides only enough space for one or a few of the values. For example, regardless of how many different types of illustrations are included in an item, the Illustration portion of the fixed field will only accommodate four illustration codes, which gives the misleading impression that only those types of illustrations are included, and other types are not.

Database: Text of the MARC Record

Errors within the text of a record can result in problems in searching, filing, display, or other uses of the record. Some of the most common text errors are transposed letters or numbers, misspelled words, extra or missing spaces or punctuation, the number *1* being input as a lowercase *l* (or vice versa) or the number *0* being input as the letter *o* (or vice versa). Computer programs interpret the text of the record very literally. For example, if a space is omitted between two words which should be two separate words, the computer will interpret those two words as one word and will index and file the "word" accordingly.

Methods for detecting and rectifying problems with record text are generally the same as the methods described in the discussion above on mistakes in MARC coding: quality control in the creation of records, a specific procedure for the reporting of such errors and the systematic seeking out of such errors by bibliographic maintenance staff.

Common Database Problems and Possible Resolutions

Some of the most common problems in the use of a library's database within an online system are missing records, missing data, and misfiled entries. Each of these problems is discussed below, with possible explanations and resolutions.

Missing Records

The first step in problem solving for missing records is to determine whether records are actually missing. In some cases, existing records are not retrieved simply because the correct search key has not been entered. In other cases, existing records are not retrieved because of typographical errors or coding errors within the record that prevent the record from being retrieved when the correct search strategy is used. In still other cases, a glitch in the searching or filing programs can prevent the item from being retrieved, even though it actually exists in the database. To determine whether a particular record does in fact exist in the database, the record should be searched through as many search strategies as possible, such as author, title, subject, and ISBN.

Once it has been determined that a record or a group of records is actually missing, a cause should be determined. Some of the most common explanations for missing records are a time lag in loading the records, overlooked tapes, tapes or disks loaded in the wrong order, and records deleted in preprocessing.

In some cases, records for items that have been cataloged may simply not have been loaded into the database yet. Also, records may not have been received from the database vendor, or there may have been an interruption to library workflow that prevented the records from being loaded.

Particularly when significant numbers of older records are involved, the possibility should be considered that all or part of the contents of a tape or disk have not been loaded. Unfortunately, it is not unheard of for a vendor or library to misplace such items. In investigating such a possibility, libraries should determine whether the missing records would have been on the same tape or disk. For example, records on tape are sometimes arranged in chronological order by date of cataloging or in numerical order by record number (001 field).

In some cases, records need to be loaded in a particular order, such as chronological order by date of inputting or in record number order. Loading the records out of the order specified by the system vendor or record supplier may cause the apparent deletion or dropping of records from the system.

If records have received preprocessing, such as deduping (duplicate resolution) or special select procedures, the resulting file may not have included all of the records that the library had expected it to include. For example, if the library requested that only some branches (or holding libraries) be included, a typographical error or omission in the libraries' specifications (or the vendor's computer programs) may have resulted in some records' being omitted. Another example relates to duplicate resolution procedures. Because records with the same record number (e.g., OCLC number) are generally considered duplicates, a library that has used the same record for cataloging various items will find that all but one of those items have been omitted from the database during the duplicate resolution process. If libraries fully investigate and understand the processes to which they submit their records (and prepare their specifications carefully), such unpleasant surprises will be much less likely to occur. (Of course, not all such occurrences are the result of the library's error; vendors also may make the same types of mistakes.) More complete information on record processing is included in chapter 6, MARC Database Processing.

Missing or Incorrectly Displayed Data

In some instances, libraries find that information they expected to display as part of a record is not displaying or is displayed incorrectly. For example, a call number prefix may not display as part of a call number, or a contents note may be displayed as a series statement. Probable explanations for such omissions or errors include the following: the data is not actually part of the record; errors or omissions have been made in library specifications; there are inconsistencies in the library's database; or there are errors in the vendor's computer programs.

Some information displayed or printed as part of a catalog record is not actually part of the record but has been generated by a computer program. For example, OCLC can automatically print call number prefixes (such as "Ref" or "Serials") on cards when the record includes the holding code for a particular collection. If the library wants this same information to appear as part of an online system display, the library must specify this to the vendor. Otherwise, the vendor will not know to generate the "automatic" prefixes.

A similar instance is the case of MARC "display constants," which are terms, phrases, or punctuation that, according to the MARC format, can display whenever a particular piece of information is displayed. For example, a library may be used to having series statements enclosed by parentheses when they are printed on card, even though the library has not actually input the parentheses and they are not part of the record. Libraries may or may not opt to have the same "constants" that were printed on their cards generated as part of an online catalog display.

Sometimes, library specifications involve errors or omissions that result in missing or incorrect data. For example, if the library has specified that none of the MARC 0XX fields should display on the screen, the ISBN note (MARC 020 field) will not display, regardless of the fact that it usually is printed as the last note field (out of numerical order, after the last 5XX field). And, if the library specifications have mistakenly stated that the MARC 505 field (contents note) be labeled on the screen display as a "series note," then the system will do so.

In some cases, inconsistencies in the library's bibliographic records will cause data to be omitted from displays or to be displayed in a way that the library does not expect. The inconsistencies may be the result of varying library practices, variations in cataloging rules or MARC format codes, or simply the result of error. For example, if library procedures have changed from inputting the call number prefix "Ref" to inputting the prefix "R," and the previously input prefixes were never rectified, then the prefixes will display inconsistently. In some cases, such changes in procedure have not been documented or considered by the library as part of system implementation; however, such history does eventually impact upon the use of the database.

Sometimes, errors in the vendor's computer programs cause the omission of data or incorrect display of data. Before assuming that the vendor's error is responsible for problem data, libraries should rule out other possibilities, such as those noted in the above paragraphs. If the library does determine that the computer programs are in error, the library should provide the vendor with documentation of the problem, such as printouts of records, and it should provide a complete and clear explanation of the problem—and the resolution—to the vendor.

Misfiled Entries

Misfiling of entries may involve such situations as double entries for the same name (next to each other in a list or filing order); entries that file under initial article rather than the first filing word; or entries that file out of order because of typographical errors, incorrect coding, or inappropriate software.

In some cases, an online catalog may include two separate filing entries for the same person's name, which requires that users search through both files for the person's works, instead of simply referring to one file. Although the two entries may look the same at first glance, closer inspection may reveal a seemingly insignificant difference in punctuation (such as a comma, space, or period) between the two entries. A difference in the MARC coding in the bibliographic record (MARC codes are usually not part of the public display) may have caused the system to treat two occurrences of the same heading differently. An example of such a situation would be an occurrence of a name in which the MARC subfield code for the birth date was omitted, causing the system to treat the dates as part of the name and thus file that occurrence separately from other instances in which the field was coded correctly.

Entries that file under initial article generally just need to have the MARC filing indicator reset to the correct number in the bibliographic record; in the case of a few fields, the initial article may need to be removed, according to cataloging rules and/or the MARC bibliographic format.

An automated system is not nearly as forgiving as humans are in regard to typographical errors. Library staff members who are filing cards may overlook misspellings or typographical errors when filing, or manually correct the errors at the time or return the cards to catalogers for correction. The automated system will simply file the entries as found. Correction of such errors will usually involve several steps: detection of misspelled words or other errors; reporting of the problem to appropriate personnel; and correction of the error in bibliographic maintenance mode.

A blank space at the beginning of a field of data may require that the field be searched with the blank space as part of the search key. Other inappropriate data that may occur at the beginning of a field include MARC tags that have been input inadvertently as part of the field data (such as a 650 keyed in as the first element of the text of a subject heading field) or Arabic or Roman numerals that have been input inadvertently to precede subject headings or tracings on cards (such as the number *1.* before the first subject heading).

RELATED READINGS

Byrne, Deborah. "Vendors, librarians, automation & communication." *Action for libraries* 11 (10): 1-2 (October 1985).

Epstein, Susan Baerg. "Contracts & testing: How to get what you think you've paid for." *Library journal* 1334-35 (July 1983).

Hildreth, Charles R. "To Boolean or not to Boolean?" *Information technology and libraries* 2 (3): 235-37 (September 1983).

Hudson, Judith. "Bibliographic record maintenance in the online environment." *Information technology and libraries* 3 (4): 388-93 (December 1984).

Lipow, Anne Grodzins. "The online catalog: Exceeding our grasp." *American libraries* 20 (9): 862-65 (October 1989).

McCombs, Gillian. "Public and technical services: Disappearing barriers." *Wilson library bulletin* 61 (3): 25-28 (November 1986).

Price, Bennett J. "Printing and the online catalog." *Information technology and libraries* 3 (1): 15-20 (March 1984).

9

MARC Authority Format

INTRODUCTION

In order to understand the structure and function of the MARC authority format, it is first necessary to understand the concepts of "authority control" and "authority work." Authority work and authority control are necessary aspects of database integrity; they provide for database quality that will enable libraries and their patrons to use their catalog records and library collections effectively.

There are two major goals of authority control within a library catalog. One is to provide uniformity in the forms of names and some types of titles and subject headings that are used. By determining a standard form of a word or phrase to use in a catalog, libraries can assure that catalog users can find related items. For example, many authors have written works using different forms of the same name, such as "Rose M. Miller," "Rose Mary Miller," and "Rose Miller." Without authority control, catalog users seeking works by this author would have to know all forms of the name that the author had used in her works in order to find them in a library catalog. The use of authority control provides for establishing and using one form of a person's name within a library catalog, so that users will be able to find all works by one person under the same heading. In addition to clarifying the relationship between different names used by the same author, authority control serves to distinguish between different authors using the same name. For example, there are two authors with the name *Marc Brown* represented in the Library of Congress name authority file. Authority control provides for establishing different forms of names in such instances, to avoid the interfiling of works by two different authors under the same name, which would be confusing and misleading to catalog users. In the case of the two Marc Browns, one of the authors used his middle name, *Tolon*, in a number of his works, so the heading established for him was his full name, *Marc Tolon Brown*. The other author used the name *Marc H. Brown* in his works (according to information provided by his publisher), so that name heading was established to differentiate him from Marc Tolon Brown and other authors with the name *Marc Brown* who may publish works in the future. Usually the form of name established for an author is the one that has been used most often in the author's works. In some cases, when different authors use the exact same name in their works, a birth year or other identifying feature is used within the established form of the name to differentiate one author from another.

The second goal of authority control is to provide cross-references from related terms to the "established" form of the heading. For example, if a catalog user were to search under "Rose M. Miller" and the established form of the name used by the library was "Rose Miller," a cross-reference from the alternate form ("Rose M. Miller") would direct the user to the established form. The cross-reference function of authority control directs the user from the variant form of the name to the established form of the name, thereby ensuring that the user will find materials that might otherwise not have been found. In addition, the cross-reference function can help to avoid confusion on the part of the user because it provides an explicit link between the variant and established forms of the name, rather than leaving the user to guess about the relationship of two different forms of the same name.

The concept of authority control applies generally to other types of access points besides personal names, including corporate and geographical names, series and uniform titles, as well as subject headings. For example, items in a series are sometimes published using different forms of the series title, which would be filed separately, such as "Contemporary art and culture" and "Contemporary arts and culture." The only difference between these two forms of title for the same series is the pluralization of the word *art*; however, without authority control, these two different forms would be filed into two separate files. Users would need to look at both lists to find a specific volume number for the series. Authority control provides for establishing one uniform title for the series (usually based on the title that has been used most often by the publisher) and then filing all items in a single file, using one established form of the title, with cross-references from alternate forms. And, for subject headings, authority control means that one standard term will be used for subject entries, with cross-references from variant forms of the subject heading and from related subject headings. Authority control for subject headings also provides for differentiation between the same word used to identify different things. For example, the *Library of Congress subject headings* uses the term *Lime* to refer to the mineral form of calcium oxide, *Limestone* to refer to the sedimentary rock, and *Lime fruit* to refer to the fruit. *LCSH* differentiates between the fruit and the color referred to as "orange" by using the terms *Orange* to refer to the fruit and *Orange (Color)* to refer to the color.

Authority control and authority work are two different functions. Basically, authority work involves the research and decision making that are required to establish a form of name (or subject heading) and cross-references. Authority work also includes the documentation of other information related to the name or subject heading such as sources in which the person's name (or subject heading term) were found. Authority work to establish headings and cross-references must be completed before authority records can be created. Authority control is based on the use of authority records.

Generally speaking, the structure and content designation of the MARC authority format is based on the structure and use of authority records that traditionally have been used in manual files, such as authority files used by library catalogers and cross-reference cards in public card catalogs. Examples shown below include a traditional cataloging authority card (figure 9.1), a corresponding MARC authority record (figure 9.2), and the public-use cross-reference generated by the authority records in either a card catalog or online catalog (figure 9.3).

```
      Simmons, Dennis L. (Dennis Lee)
        x Simmons, Dennie
```

Fig. 9.1. Example of a name authority card traditionally used by catalogers within a manual file.

```
100 10   ‡a Simmons, Dennis L. ‡q (Dennis Lee)
400 10   ‡a Simmons, Dennie.
```

Fig. 9.2. Example of name authority information as used in a MARC authority record.

```
            Simmons, Dennie
              search under
      Simmons, Dennis L. (Dennis Lee)
```

Fig. 9.3. Example of a public-use cross-reference supplied from information provided in the name authority record.

The three figures illustrate the case of an author who has used his full first name and middle initial in most of his works. In a few cases, he used the nickname *Dennie*. The established form of the heading includes his full name and middle initial, as used in most of his works. Because some users may only be familiar with the works in which the author used his nickname and thus search for works only under that name, the form of name using his nickname has been supplied as a cross-reference to direct library patrons to the established form of the name, under which all the works have been entered.

MARC AUTHORITY RECORDS: NAMES AND SUBJECTS

The MARC authority format is used to code the information contained in authority records. There are two primary categories of authority records: name authority records and subject authority records. These two categorizations and the types of headings that they include are detailed below.

Name Headings

Name headings include personal names, corporate names and names of jurisdictions, meeting names, name/title combinations, and uniform titles. Each of these types of headings is defined in the following paragraphs, with examples provided in each case.

Personal Name

A personal name may be a surname and/or a forename; letters, initials, abbreviations, phrases, or numbers used in place of a name; or a family name. The personal name used as a heading is usually based on the form of name that has been used by the person.

Examples of personal names are the following:

> Thomas (Anglo-Norman poet) [Forename]
>
> Stoodt, Dieter [Surname and forename]
>
> Plantagenet, House of [Family name]
>
> W. P., Esq. [Initials]

Corporate Name or Jurisdiction Name

A corporate name is the name of a corporate body (e.g., a group of two or more people working together, not necessarily as a "corporation" *per se*); a jurisdiction (political or otherwise) under which a corporate body, city section, or a title of a work is entered (e.g., the name of a ship whose personnel may issue publications); or a jurisdiction name that is also an ecclesiastical entity (e.g., an organized religious group).

Examples of corporate names are the following:

> Nigel Brooks Chorale [Corporate body]
>
> J. Paul Getty Museum [Corporate body]
>
> Discovery (Ship) [Jurisdiction]
>
> Texas. Dept. of Human Services [Jurisdiction]
>
> Cyrus (Archdiocese) [Ecclesiastical entity]

Meeting Name

A meeting name is the name of a meeting or a jurisdiction name under which a meeting is entered. A meeting is an activity that has a definite beginning and ending, as opposed to a corporate name, which indicates an ongoing entity.

Examples of meeting names are the following:

> IASTED International Symposium [Meeting name]
>
> Venice (Italy). International Biennial Exhibition of Art
>   [Jurisdiction name under which a meeting is entered]

Name/Title Combination

A name/title combination includes the name of a person connected with a work or series (e.g., an author or a composer) and the title of the work or series.

Examples of name/title combinations are the following:

> Law, Felicia. Ways we move.
>
> Wagner, Richard, 1813-1883. Overture.

Uniform Title

A uniform title heading is used to bring together catalog entries for a work when various issues have appeared under different titles. This heading is generally used for works that have been published in many different versions or languages, including religious works, folktales, and anonymous works, or other works generally entered under title rather than a single author's name, such as treaties, names of motion pictures, and series titles. Although it may seem inappropriate to consider titles as part of the "name" category of authorities, this is probably most simply explained by the idea that the title of the work is the "name" by which it is known.

Examples of uniform titles are the following:

> Ten commandments. [Religious work]
>
> Arabian nights [Folktale]
>
> Beowulf [Anonymous work]
>
> Treaty of Utrecht (1713) [Treaty]
>
> King Kong (1933) [Motion picture]
>
> Mineral resources series (Morgantown, W. Va.) [Series]

Name headings may be used as a main, added, or series added entry in bibliographic records. Subject headings, the other category of authority heading, may only be used as subject headings in bibliographic records. Nevertheless, a name heading is used as a *name* heading when it is related to the authorship or publication of a work, but may also be used as a *subject* heading when the person or other entity is the subject of a work. For example, a bibliographic record for a book *by* Mark Twain would include Twain's name as a "name" heading in a "name" heading field. On the other hand, a bibliographic record for a book *about* Mark Twain would include Twain's name as a "subject" heading in a "subject" heading field. The form of the name used is the same, regardless of whether it is used as a "name" heading or a "subject" heading. And, the "name" heading is still considered as a name even when it is used as a subject. On the other hand, words or phrases that are devised as "subject" headings are used only as "subject" headings. Since they include entities or concepts that are not capable of authorship or publication, they could not be used as main, added, or series entries, as "name" headings are.

Subject Headings

The category of subject headings (as opposed to name headings) includes topical subject headings, geographic names that are not jurisdictions, name headings with subject subdivision terms, and terms and names used as subject subdivision terms. Each of these types of headings is defined in the following paragraphs, with examples provided in each case.

Topical Subject Heading

Topical subject headings are general subject terms including names of events or objects. A title, a geographic name, or the name of a corporate body used in a phrase subject heading is also considered as topical subject headings.

Examples of topical subject headings are the following:

Blood [Object]

Bull Run, 2nd Battle, 1862 [Event]

Bible and atheism [Title in phrase]

Iran in the Koran [Geographic name in phrase]

Catholic Church in motion pictures [Corporate name in phrase]

Geographic Name That Is Not a Jurisdiction

Geographic names that are not jurisdictions can only be used as subject headings, not name headings. In some cases, the geographic names that are not jurisdictions are the same as the names that are used for jurisdictions. For example, the geographic name *Pennsylvania* is used as a subject heading to refer to the geographic area of the state of Pennsylvania. On the other hand, when the state name *Pennsylvania* is used to refer to the political jurisdiction (e.g., for publications or laws of the state), it is considered a name heading. When the name of an area is used only to refer to the geographic area, it is considered to be a "geographic name that is not a jurisdiction," even though there is a corresponding "name" that is used to refer to a jurisdiction. The distinction is in the way in which the name is used and the characteristics to which it refers (i.e., geographic or jurisdictional).

Examples of geographic names that are not jurisdictions are the following:

> Amazon River [Geographic entity]
>
> Communist countries [Geographic entity]
>
> Leesville (S.C.) [Geographic entity that has a corresponding "jurisdictional" entity that can be used as a name heading]

Name Heading with Subject Subdivision Term

Name headings used with subject subdivision terms can only be used as subject headings.

Examples of name headings with subject subdivision term are the following:

> Washington, George, 1732-1799 — Biography [Personal name heading with subject subdivision]
>
> United States — Census, 2nd, 1800 [Corporate name heading with subject subdivision]

Terms and Names Used as Subject Subdivision Terms

Terms and names used as subject subdivision terms can be used in this manner only as part of a subject heading in a "subject" field. Some terms can be used only as a subject subdivision, not as a subject heading (the subject heading being the first and main term in a subject field). In other cases, terms and names that can also be used alone as subject headings may be used also as subject subdivisions.

Examples of terms and names used as subject subdivision terms are the following:

> 20th century [Subject subdivision term that can be used only as a subdivision of a subject heading, but not alone as a subject heading]
>
> Real property — Mississippi ["Mississippi" is used here as a subject subdivision, but it can also be used alone as a subject heading]

STRUCTURE AND CODES OF THE
MARC AUTHORITY FORMAT

The structure and codes of the MARC authority format are essentially the same as that of the MARC bibliographic format (as explained in chapter 2, MARC Format Structure and Content Designation and chapter 4, Major MARC Bibliographic Codes) in that they include fixed and variable fields, with the variable fields being subdivided into subfields. Just as the fields and subfields of the MARC bibliographic format are based on the structure of library catalog records and their uses, the fields of the MARC authority format are based on the fields used in manual authority files. For example, the MARC authority format includes specific fields for headings and different types of cross-references (e.g., "see" and "see also" references), as well as notes fields for documentation of research performed to establish an authority heading. In addition, like the MARC bibliographic format, the MARC authority format accommodates the inclusion of additional information beyond that traditionally included in manual files, which can be used to great advantage within automated systems.

Figure 9.4 is an example of a MARC authority record, taken from the *USMARC format for authority data*.

LDR	*****nzƀƀ22*****nƀƀ4500
001	exƀ82221219ƀ
005	19860107072428.3
008	ꓲ 860107 ꓲ inƀac ꓲ nnnaa ꓲ bnƀƀƀ ꓲ ƀƀƀƀƀ ꓲ ƀƀsaƀ ꓲ anaƀƀ ꓲ ƀƀƀu ꓲ
040	ƀƀ‡cDLC
110	20‡aOklahoma Council on Juvenile Delinquency
410	10‡aOklahoma.‡bCouncil on Juvenile Delinquency
410	10‡aOklahoma.‡bOklahoma Council on Juvenile Delinquency
510	20‡wa‡aOklahoma Council on Juvenile Delinquency Planning
510	20‡wb‡aOklahoma Council on Juvenile Justice
670	ƀƀ‡aOklahoma Council on Juvenile Delinquency Planning. Youth in trouble, 1971–1982:‡bv. 2, t.p. (Oklahoma Council on Juvenile Delinquency) p. 3 (organized as Oklahoma Council on Juvenile Delinquency Planning in 1969)
670	ƀƀ‡aOklahoma Council on Juvenile Justice. Report, 1983:‡bp. 5 (Oklahoma Council on Juvenile Justice ... previously the Oklahoma Council on Juvenile Delinquency)

Fig. 9.4. Example of a MARC authority record for an established corporate name heading.

Some of the major MARC authority codes are discussed below. Definitions of some of the codes are presented from the *USMARC format for authority data*, published by the Library of Congress. A discussion of each code is included.

Major MARC authority codes are discussed in the following order: leader codes, 008 codes, and variable data fields. Variable data field information is generally presented in order by the predominance of use of the fields within authority records. For this reason, the fields are not presented in strict numerical order. For comprehensive information in regard to MARC authority codes, consult the *USMARC format for authority data*, which is available from the Library of Congress.

Major Leader Codes

Record Status (Offset Character 5)

> USMARC Definition
>
> The Record status character position contains a single-character alphabetic code that indicates the relationship of the record to a file for file maintenance purposes.

Discussion

The primary Record status codes are *c* (corrected or revised record), *n* (new record), *s* (record deleted because heading has been split into two or more headings) and *x* (record deleted because heading is replaced by another heading).

Libraries that follow Library of Congress practice for headings will want to be aware of record status, particularly in regard to corrected or revised headings. The *c* status code will often be the primary indication that an established heading has been changed in some way. Libraries will need to know when a heading has been changed so that they will be able to rectify the heading in bibliographic records that include the previous form of the term. The *c* status code helps to avoid confusion about an apparently new heading that is actually a revision of an old heading.

A record that includes status code *s* (which will usually have previously been a code *n* or *c*) indicates that the record has been deleted from a file because the heading has been split into two or more headings, requiring a new authority record for each. For example, the former heading "Buddha and Buddhism" was split into two separate headings, one for "Gautama Buddha" and one for "Buddhism," each of which was included in a new authority record. The heading from the deleted record (in this case, "Buddha and Buddhism") is included in each of the new authority records as a tracing in a cross-reference ("see from") field. The *USMARC format for authority data* includes the following suggestion for use of this type of record in an automated authority control system:

An automated authority control system can scan other authority records until it locates two records which contain the deleted heading used as a 4XX See From Tracing. At that time, the system can display the deleted heading and the two replacement headings for review or take other automatic actions. (When a heading is split, a computer cannot automatically replace the old heading in bibliographic records Manual intervention is required to determine which of the new headings is appropriate in each bibliographic record containing the old heading.)

Code *x* indicates that the record has been deleted from a file and has been replaced by a new authority record in which the heading from the deleted record appears as a cross-reference ("see from") field. The *USMARC format for authority data* includes the following suggestion for use of this type of record in an automated authority control system.

In a system where authority control is linked to the bibliographic file, a computer can effect the one-to-one replacement indicated by code x without manual intervention.

Libraries should be aware that these codes have not always been a part of the USMARC authority format; libraries with older authority records or files may not be able to use records in the manner suggested. Also, it has not always been a practice for the Library of Congress to use a deleted heading as a cross-reference to a new replacement heading; in this case, as well, libraries may not be able to rely on older records to be able to perform the suggested functions.

Type of Record (Offset Character 6)

USMARC Definition

The Type of record character position contains a single-character alphabetic code that specifies the characteristics and defines the components of the record.

Discussion

Code *z* is the only Type of record code used in authority records. The specific kind of authority record is identified by a code in the 008 field. Within an automated library system that utilizes bibliographic and authority records, this code allows the system to easily differentiate between those two types of records.

Major 008 Codes

Direct/Indirect Geographic Subdivision Code (008/06)

USMARC Definition

A single-character code indicates whether the 1XX [established name or subject] heading can be subdivided geographically by the name of a country or other jurisdiction, region or geographic feature. If the heading can be subdivided geographically, the code identifies the method of subdivision that is used. In extended subject heading records, 008/06 coding is based on the entire heading, including the subdivisions.

Code ƀ, d, or i is used only in an established heading record (008/09, Kind of record, code a or f) that also is appropriate for use as a subject added entry in bibliographic records (008/15, code a). Code n is used in an established heading record that is not appropriate for use as a subject added entry in bibliographic records (008/15, code b) and in a reference, subdivision, or node label record (008/09, code other than a or f).

Discussion

The direct/indirect subdivision code provides instructions to catalogers as to whether it is appropriate to create geographic subdivisions for subject headings and how to create appropriate geographic subdivisions for subject headings, when those subdivisions are allowed.

Code ƀ indicates that the heading cannot be subdivided geographically, such as for a personal name heading. Code *d* indicates that the established heading can be subdivided geographically using the direct subdivision method. In this subdivision method, the heading is followed by the name of the specific place (e.g., the name of a city) to which the heading is limited without the interposition of a subdivision for the name of the larger geographic entity (e.g., the name of the state or country in which the city is located). Code *i* indicates that the established heading can be subdivided geographically using the indirect subdivision method. In this subdivision method, a subdivision for the name of the larger geographic entity (e.g., a state or country) is interposed between the heading and the subdivision for the specific place to which the heading is limited. Code *n* ("not applicable") indicates that the main heading in the authority record is an unestablished heading or is an established heading that is not appropriate for use as a subject added entry in bibliographic records.

Kind of Record Code (008/09)

USMARC Definition

A single-character alphabetic code indicates whether the authority record represents an established or unestablished 1XX [main] heading. The 1XX [main heading] field in an established heading record or an established heading and subdivision record contains an established heading. Reference, subdivision, and node label records contain an unestablished heading in field 1XX. If the record is a reference record, codes b and c indicate whether the 1XX heading is traced as a 4XX See From Tracing field in authority records for each heading referred to in the reference record....

Discussion

Code *a* indicates that the 1XX field contains an established heading, that is, a heading that has been created as an appropriate heading by the Library of Congress or other agency. An established heading record may also contain "see" and "see also" tracing fields for variant and related headings, and notes recording information such as the source used to establish the heading and information explaining scope and usage. Subject subdivision subfields, including general, chronological, and/or geographical subdivisions, may be present in the 1XX field in an extended subject heading. Code *c* indicates that the 1XX field contains an unestablished heading and that the 1XX heading is traced as a 4XX See from tracing field in the established heading record for each heading referred to in the reference record. The reference record contains a Complex see reference (664) field to guide the user to an established heading. Code *d* indicates that the 1XX field contains an unestablished heading that may be used as a subject subdivision with an established heading. Code *f* indicates that the 1XX field contains an established heading that may be used as a main term and as a subject subdivision. When code *f* is used, this means that a single authority record is used to describe this dual function. If, for whatever reason, a library prefers or needs to use two separate records, one for the term as an established heading and one for the term as a subject subdivision, then the records would be coded *a* and *d*, respectively.

Heading Use Code — Main or Added Entry (008/14)

USMARC Definition

A single-character alphabetic code indicates whether the 1XX [established name or subject] heading is appropriate for use as a main (1XX field) or added entry (7XX field) in bibliographic records. An appropriate heading is a 1XX heading in an established heading record (008/09, Type of record code, code a or f) that conforms to descriptive cataloging rules (008/10, any code except n). An inappropriate heading would be any unestablished 1XX heading or any heading that does not conform to descriptive cataloging rules (008/10, code n).

Discussion

Code *a* indicates that the heading in the authority record is appropriate for use as a main or added entry. Code *b* indicates that the heading is not appropriate for use as a main or added entry. Generally speaking, the headings coded as *a* are those that fall under the category of name headings (as described above) and the headings coded as *b* are those that fall under the category of subject headings (as described above). There are other, finer distinctions in the case of some authority records.

Heading Use Code — Subject Added Entry (008/15)

USMARC Definition

A single-character alphabetic code indicates whether the 1XX [established name or subject] heading is appropriate for use as a subject added entry (6XX field) in bibliographic records. An appropriate heading is a 1XX heading in an established heading record (008/09, Type of record code, code a or f) that conforms to subject heading system thesaurus rules (008/11, any code except n). An inappropriate heading would be any unestablished 1XX heading or any heading that does not conform to subject heading system/thesaurus rules (008/11, code n).

Discussion

Code *a* indicates that the heading in the authority record is appropriate for use as a subject entry. Code *b* indicates that the heading is not appropriate for use as a subject entry. Most authority headings, whether they are name or subject headings, can be used as subject entries, but there are a number of exceptions to this generalization. One major exception is in the case of names of jurisdictions that have changed over time. For example, the country of Sri Lanka was formerly Ceylon. For the purposes of subject entry, all books about that country are entered under the current name, *Sri Lanka*, regardless of the time period covered. For purposes of main or added entries, which are used for publications that were produced *by* that jurisdiction (i.e., authorship was involved) rather than *about* that country, the name of the jurisdiction that was used at the time of publication is used as the main or added entry.

Heading Use Code — Series Added Entry (008/16)

USMARC Definition

A single-character alphabetic code indicates whether the 1XX [main] heading is appropriate for use as a series added entry in bibliographic records (4XX Series Statements (Traced); 8XX Series Added Entry). An appropriate heading is a 1XX heading in an established heading record (008/09, Type of record code, code a) that represents a monographic series, a multipart item, an occasionally analyzable item, or a series-like phrase (008/12, code a, b, z, or c). An inappropriate heading would be any unestablished 1XX heading or any established heading that does not represent a series heading (008/12, code n).

Discussion

Code *a* indicates that the heading in the authority record is appropriate for use as a series added entry. Code *b* indicates that the heading is not appropriate for use as a series added entry. In the majority of cases, headings that are appropriate for use as series added entries are those headings that fall under the subcategory of uniform title headings, discussed above under the category of name authority headings. Within the subcategory of uniform title headings, only those headings defined as series headings (as opposed to uniform title headings for anonymous works, folktales, religious works, motion pictures, etc.) are appropriate for use as series added entries.

Variable Data Fields

1XX Headings

The 1XX field within an authority record contains a heading that is either an established heading or a reference. A list of 1XX fields and the type of heading that is contained within each field is given below.

    100 - Personal name heading

    110 - Corporate name heading

    111 - Meeting name heading

    130 - Uniform title heading

    150 - Topical term heading

    151 - Geographic name heading

Discussion

The types of headings listed above correspond to the headings described above within the categories of "name" and "subject" headings. All the types of headings can be used within bibliographic records as subject headings (6XX fields), although there are specific exceptions to this within each heading type. Only the types of headings included within the category of "name" headings (100, 110, 111, and 130) can be used as main or added entries within bibliographic records (1XX, 4XX, 7XX, or 8XX, as appropriate). The indicators and subfield codes used within each 1XX field within an authority record are in many cases the same as those used for the same headings within bibliographic records (as described in chapter 4, Major MARC Bibliographic Codes). There are also many differences; for specific and comprehensive information, consult the *USMARC format for authority data*, published by the Library of Congress.

4XX and 5XX Tracing Fields

4XX and 5XX fields within an authority record contain "see from" and "see also from" tracings, respectively. Tracing fields lead directly from one heading to a single other heading. A 4XX See from tracing field leads from an unestablished heading (such as a variant form of an author's name, a 400 field) to an established heading (for example, the form of an author's name that has been established for use for all works by that author, the 100 field). A 5XX See also from tracing field leads from an established heading to another established heading. For example, two related subject headings, each of which is used as an established heading within a 150 field in its own authority record, may also be found in a 550 See also from field within the record for the other heading, which can help to direct users interested in one of the topics to the other related topic.

Discussion

The types of headings listed above correspond to the headings described above within the categories of "name" and "subject" headings. The indicators and subfield codes used within each 4XX and 5XX field within an authority record are in many cases the same as those used for the same headings within bibliographic records (as described in chapter 4, Major MARC Bibliographic Codes). There are also many differences; for specific and comprehensive information, consult the *USMARC format for authority data*, published by the Library of Congress.

The ≠w subfield (which is not used in the same way within bibliographic heading fields) is one of the most significant subfields that is included within the USMARC authority format for the 4XX and 5XX fields. The ≠w subfield includes information regarding the cross-reference headings found in the 4XX and 5XX fields; generally this is information that describes the relationship between the 4XX or 5XX cross-reference heading and the main 1XX established heading. The ≠w subfield includes four character positions, each of which can include a code or a blank character, as is appropriate.

Definitions of the four character positions and examples of some of the codes are as follows. The four character positions are identified as ≠w/0, ≠w/1, ≠w/2, and ≠w/3.

The character position ≠w/0 contains a code that describes a relationship between a 1XX heading and a 4XX or 5XX heading that is more specific than the relationship implicit in the tag. The codes may be used to generate a special reference instruction phrase in a cross-reference display.

Codes a and b are used primarily for fields that include name headings, as opposed to subject headings. Code a indicates that the established heading in the tracing field (5XX field) is an earlier name for the 1XX heading. This is used most often in the case of corporate bodies, such as state government departments or universities, that have changed names over time. This code, or a special reference instruction phrase that can be generated for public use, allows catalogers and library users to understand the relationship between the two headings. For the same purpose, code b indicates that the heading in the tracing field (5XX) is a later name for the 1XX heading.

Examples of records using codes a and b are given below. They illustrate the relationship between the headings for the institution currently known as the Anytown College, which was formerly Anytown Woman's Institute.

110 10 ≠a Anytown College

510 10 ≠w a ≠a Anytown Women's Institute [Earlier heading]

110 10 ≠a Anytown Women's Institute

510 10 ≠w b ≠a Anytown College [Later heading]

Codes g and h are used primarily for fields that include subject headings, as opposed to name headings. Through the use of these codes, catalogers can determine the relationship between established headings. The codes can also be used to generate special reference instructions phrases for use by library users within an online catalog. Code g indicates that the heading in the tracing field is a broader term than the 1XX heading. The code may be used to generate a special reference instruction phrase such as "search under the narrower term:" in a cross-reference display. Code h indicates that the heading in the tracing field is a narrower term than the 1XX heading. The code may be used to generate a special reference instruction phrase such as "search also under the broader term:" in a cross-reference display.

Examples of records using codes g and h are given below. They illustrate the relationship between the broader subject heading *Foot* and the narrower subject heading *Toes*.

150 ƀ0 ≠a Toes

550 ƀƀ ≠w g ≠a Foot [Broader term]

150 ƀ0 ≠a Foot

550 ƀƀ ≠w h ≠a Toes [Narrower term]

The character position $\neq w/1$ contains a code that specifies the authority reference structure in which the use of a 4XX or 5XX tracing to generate a cross-reference is appropriate. Code *a* specifies that the tracing can be used to generate a cross-reference within a name reference structure only. Code *b* specifies subject reference structure only. Code *c* specifies series reference structure only. Code *d* specifies name and subject reference structures. Code *e* specifies name and series reference structures. Code *f* specifies subject and series reference structures. And, code *g* specifies that the tracing is appropriate to generate a cross-reference within name, subject, and series reference structures.

The character position $\neq w/2$ contains a code that specifies whether the 4XX tracing is a form in which the heading was established under earlier descriptive cataloging rules. Code *a* indicates that the unestablished heading in the tracing field contains a form of the 1XX heading that was established under earlier descriptive cataloging rules. Code *n* indicates that the tracing is not a form of the 1XX heading established under earlier descriptive cataloging rules. One of the primary uses of code *a* is in the case of older (pre-1981) authority records in which the headings were originally devised according to pre-*AACR2* rules. The old form of the heading, which formerly would have been contained in the 1XX field, has been placed in the 4XX field, and the new form of the name, devised using current cataloging rules, is the 1XX heading. Among other uses, this code can be used in automated authority flips that are accomplished to replace obsolete headings in libraries' bibliographic files with the currently used headings.

The character position $\neq w/3$ contains a code that enables the generation or suppression of a cross-reference from a 4XX or 5XX field. Generally, this code is used in cases where a simple cross-reference from the field does not provide enough information about the heading and its use. In most cases, the information is provided from another record or field, as indicated by the code. Code *a* indicates that the generation of a cross-reference display from a tracing field should be suppressed. Code *b* indicates that the generation of a cross-reference display from a tracing field in an established heading record should be suppressed because of the existence of a separate reference record containing field 664 (Complex see reference — Name). Code *c* indicates the generation of a cross-reference display from a tracing field in an established heading record should be suppressed because the record also contains a 663 field (Complex see also reference — Name). Code *d* indicates that the generation of a cross-reference display from a tracing field in an established heading record should be suppressed because the record also contains a 665 field (History reference).

260 and 360 Complex See References
for Subjects Fields

260 and 360 fields within an authority record contain reference notes that lead from one heading to one or more other headings. A reference note field is used when more complex reference instruction is needed than can be conveyed by one or more simple cross-references generated from 4XX and/or 5XX tracing fields. Cross-reference displays constructed from the reference note fields are "complex cross-references." In a complex

cross-reference display, the content of the 1XX field is the "heading referred from," and following a reference instruction phrase, the reference note field contains the "heading(s) referred to." In fields 260 and 360, the complete reference instruction may be a combination of a phrase implicitly associated with the field tag and explicit text in subfield ≠*i* (explanatory text). Field 260 is used in reference records to lead from an unestablished heading to established headings. Field 360 is used in established heading records to lead from an established heading to other established headings.

663 Complex See Also Reference – Name

This field contains the "explanatory text" and the "headings referred to" that are required when relationships exist between an established name and other established names that cannot be adequately conveyed by one or more simple cross-references generated from 5XX See also from tracing fields. Subfield ≠*a* includes the explanatory text of the see also reference. The text includes a reference instruction phrase such as "see also" or "search also under." Subfield ≠*b* contains the related established headings to which the heading in field 1XX of the record refers. An example of a 663 field is given below.

663 ᵇᵇᵇ ≠a　For works of this author written under pseudonyms, see also ≠b Gray, E. Condor, 1839-1905 and Page, H. A., 1839-1905.

664 Complex See Reference – Name

This field contains the "explanatory text" and "headings referred to" that are required when relationships exist between an unestablished name and one or more established names that cannot be adequately conveyed by simple cross-references generated from 4XX See from tracing fields in the established heading records. Subfield ≠*a* includes the explanatory text of the see reference. The text includes a reference instruction phrase such as "see" or "search under." Subfield ≠*b* contains the established headings to which the heading in field 1XX of the record refers. An example of a record including a 664 field is given below.

100 10 ≠a Reger, Max, ≠d 1873-1916. ≠t Dies irae

664 ᵇᵇᵇ ≠a　For this movement included in the composer's unfinished Requiem search under ≠b Reger, Max, 1873-1916. ≠t Requiem (Mass)

665 History Reference

This field contains the text for a history reference for names. It is used when more information is needed about the relationships that exist among three or more established names (usually corporate names) than can be adequately conveyed by simple cross-references generated from 5XX See also from tracing fields in the established heading records. The 665 field may also contain text describing the subject entry treatment for works about the various related headings. Subfield ≠*a* contains text describing the relationships and the headings to which the heading field 1XX of the record refers. Subfield ≠a may be repeated to allow the generation of paragraphs and/or a list of the headings in a cross-reference display. An example of a 665 field is given below.

> 665 ᑲᑲ ≠a In Jan. 1979 the Connecticut Dept. of Social Services split to form the Dept. of Human Resources and the Dept. of Income Maintenance. ≠a Works by these bodies are found under the following headings according to the name used at the time of publication: ≠a Connecticut. Dept. of Social Services. ≠a Connecticut. Dept. of Human Resources. ≠a Connecticut. Dept. of Income Maintenance. ≠a SUBJECT ENTRY: Works about these bodies are entered under one or more of the names resulting from the separation. Works limited in coverage to the pre-separation period are entered under the name of the original body.

667 Name Usage or Scope Note

This field contains information about a 1XX name or uniform title heading that is not from a source cited in field 670 (Source data found) but is needed in the record to clarify the usage or scope of the heading in an established heading record. Subfield ≠a contains a usage or scope note. An example of a record containing a 667 field is given below.

> 110 20 ≠a Mennonite Brethren Church

> 667 ᑲᑲ ≠a Not the same as the Mennonite Brethren Church of North America

POTENTIAL USES FOR MARC AUTHORITY RECORDS

There are five main uses for MARC authority records. All these uses are currently either in practice or under development by a number of libraries and vendors. The five uses are (1) online authority file, (2) offline batch authority control, (3) cross-referencing for public access catalogs, (4) editing and exceptions list production for new and changed headings, and (5) global changes within offline products or online systems. A discussion of each use follows.

Online Authority File

A file of MARC authority records can be used to provide an online authority file for use by library staff and/or patrons. In both cases, the simplest use would involve a file that is separate from the bibliographic (catalog record) file. For library cataloging functions, an online authority file within a library's system or provided by a bibliographic utility, such as OCLC, can assist in checking, supplying, and creating authority headings for use in bibliographic records. In some cases, such as with the OCLC and RLIN online name and subject authority files, MARC authority records can be transferred from the utility to a library's online system. An online authority file within a library's in-house system could be used to provide patrons with information about established headings and cross-references for names, uniform titles, and subject headings. A display of the record in the MARC format (including all MARC coding, with its implicit meanings) would suffice for use by library cataloging staff. The use of an online authority file by library patrons, however, would call for a more user-friendly display (without the MARC codes) with explicit labels for specific fields and reformatting of the information where necessary.

Offline Batch Authority Control

Libraries that have MARC bibliographic databases that have not received consistent authority control (e.g., not all bibliographic records have been updated for heading changes) often choose to have some updating of their MARC file accomplished prior to loading the records into an online system. There are some aspects of authority control (such as replacing pre-*AACR2* name headings with their current counterparts) that can be accomplished in a batch process. By comparing headings in the bibliographic records with headings and cross-references in the authority records, some obsolete name and subject headings can be flipped to the current forms. This process and its benefits and limitations are explained in chapter 6, MARC Database Processing.

Cross-referencing for Public Access Catalogs

MARC authority records can be used to provide cross-references and explanatory notes within public access catalogs. Ideally, the library should have an authority record for each heading found in its MARC bibliographic database. Within systems that provide such a function, the use of this authority function is based on some type of link between the bibliographic records and the authority file, either through indexing of all headings and cross-references within the same index, or by some other means. Generally speaking, the provision of cross-references and explanatory notes means that, when a library patron searches the catalog using a variant or alternative form of a name, or a broader or narrower subject heading, the catalog will direct the user to other headings/records through the use of a "search under:" or "search also under:" term. The automated system may automatically direct users to the other forms of names or other subject headings, or it may require the user to re-enter the search request using the other terms. The use of cross-referencing within an automated catalog can provide for much more successful use of the catalog and the library's collection. This is accomplished in part because cross-references can provide an alternative to dead-end searches that result when the user does not know the exact established name heading or subject term used in the catalog.

Editing and Exceptions List Production

A MARC authority file within a library's online system can be used as the basis for quality control when headings in newly entered MARC bibliographic records are compared to headings in the MARC authority records. An edit list or exceptions list can be produced for name or subject headings that do not match headings in any of the MARC authority records. In some cases, a nonmatching heading will be a heading that is new to the file, which will require the creation of an authority record for that heading. In other cases, however, the nonmatching heading will simply be a heading that includes typographical or coding errors that require correction. Instead of being a new heading, the heading does not match the authority file heading simply because it has been incorrectly entered. Once corrected, the heading will match the authority file heading and will not occur again within an edit or exceptions report.

Global Changes

A MARC authority file within an online system can enable libraries to make global changes to headings within bibliographic records in the system. The term *global change* refers to the function of having all occurrences of a particular heading (within all bibliographic records that include the heading) changed at the same time from one form to another by an automatic function. This option is preferable to manually searching and changing each individual occurrence of the heading within the bibliographic records.

An example of a situation in which a global change could be used within an online system is the case of a subject heading that has been declared obsolete and replaced with another term. For example, the former Library of Congress subject heading *color-sense* has been changed to the more timely term *color vision*. All Library of Congress bibliographic records used by libraries and all bibliographic records created by libraries after the change include the subject heading *color vision*; however, previously cataloged items in a library's database (either from the Library of Congress or locally created) still include the obsolete form of the term. These items need to be changed to the current form so that catalog users can find all relevant items under that term. Without global change capabilities, each individual record with the term *color-sense* would have to be manually searched and the old subject heading would have to be manually replaced within each record with the new heading *color vision*. With global change capabilities, however, an online system can be programmed to automatically seek out all occurrences of the old term and replace them with the new term. An automatic global change can be accomplished within a fraction of the time required for a manual change, particularly when a large number of bibliographic records is involved.

There are limits to global change capabilities for most online systems and batch processes. In many cases, only the first subfield of a field (particularly topical subject headings) can be changed through a global change operation. In other cases, an online system or processing vendor may be able to change subdivision subfields or other parts of a field with varying degrees of success. For portions of a record other than traditional access points (1XX, 4XX, 6XX, 7XX, and 8XX fields), global change capabilities are not well-developed.

There are two primary methods for effecting global changes within online systems. The methods are at least partially dependent on the way the bibliographic and authority databases are constructed and used by the system. One method involves "unlinked" authority and bibliographic records, which means that the authority and bibliographic records are used and maintained separately and that there is no permanent link between a heading within a bibliographic record and its counterpart in the authority file. When bibliographic and authority records are unlinked, a global change involves programming the system to compare the old heading to all subject headings in the bibliographic file. The system must look at each heading field in each bibliographic record and determine which ones are the same as the old heading. Then, the text is replaced with the new heading.

With "linked" bibliographic and authority files, the headings in the bibliographic records are permanently linked to their counterpart in an authority record. This involves a relationship and interdependence between the bibliographic and authority files that is not found with "unlinked" databases. One method of establishing a permanent link between authority and bibliographic records involves placing, within each field in a bibliographic record, a "pointer," generally a record number, that directs the system to look at the authority record with that number. The bibliographic record in the database does not actually contain the text of the heading in the field; the text is retrieved from the authority record when the record is used for display or other purposes. When "linked" records are used, a global change is automatically effected by simply changing the authority record to which the bibliographic record is linked. After the authority record has been changed, the new heading will automatically be retrieved and placed in the bibliographic record when the bibliographic record is used.

The option of using "linked" or "unlinked" records is not related simply to authority control or global changes. In fact, automated system vendors may choose to use either method regardless of whether authority control is accomplished by the system. There is not a consensus among automation vendors as to whether a "linked" database is preferable to an "unlinked" database; both methods have their own advantages and disadvantages. For example, vendors that use "linked" databases argue that a bibliographic database that includes fewer characters (i.e., pointer numbers instead of full text in each record) will provide faster response time (for searching and other purposes) because the database is smaller. (Database size can impact upon response time.) On the other hand, vendors that use "unlinked" databases argue that response time can be faster for unlinked databases because, when a record is retrieved, the system can simply retrieve the full text bibliographic record in one step, rather than having to refer to pointer numbers for headings, retrieve the headings from the record, and assemble them into a bibliographic record display. The options of linked or unlinked records are dependent on many factors, including hardware, operating software, applications software, database construction, and uses of the system by the library.

LSP—THE LINKED SYSTEMS PROJECT

The LSP (Linked Systems Project) was devised as a way to facilitate the creation of a national name authority file for use by all libraries in the United States and elsewhere. The LSP accommodates this effort in two ways. First, it provides for the creation of "Library of Congress" authority records by other libraries that are trained and authorized to provide such a service; in this way the LC name authority file can be expanded at a much greater rate than if only a few government agencies are involved in its creation. The second way in which LSP accommodates the creation of a name authority file involves the fact that the creation of name authority records sometimes requires a significant amount of research into the background of the person or institution that is the focus of the authority record. For persons or organizations that have been based in a particular geographical area, it is usually much easier for local researchers to do the research than for one centralized agency, such as the Library of Congress, to try to research information that is available only in other regions of the country.

The article "NACO LSP Libraries now number 22" in *Library of Congress information bulletin* 48 (48): 418 + dated November 27, 1989, provides this information in regard to the Linked Systems Project:

The National Coordinated Cataloging Operations (NACO) expanded the authority application of the Linked Systems Project (LSP) with the addition of four more libraries in September 1989: Louisiana State University; Texas State Library; University of California, San Diego; and University of Pittsburgh. A joint project of the Library of Congress, the Online Computer Library Center (OCLC), and the Research Libraries Group, Inc. (RLG), LSP is a computer-to-computer link allowing for online contribution and distribution of authority records.

LSP Record Transfer provides OCLC and RLG with up-to-date copies of the Library of Congress Name Authority File, and in addition provides a mechanism for OCLC and RLG NACO participants to contribute name authority records directly to the Library of Congress from their respective input-update systems.

Records are transmitted between systems and loaded within a 24-hour period. LSP provides more timely and accurate access, eliminates duplicate work, and makes contributed records available to library users more quickly. The contributed authority records are also available to MARC tape subscribers....

In addition to the Serial Record Division at the Library of Congress, there are now 22 institutions contributing authority records to the national authority file via LSP: American Antiquarian Society; Columbia University; Getty Art History Vocabulary Group; Eighteenth-Century Short Title Catalogue/North America; Indiana University; Louisiana State University; Minnesota Historical Society; NACO-Music Project at the Indiana University Music Library and the Sibley Library of the Eastman School of Music; OCLC; University of Pittsburgh; Princeton University; St. Louis University School of Law; Stanford University; Texas State Library; U.S. Department of the Interior; U.S. Government Printing Office; University of California, Los Angeles; University of California, San Diego; University of Illinois, Urbana/Champaign; University of Maryland; University of Michigan; and Yale University.

RELATED READINGS

Clack, Doris H. *Authority control: Principles, applications, and instructions*. Chicago: ALA, 1990.

Johnston, Sarah Hager. "Current offerings in automated authority control: A survey of vendors." *Information technology and libraries* 8 (3): 236-64 (September 1989).

Kruger, Kathleen Joyce. "1984 automated authority control opinion poll: A preliminary analysis." *Information technology and libraries* 4 (2): 171-78 (June 1984).

10

MARC Format for
Holdings Data

INTRODUCTION

The USMARC format for holdings data is the youngest of the three USMARC formats, being published in 1990, more than 20 years after the implementation of the bibliographic format.[1] The time lag between the initial research of the holdings format and its publication in a finalized status has also been longer than for the other two formats: more than eight years. The format was originally called the "MARC format for holdings and locations." The purpose of the MARC holdings format is to record item-specific information, such as the call number; the branch, collection, and/or location in which an item is held; and the number of copies or volumes held. The USMARC format for holdings data is based largely on ANSI standards Z39.44 (detailed and summary serials holdings) and Z39.57 (nonserial holdings, most notably, holdings for multipart items such as kits).

The holdings format differs from the bibliographic and authority formats in a number of ways, some of which explain the delays in its implementation.

Unlike the bibliographic and authority formats, which were based on well-established standards for catalog and authority records, the holdings format had no established model in the manual environment.

In the absence of a standard for holdings data, a wide variety of localized holdings formats have been implemented and used by individual libraries, tape processing vendors, system vendors, and bibliographic utilities.

In most cases, a MARC holdings record cannot be used as an independent entity, as bibliographic and authority records can. MARC holdings records provide information in regard to a particular bibliographic item, which is represented by a bibliographic record.

MARC holdings fields can be used as part of a bibliographic record or as a separate record that is linked to the bibliographic record through the use of a linking number field.

In addition to being a communications format, the MARC holdings format has been developed as a processing format to support some very specific applications.

To a large extent, information in MARC holdings records is formatted, as compared to the free-text information or information transcribed directly from the source that is found in bibliographic and authority records.

PRE-MARC HOLDINGS FORMATS AND USES

A number of localized holdings formats have arisen in the absence of a standard format. The existence of a number of disparate formats has had its advantages in that MARC research could benefit from the experience gained in the use of such formats. On the other hand, the existence of widely differing coding for holdings information has meant that the holdings statements were not transferable to other systems or other uses. It also means that libraries that have used other formats may find it difficult or impossible to transform their existing records into the MARC standard.

Some of the most commonly used fields for holdings information have been the OCLC-MARC 049 field, and the 590, 599, 910, and 949 fields, all of which are local-use fields. Subfield codes for use within these fields have been locally defined as well. The holdings records or fields have included, among other information, a barcode number for each individual item, the call number, call number prefixes or suffixes, library branch code (when branches are involved), a collection code (such as "Ref" for reference), the cost of the item, and volume numbers, and other numbering.

Holdings records have been used for two main purposes to date: to support circulation functions and to provide displays of item information within online catalogs. These functions have generally been performed through the use of individual "item" records, one per physical volume, that include information for that volume. The item records are permanently linked to corresponding bibliographic records within an online system. Multiple item records can be linked to a single bibliographic record, when necessary. When a particular volume is checked out, the barcode number on the physical item is matched up to the barcode number in the item record. The status of the item is changed (to "checked out") in the online catalog and the item record is temporarily linked to the record of the patron who has checked it out. Users of the online catalog can tell, through the use of holdings records, which volumes of an item the library holds, as well as which are checked out. (Patron information is generally not given through the online catalog, however.)

Other lesser-used but significant and sophisticated functions of holdings records have been to support serials control, including such operations as serials check-in, claiming, production of bindery slips, and fund accounting.

USES OF THE MARC HOLDINGS FORMAT

The MARC holdings format has been designed with specific uses in mind, including both the functions described in the above section and other uses. An understanding of those uses will help in understanding the purpose of some of the codes in the format. One of the primary uses of the MARC holdings format, of course, is as a "communications" format to exchange holdings information between systems. The transfer of holdings data from one system to another is most likely to happen when a library replaces its online system or when a library participates in union catalog activities, such as a serials union list.

The format provides flexibility in describing holdings in that it provides for both summary and detailed holdings statements, with several levels of detail allowed. The option of "compressing" detailed holdings into briefer statements and "expanding" brief statements into more detail is also built into the MARC holdings format.

MAJOR MARC HOLDINGS CODES

The MARC holdings format is a very detailed and complex format that has been designed to accommodate a wide variety of descriptions and a number of functions within the automated environment. Many of the codes will be used only rarely within a given library (or perhaps not at all). As was noted in the introduction to this chapter, the USMARC holdings fields can be used as a separate record that is linked to bibliographic records or as fields within a bibliographic record. The major MARC holdings fields are discussed below. For more comprehensive information, see the *USMARC format for holdings data*, published by the Library of Congress.[2]

Leader

The Leader is the first field of a separate holdings record. It is similar to the Leader in the bibliographic format. Among other codes, there is a code to indicate whether the record is for a "single-part item" or a "multipart or serial item." Another code indicates which "holdings level," or level of detail is used within the record (levels range from *1* to *4*, with *4* being the most detailed).

008 Field

The 008 field includes, among others, codes to indicate the receipt or acquisition status, method of acquisition, general and specific retention policies, completeness, lending policy, and reproduction policy.

Notes Fields (583, 841, 843, 845 Fields)

Notes fields within MARC holdings records include the 583 Action Note field, which may include information on processing action, preservation actions, review of condition, queuing for preservation, completion of preservation, and public and nonpublic notes. Other notes fields are the 841 (Holdings coded data values), 843 (Reproduction note), and 845 (Terms governing use and reproduction note).

852 Field (Location)

The 852 field includes location information, with the first indicator being coded for the "shelving scheme," which is usually the type of classification used, such as LC or Dewey. Subfields are included for a location, sublocation or collection, location qualifiers, call numbers, call number prefix or suffix, piece designation, piece physical condition, and public and nonpublic notes. The use of multiple 852 fields for multiple copies of an item held at different branches solves a long-standing problem for multi-branch libraries using MARC records. Although the MARC bibliographic format does allow for multiple call numbers of the same type within bibliographic records, there has been no clear-cut or standardized way to show which call number had been used at each branch.

Captions and Pattern Fields
(853, 854, 855 Fields)

The fields numbered 853, 854, and 855 include captions and pattern information for basic bibliographic units, supplementary material, and indexes, respectively. Subfields ǂa through ǂf include increasingly specific "enumeration captions," that is, the terms used on the item to designate the levels of enumeration, such as "vol." or "pt." Subfields ǂi through ǂl include increasingly specific "chronology captions," that is, the terms used to designate the levels of chronology, such as "year" or "month."

Enumeration and Chronology Fields
(863, 864, 865 Fields)

The fields numbered 863, 864, and 865 include enumeration and chronology information for basic bibliographic units, supplementary material, and indexes, respectively. Subfields ǂa through ǂf include numbers of volumes, parts, and so forth, of a publication, in increasing levels of specificity. Subfields ǂi through ǂl include the time period involved, in increasing levels of specificity, such as "1970" and "June." In most cases, one 853 field, which designates the captions and patterns, will be used with numerous 863 fields, in which are recorded the information for individual issues, volumes, and so on. Figure 10.1 provides an example of multiple 863 fields with the corresponding 853 field.

```
853 20 ǂa vol. ǂb no. ǂi (year) ǂj (month)
863 41 ǂa 8 ǂb 1 ǂi 1987 ǂj Jan
863 41 ǂa 8 ǂb 2 ǂi 1987 ǂj Feb
863 41 ǂa 8 ǂb 3 ǂi 1987 ǂj Mar
863 41 ǂa 8 ǂb 4 ǂi 1987 ǂj Apr
```

Fig. 10.1. Multiple 863 fields with corresponding 853 field.

The 863 fields shown in figure 10.1 represent numbers 1, 2, 3, and 4 of volume 8 of the publication, published in January, February, March, and April of 1987, respectively. The process of "compression" of holdings statements would allow for the four 863 fields to be displayed as an inclusive statement, such as "vol. 8, no. 1 (1987:Jan)-vol. 8, no. 4 (1987: Apr)." If individual issues do not need to be represented by separate fields, then the holdings format also provides for a single, inclusive ("compressed") holding statement within a field, such as "ǂa 8 ǂb 1-4 ǂi 1987 ǂj Jan-Apr."

Textual Holdings Fields (866, 867, 868 Fields)

The 866, 867, and 868 fields include textual holdings information for the basic bibliographic unit, supplementary material, and indexes, respectively. Textual holdings information is free-text information (as compared to the coded information in fields

863-865), which is input into one subfield. Free-text holdings information can be used in combination with other fields for display purposes or it can be used in place of other 8XX fields for display.

NOTES

1. Thanks go to Rebecca Guenther, Library of Congress Network Development and MARC Standards Office, for supplying the author with the most up-to-date USMARC holdings information.

2. *USMARC format for holdings data* (Washington, D.C.: Library of Congress, Cataloging Distribution Service, 1990).

RELATED READINGS

Baker, Barry G. *The USMARC format for holdings and locations: Development, implementation and use.* New York: Haworth Press, 1988.

11

MARC Use in Different Types of Libraries

INTRODUCTION

This chapter focuses on the use of MARC records and MARC-based systems within different types of libraries. Three types of libraries are considered: academic and research libraries, public libraries, and school libraries. Of course, all types of libraries share many things in common, and categorization of libraries into types is a matter of generalization that may not effectively define individual libraries within each type. For example, a large public library may have more in common with an academic library than it does with a small public library. Likewise, a regional public library with many branches may have more in common with school libraries than it does with a single-building public library. The generalizations used in this chapter are not meant to restrict useful information through the use of categorization. Readers within a library of any type will almost certainly benefit from the information provided regarding the use of MARC by other types of libraries.

ACADEMIC AND RESEARCH LIBRARIES

For the purposes of this chapter, "academic and research libraries" refers generally to community college libraries, college and university libraries, and large research libraries.

MARC Implementation

The use of MARC format and MARC-based systems within academic libraries often takes place in phases, which can be a distinct advantage. For example, many academic libraries first use MARC for cataloging purposes, through an online utility such as OCLC, RLIN, or WLN. When the library later implements an online system that uses MARC records, they have two advantages from their previous use of MARC. One of these benefits is that the library may be able to obtain a machine-readable database of materials cataloged through the utility, which reduces the number of items that must be input through retrospective conversion. The other benefit is that library cataloging staff are knowledgeable about MARC format and can provide valuable input relating to system specifications for use of the MARC records within an online system. In addition, academic libraries often have had experience, through use of other systems, to assist them in their understanding and use of similar activities (such as keyword searching) within MARC-based online searching.

Another benefit academic libraries can take advantage of regarding MARC use has to do with the large amount of published information available concerning automation of academic libraries (much of which does not have the same value for use by other types of libraries, because of differing needs). There are two reasons for this comparatively large "share" of published information. One reason is that more academic libraries than other types of libraries have implemented the use of MARC and MARC-based systems. The other reason is that, within the academic community at large, staff members work in a "publish or perish" environment that requires them to publish, or at least work within an environment in which publication is rewarded or expected. Also, academic library staff are more likely to be supported (either financially or through professional release time) by their institutions for travel to conferences that provide information in regard to MARC use.

Collections

Compared to the types of materials used by other types of libraries, academic library collections consist primarily of print materials (as opposed to audiovisual materials and kits). On the other hand, these print materials often fall into a broader range of types than those used by other types of libraries, which means that academic libraries are required to deal with a broader range of concerns or questions regarding the cataloging and use of print materials within MARC-based systems. A listing of various types of print materials used by academic libraries is given below, with discussion of each type as it pertains to MARC use.

Serial Publications

As part of their role in supporting research, academic libraries must provide both up-to-date and historical information about issues in a wide variety of fields, much of which is provided through serials collections. Serial publications, such as journals and monographic series, generally represent a significant proportion of the library's collection, as well as its acquisitions budget. There are a number of factors that impact upon the library's use of serials with MARC and MARC-based systems. These factors generally fall into the two categories of "cataloging" and "use" of serials.

Cataloging of serials using the MARC format requires the use of the serials format, probably the most complex of the format types. Using the serials format involves knowledge of such complex issues as "linking fields," which serve to link related publications, such as the same journal published under different names at different times. A comparatively large number of interdependent fields, with multiple options for display constants, also are a part of the serials format. In addition to cataloging serials as a unit, using the serials format, libraries also have the option of using the MARC books format for cataloging individual issues of serials or an individual article within a serial item. This requires the use of fixed field codes (such as Leader code 007/07 for monographic component part or serial component part) and variable data fields (such as MARC field 773 (Host item entry)) that are not used as often for cataloging monographs.

Cataloging of serials also involves much more detailed information relating to holdings than does the cataloging of books, which generally just involves information regarding the number of copies available. To provide explicit information about the specific issues held by the library, it is necessary to provide information in regard to each volume and subunit (e.g., "number 2," "part A," "Bd. 5"), as well as the dates involved. Generally speaking, libraries have two options for presenting this information. Summary notes can be used, such as "vol. 1, no. 1 - vol.13, no 4" with an additional note presenting exceptions to the summary note (such as "vol. 5, no. 3 missing"). In addition to or in lieu of presenting summary notes, libraries may present detailed holdings, basically a listing of each individual issue held. For patron use, a summary statement may suffice; for serials check-in and control (discussed in more detail below), detailed holdings are usually necessary. Because there has formerly been no national standard for holdings information, libraries have had to use the individual holdings formats devised by cataloging or automation vendors to represent this information. The current implementation of a standard, the *USMARC format for holdings data* (which is the topic of chapter 10, MARC Format for Holdings Data) will provide for a single standard that can be used for all purposes within all systems.

Serials control involves such factors as ordering of serials (in some cases through online transmission of orders to vendors); serials check-in (for each issue); serials fund accounting (particularly useful for libraries that have a large serials budget and receive subscriptions for materials that may suddenly increase greatly in price); automatic notification (by a serials module or system) of issues not received; production of claim notices (for issues not received); and production of bindery slips for groups of individual issues to be bound. Automated serials control may be accomplished through an integrated system that includes other modules (such as circulation and an online catalog) or through the use of an individual serials control system.

Serials Union Listing

Serials union listing involves a cooperative effort of groups of libraries to make information about their serials holdings available to each other and other libraries. Serials union lists have been used for many years to facilitate interlibrary loan requests for periodical articles. Initially, serials union listing took place through the use of printed union lists, and such printed lists are still used. Increasingly automation is being used to facilitate both the provision of information about holdings (e.g., via an online union catalog) and the communication of interlibrary loan requests for articles (i.e., via E-MAIL or cooperative online systems).

Microforms

Academic library collections often include a significant number of materials in microform, usually either on microfiche or microfilm. These materials may have been initially published in microform or they may be microform copies of materials initially published in a paper format. Often, microform materials are not included within card catalogs or online catalogs. In part, this is because they are not used as much as books and serials. On the other hand, it should be questioned whether lack of entry of these materials within library catalogs is part of the reason that they are not used as much as other types of materials. In many instances, access to materials in microform is provided through other means, such as periodical and newspaper indexes or databases such as the ERIC online and CD-ROM databases.

In any case, the MARC format does provide for the inclusion of microforms within a MARC database. The *USMARC format for bibliographic data* states that "Microforms, whether original or reproductions, are not identified by a distinctive Type of record code. The type of material characteristics described by the codes [e.g., for music or printed language materials] take precedence over the microform characteristics of the item." There is no record type code for microform materials; the type of material represented on the microform, such as printed music or printed maps, determines the record type. The 008 field character position for Form of item provides for a code that indicates whether the material is microfilm, microfiche, or microopaque. The MARC format also contains a field 007 (Physical description fixed field) for comprehensive and detailed coded information about the microform item being cataloged. For materials that were originally produced as hardcopy material (such as books), cataloging rules and the MARC format for that type of material allow for creation of a record for the original item, with a 533 field (Reproduction note) that includes the details in regard to the microform edition.

Technical Reports

Academic library collections often contain a considerable number of technical reports, which are reports of research funded or sponsored by government agencies or other organizations. There are a number of MARC codes and fields that have been included within the formats to identify information needed to describe technical reports. For example, the 536 field (Funding information note) contains information on contract, grant, and project numbers, and it may also contain information concerning the sponsors or funding agencies. Although many technical reports are actually U.S. government publications distributed to federal depository libraries, they do not receive the same priority for MARC cataloging by the Government Printing Office (GPO, which serves as a cataloging agency for government publications) as do other types of government documents, and they are not included in the GPO MARC tapes. Most technical reports are cataloged by other agencies according to the COSATI (Committee on Scientific and Technical Information of the Federal Council for Science and Technology) format, a non-MARC format created specifically for technical reports prior to the development of the MARC format. (Development of the MARC format has only recently, within the past decade, provided for codes and fields deemed necessary for cataloging of technical reports.) In many cases, the agencies that catalog technical reports in the COSATI format provide the capability to transform (through computer software) COSATI format records into the MARC format.

Government Documents

Government publications from many nations and from many levels of government (e.g., federal, state, local) constitute a significant portion of many academic library collections. In some cases, indexes produced by the publishing agencies (such as the Government Printing Office *Monthly catalog* or state government document checklists) provide access to these materials, but they are not often included as part of a library's card or online catalog. The MARC format does provide for cataloging of government publications of all types and includes such fixed field codes as the 008 field Government publication code to indicate the level of government involved, as well as call number fields to accommodate classification schemes used by such agencies as GPO, the National Agricultural Library, and the National Library of Medicine. GPO MARC records, for all publications cataloged by GPO, are available on OCLC, from the Library of Congress, and through a number of MARC record vendors. GPO has been producing MARC records for a number of years, and currently there are projects to coordinate automatic distribution of these records to federal depository libraries.

Analytical Entries

Analytics involve the creation of a separate record for a part of an item, such as a single play within a book that includes a collection of plays or a single article within a journal that includes a number of articles. The MARC format provides for these types of records through the use of fixed field codes (such as the Leader 007/07 code—*a* for a monographic component part and *b* for a serial component part) and variable data fields (such as field 773, which includes a note that indicates the "host" item within which the component part can be found).

Archival and Manuscript Materials

Academic library collections often include published and unpublished archival materials and manuscripts (either handwritten or typed). In some cases, the archival materials are published items that document the history of a person or an institution; in other cases, the archival materials may be "unpublished" memos, papers, or other such materials, also collected for their historical value. Manuscript materials may include such items as notes, drafts, or final drafts of works by an author that may or may not have been published. Archival and manuscript materials may be bound or unbound. Often, these types of materials are unbound items organized by the library and placed in folders or boxes. Within the last decade, the MARC format has evolved to include fixed field and variable data field elements that accommodate the description and use of such materials. For example, the Leader 007/07 code *d* indicates that a record is for a part of a collection, particularly an archival unit that is described collectively within another record. Another example is the variable data 540 field (Terms governing use and reproduction note), which contains information about terms governing the use of materials, such as restrictions of the right to reproduce or quote from archival or manuscript materials. Additional subfields were created during the mid-1980s for the MARC 300 field (Physical description) to accommodate physical description of archival materials. The subfields include subfield ≠*f* (Type of unit), which allows for describing materials in terms of boxes, cubic feet, linear feet, and so forth, and subfield ≠*g* (Size of unit), which contains the size of the type of unit given in subfield ≠*f* (e.g., the size of a box). In addition, many other codes and fields have been supplied to accommodate the creation and use of records for archival and manuscript materials.

Special Collections

Academic libraries often have one or more collections designated as "special collec-tions." Most of the types of materials included in these special collections can be cataloged using the existing MARC formats. One instance that may impact upon MARC-based automation is the situation in which a special collections item is basically a duplicate of an item in the library's circulating collection. The special collections item may contain an autograph or margin notes or some other aspect that resulted in its being included within "special collections." Within a card catalog, two such items have gener-ally been accommodated by using two card sets, one for the "stacks" copy with the appropriate call number and one for the "special collections" copy, including a note regarding the autograph or other differentiating information as well as the appropriate call number. Within automated catalogs, however, the rule is generally to use one biblio-graphic record to represent all copies held within the institution. There are at least two methods for indicating the difference between the two copies. One is to include a note within the bibliographic record that describes the differences. The other method is to use the "item holding record" (a type of record used within automated systems to represent each physical volume in the system, including the specific call number of the item, etc.) to include a note indicating the autograph or other differentiating information, as well as the separate call number.

Foreign Language Materials

Academic and research library collections often include a great many materials in non-English languages and non-Roman alphabets (e.g., Cyrillic alphabets and oriental scripts). For non-English languages that use the Roman alphabets, the ALA character set (which essentially corresponds to ANSI standard Z39.47) is used. It includes diacritical marks, such as umlauts, accent marks, tildes, and other such characters used within other cultures. It should be noted that, although these special characters are included within MARC records when they are cataloged, many automated systems delete these characters from the records when they are used in online catalogs. Current technology does provide for the inclusion of these characters within online catalogs. Because these special characters are initially included within the records when they are cataloged, the deletion of such characters by automated library systems actually devalues the records and "deculturizes" library resources. Libraries should be aware of this aspect of library automation and should consider requiring that the system vendor(s) respect the needs and purposes of libraries and their users. As noted in the Library of Congress *Cataloging service bulletin*, "the need for accurate recognition, clarity, and uniform rendition of diacritics and special characters cannot be stressed too strongly...."[1]

Non-Roman alphabet materials within a library collection are generally handled one of two ways. Either the alphabetic characters are translated into Roman alphabetic characters (this is called "romanization") or the original alphabet (such as Cyrillic and Hebrew alphabets) is used, often with romanized or English language notes. The Library of Congress regularly publishes in the *Cataloging service bulletin* "romanization tables" (generally referred to as the "ALA/LC romanization tables") for use with a wide variety of alphabets, including those used in such languages as "Kashmiri in Perso-Arabic script," "Lepcha," "Limbu," "Divehi," and "Moplah."

In regard to oriental language materials, it should be noted that the Library of Congress recently ceased its distribution of CJK (Chinese-Japanese-Korean) catalog cards. This was not caused by lack of interest, however. As noted in the *Library of Congress information bulletin*, "This step has been taken due to the high cost of producing these cards with printed vernacular as well as romanized fields to libraries. Now other vendors are capable of supplying such cards, and many CJK collections are cataloged on an online system [which accommodates such vernacular]."[2]

Classification and Call Numbers

Academic libraries include a variety of collections that may use differing classification schemes for these collections. For example, an academic library that uses the Library of Congress (LC) classification for its main collections may also use the National Library of Medicine (NLM) classification for its medical branch. The federal government documents collection within an academic library may be classified according to the Superintendent of Documents (SuDocs) classification, which serves to organize publications of government agencies together.

In some cases, the use of different classification schemes is not an intentional situation. For example, many academic libraries that formerly used the Dewey classification schedules have since adopted the LC scheme for current acquisitions but have not had the resources to undertake a reclassification project to change the Dewey numbers on older materials to LC call numbers.

When differing types of call numbers are used within a library, automation of the collection may present unforeseen situations that the library may want to examine and rectify. For example, within the "shelflisting" or "call number browse" function of an automated system, will all different call numbers be filed together in one file, or should they be separated into individual files according to the classification scheme used?

The use of MARC records within an automated system does provide new opportunities, as well as problems, regarding call number schemes. For example, many MARC records include multiple types of classification numbers (e.g., both Dewey and LC) that apply to the item in the record. A library that has formerly used Dewey numbers but has switched to LC may find that the MARC records used to catalog those items may in many instances also include the LC numbers. This could serve as a basis for an automated process whereby the records for Dewey items could be processed to produce new spine labels according to the LC number in the record. The process could produce the spine labels in order by the previously used Dewey number, so they would be in order by their arrangement in the stacks, in order to facilitate relabeling.

Patron Needs

Academic library patron needs tend to be more research oriented, as compared to the informational and recreational reading needs fulfilled by public libraries. In many cases, fulfillment of research needs involves interlibrary lending (ILL) activities to acquire materials on a given topic that are not owned by the library. MARC-based union systems, most notably OCLC, have greatly increased the capabilities of libraries to take part in ILL, the number of materials to which libraries have access and the speed with which materials can be obtained. Other MARC-based technologies, such as CD-ROM and

COM union catalogs, have also broadened the scope and capabilities for interlibrary lending. Although ILL and public services staff do not necessarily use the MARC format, it should be pointed out that the cooperative endeavors in existence today have, in the majority of cases, been made possible by the fact that MARC is a common standard used by all participating libraries. Most of the automated systems in existence today would not be a reality without the development of MARC.

Another aspect of patron needs has to do with the patron's age level and relative understanding of automation. By and large, academic library patrons are adults with a comparatively high degree of sophistication regarding automation. This generally translates into the fact that the bibliographic instruction needs of patrons and the enhancements to automated library systems may be somewhat less demanding in the academic library than in other types of libraries, whose patrons' ages and levels of sophistication are more varied.

PUBLIC LIBRARIES

There are public libraries of many types, including single-building libraries and multibranch libraries. The geographical areas and populations served vary widely from one public library to the next. Public libraries that must serve as "research libraries" as well as providers of general research, informational, and recreational reading needs, would benefit from information in the section above regarding academic libraries. Public libraries that serve multicultural and multilingual populations would also benefit from that information. Public libraries that have many branches or have collections that include a significant proportion of multimedia items would benefit from discussions in the section on school libraries, given below.

MARC Implementation

Within many public libraries, the use of MARC format is implemented at the same time that automated circulation and catalog systems are implemented. This often means that libraries are faced with selecting, providing specifications for, and implementing systems that require the use of MARC without having a familiarity with MARC. In many cases, this also means that libraries will be implementing centralized cataloging for the first time. In the case of implementation of stand-alone micro-based systems that use individual databases (instead of a networked system with a single, union database), libraries should understand that a future move to a networked system may not necessarily mean simply moving the individual databases to the new system. The databases will probably not be in a format compatible with the new system and, even if they are, a good deal of database processing will be necessary prior to loading the records into another system.

One topic that often requires scrutiny when public libraries automate is that of accession numbers. Public libraries that use accession numbers usually rely on them to differentiate one copy of a title from another; however, barcode (or OCR-optical character recognition) numbers that serve as unique identifiers within an online system will serve that same function. The use of accession numbers is a labor-intensive activity that should be reconsidered in great depth when libraries automate, particularly if the library intends to enter the accession numbers into the system. Many libraries that have automated with the intention of maintaining accession numbers have eventually come to the conclusion that the accession numbers were not useful enough to justify the work that they involved.

Library staff should attend relevant conferences and workshops and contact as many other automated public libraries as possible, to avoid reinventing the wheel. Public libraries will benefit from the published literature about library automation. It should be noted, however, that much of the published information focuses on the automation of academic rather than public libraries, and it does not discuss some of the questions and problems encountered by public libraries. The discussions below will assist public libraries on such matters.

Collections

Paperback Materials

There are paperback materials and then there are paperback materials. In other words, "a paperback is not a paperback is not a paperback...." Some paperbound materials are also published in hardback format, others are not. Some are used as an integral part of the collection, while others are considered as much more expendable. The "integral" paperbound materials are usually cataloged and circulated in the same manner as hardbound materials and are replaced when they are lost or missing. Other paperbacks may be uncataloged, and these items may or may not be considered for replacement if they are lost or missing. When libraries implement automated catalogs and circulation systems, they are faced with making a choice regarding the more "expendable" paperback items. The items may not be considered as worthy of the time and effort needed to create catalog records for them in the online catalog; however, in some cases, within integrated systems, this may mean that the items cannot be circulated through the circulation system. In this case, the library is faced with the prospect of maintaining two separate circulation systems: the automated system for cataloged items and a manual system for uncataloged items. This is not always a satisfactory resolution. Libraries may want to consider one of the following methods of dealing with "expendable" paperbacks within an automated system:

1. Enter a brief catalog record for each paperback item, without providing full cataloging. The record may include just a title field that indicates that it is a paperback, without actually even entering a title in each individual record. If a brief title is entered into the record, then overdue slips will note the title; otherwise, they will just indicate the generic term used to describe the material.

2. Most integrated systems involve the use of a catalog record for each title held, to which are attached item records (including the barcode number, call number, etc.) for each physical volume held. The item records are used for circulation purposes, to indicate that a particular item is checked out. One method for dealing with paperback items within this type of system is to create a single dummy catalog record that simply includes a generic title, such as "Paperbacks." Item records for various paperbacks can be linked to the catalog record,

regardless of their individual titles. Items can be circulated through the system this way; however, overdue slips will not indicate specific information about the title of the particular paperback.

3. If the system provides for item records that do not have to be linked to a catalog record (e.g., item records that just include the barcode number and the description *PB* for paperback), then a brief "unlinked" item record can be created for each paperback. This will provide for circulation control without having to provide cataloging information for each item. Some item record structures include a notes field in which a brief title could be included, which may or may not be printed on an overdue slip, depending upon the system capabilities. Or, the library may just want to include a generic term or designation for a paperback in the notes field or other area of the item record.

Multimedia Collections

Public libraries often include a significant number of nonbook materials, including such materials as sound recordings and videocassettes, which may or may not be cataloged and/or circulated. The MARC format provides for the creation of MARC records for all such types of materials; however, there are relatively few MARC catalog records available from vendors or utilities, which requires more "original" cataloging for libraries. The database that contains the highest number of nonbook materials is the OCLC database, which includes over 20,000,000 records of all types and grows at the rate of about 1,000,000 records per year. Libraries that think OCLC is too expensive an option may want to reconsider in light of the time and expertise required to catalog nonbook materials.

Pseudonyms

Public libraries, probably more than any other type of library, include materials that have been published by authors using one or more pseudonyms. The most practical method for cataloging and classifying these materials has been to use the name used on the title page. However, the *Anglo-American cataloguing rules*, 2nd edition, which were originally published in 1978 and implemented in 1981, called for using one pseudonym as the main entry in all records, regardless of the name used on the title page. This created a problem for libraries that were using MARC records provided by the Library of Congress or other organizations that followed that practice, because public library patrons were used to searching for the title page form of the name, under which the item had been published. This also created a problem in regard to authority control and use of MARC authority records within online systems, which used only one form of the name as the established form and provided only "see" references (not "see also" references) from the various other pseudonyms. More recently, with the revision of *AACR2*, the practice has been changed to use the pseudonym used on the title page as the main entry for the item. Also, different authority records have been created for the various pseudonyms as "established" headings, with "see also" references from other pseudonyms. However, the changes have affected mostly currently cataloged materials and have not necessarily included changes to MARC bibliographic or authority records created prior to the revision of this practice. As time passes, more and more retrospective bibliographic and authority records will be changed; libraries should consider this situation and evaluate impacts upon their catalogs and users when they automate.

Classification and Call Numbers

Non-unique Call Numbers

Unlike academic libraries, which usually have a unique call number for each item, or at least for each title, many public libraries may use the same call number for a number of items. These call numbers usually include a Dewey classification number and a second line that includes the first two or three letters of the authors last name. The use of non-unique call numbers may cause "scrambled" filing of items within "shelflist" or "call number browse" functions of an online system, depending upon the way the filing programs of the system work. If the filing programs file only upon the call number and do not consider the main entry for filing purposes, then entries for all author names that begin with the same two or three letters will simply be listed in random order. If the computer filing does consider the main entry, but not the title, then entries for individual authors will be listed together, with individual titles being listed in random order.

High Duplication Rates

Public libraries with multiple branches will generally have high duplication rates of titles within the collective holdings of the branches. One question that may arise when automation is implemented, particularly if cataloging for the branches has not been centralized previously, will be the use of different call numbers for duplicate items at different branches. For pragmatic reasons, including more efficient cataloging, as well as standardization useful to library patrons, it may be advisable to use the same call number for the same item in all branches. Although many systems can accommodate different call numbers for different copies of the same item, others may not accommodate this differentiation.

Biographies

There has been a trend toward classifying biographies within subject, rather than as biographies. (For example, a biography of a football player would be classified under the Dewey number for football.) This has its advantages, and even those libraries that rely heavily on biography as a genre for their users have found that keyword searching within MARC-based system provides for locating biography materials by genre in addition to subject. Public libraries that classify by genre rather than subject often supply call numbers for biographies that include a classification line (such as "B" or "92") and then a second line with the first two or three letters of the biographee's last name. When such call numbers are filed within the library's shelflist, staff must refer to the subject heading for the biographee in order to file the cards in the correct order. Few, if any, automated systems provide for call number filing that refers to the subject heading for call number filing purposes. For this reason, biography call numbers that are the same will usually be filed randomly, without regard to the biographee's name, or they may be subfiled according to the author's name. This will not allow for grouping biographies about the same person together in "shelflist" or "call number browse" functions of an automated system. There is one method that has been used successfully by some libraries for creating biography call numbers that will cause biography call numbers for the same biographee to file together within an automated system. This method involves creating a unique Cutter number to use as the second line of the call number for each biographee. For example, the Cutter numbers for "Booker T. Washington," "George Washington," and "Martha Washington" might be "W22," "W23," and "W24," respectively. The biography call numbers for each person could then be filed together in separate sequences, in alphabetical order in relation to each other.

Patron Needs

Bibliographic Instruction

Public library patrons include an extremely varied population in regard to age, informational needs, and sophistication in regard to automation. Public libraries may find that they need to maintain a relatively high level of bibliographic instruction in regard to the use of automated library systems, particularly when enhancements and changes to the system are made over time. If the system is not extremely user-friendly, public libraries may find that they need to provide continuously updated documentation and intensive ongoing bibliographic instruction for system use.

Sears Subject Headings

Many public libraries use Sears subject headings instead of Library of Congress (LC) subject headings, sometimes because of the belief that Sears headings are simpler and/or more in line with patron needs. Because the vast majority of MARC records include LC subject and very few include Sears headings, use of Sears headings may cause problems or additional work within the MARC environment. Specifically, both cataloging and authority control may be affected. The performance of cataloging using Sears headings will generally require additional work in regard to checking the Sears documentation to determine whether it is the same as the LC heading in the record, and, in some cases, substituting Sears headings for LC headings. Even in those cases that the Sears heading matches an LC heading already in the record, staff will in all cases be required to change the subject heading indicator from *0* (which indicates that LC subjects have been used) to another code that indicates that Sears is used. In regard to authority control within the MARC environment, libraries that use Sears are severely handicapped because there is no "authoritative" source for MARC authority records for Sears subject headings, therefore automated authority control for Sears headings is almost nonexistent. (MARC authority records for LC subject headings, created by the Library of Congress, are widely available.) The lack of access to Sears MARC authority records will generally require that libraries that want to make use of authority control functions within an automated system using Sears headings will need to create their own MARC authority records, a very labor-intensive and time-consuming undertaking. Libraries may want to consider switching from Sears to LC headings for the above reasons. The experience of two libraries that have considered switching from Sears to LC (because of plans for automation) have provided the following results: One library had its subject headings flipped from Sears to LC via an automated authority control process prior to loading the database into a system. In that process, it was found that 75 percent of the Sears headings were exactly the same as the LC subject heading. A number of the Sears headings that did not match involved typographical errors or other errors that, if they had been correct, would have matched the LC heading. The other library undertook a comparison of a random sample of 100 Sears headings to the LC headings, done manually. This study showed that only 8 of the LC headings were different from their LC counterparts. In a few of these cases, the LC headings were actually simpler than the Sears headings; for example, LC uses the subject heading *Cows*, whereas Sears refers users to the term *Cattle*. In addition, it was noted that LC subject heading records included more cross-references than Sears.

SCHOOL LIBRARIES

For the purposes of this chapter, the emphasis is on school libraries within school districts and the focus is on the use of a networked system used by two or more libraries in the district rather than upon micro-based stand-alone systems used by individual libraries. However, much of the information supplied will be applicable to all types of school libraries, regardless of the configuration of the system.

MARC Implementation

Within many school libraries, the use of MARC format is implemented at the same time that automated circulation and catalog systems are implemented. This often means that libraries are faced with selecting, providing specifications for, and implementing systems that require the use of MARC without having a familiarity with MARC. In many cases, this also means that libraries will be implementing centralized cataloging for the first time. In the case of implementation of stand-alone micro-based systems that use individual databases (instead of a networked system with a single, union database), libraries should understand that a future move to a networked system may not necessarily mean simply moving the individual databases to the new system. The databases will probably not be in a format compatible with the new system and, even if they are, a good deal of database processing will be necessary prior to loading the records into another system.

One topic that often requires scrutiny when school libraries automate is that of accession numbers. This topic is discussed in the "MARC implementation" discussion for public libraries, above. The use of accession numbers is a labor-intensive activity that should be reconsidered in great depth when school libraries automate.

More than librarians in any other type of library, school librarians in general are at a disadvantage in regard to accessing information specifically in regard to automation of their particular type of library. In part, this is because relatively little automation of school libraries has taken place. Also, school librarians work in an environment where research and publishing is not given as high a priority and where financial support and release time for conferences is not as abundant as in other types of libraries. As a result, school librarians often turn to their automation vendors as a chief source of information in regard to automating their libraries. In some cases, this is a useful activity, but, in other cases, it is not in the library's best interest. Vendors do have the responsibility of supporting their own companies and interests, and the information provided by them may be lacking in quantity or quality, either purposely or due to their lack of knowledge about automation of libraries in general.

School libraries also face other disadvantages that generally do not impact upon other types of libraries to the same extent. For example, the fact that school media centers are widely dispersed geographically within a district means that the implementation of a networked system requires much more extensive consideration and implementation of hardware and telecommunications systems to fully serve all patrons. Because online catalog and circulation terminals will be required at each site, regardless of the number of patrons served, a school district with 35 media centers serving 25,000 students and staff will require at least 35 circulation terminals. In contrast, an academic library that serves the same number of students and staff generally requires only a fraction of that number of circulation terminals because of more centralized circulation functions.

In many cases, one school librarian performs all professional functions within the library (such as acquisitions, reference, circulation, and interlibrary loan) that are usually dispersed among different personnel within public and academic libraries. For this reason, it is generally necessary for each school librarian using an automated system to have expertise in all aspects of the system, instead of simply specializing in one aspect. This involves a broader range of knowledge about the system than is generally required of more specialized personnel in larger libraries and requires a particularly intensive involvement by the school librarian when changes or enhancements are made to the automated system.

Collections

Paperback Materials

School libraries generally maintain a significant proportion of paperback materials within their collections. Paperback materials are included in the discussion on collections in the section on public libraries, above.

Multimedia Collections

More than any other type of library, school libraries maintain collections that are rich in nonbook resources, including sound recordings, videocassettes, multimedia kits, and computer files, to name a few. The MARC format provides for cataloging of all of these types of materials, but school libraries are at a disadvantage in two regards in the cataloging of nonbook materials. One disadvantage is that MARC records for nonbook materials are not generally available, which means that the MARC records for such materials will have to be created by the library, instead of acquired from a vendor or utility. OCLC, with over 20,000,000 records for materials of all types, represents the richest database for records for nonbook materials. Libraries that might otherwise consider OCLC as too expensive an alternative may want to reconsider in light of the time and money required to create MARC records for nonbook materials.[3] The second disadvantage faced by school libraries in regard to the cataloging of multimedia collections was alluded to above, in that the cataloging of AV and computer files is an extremely time-consuming effort that requires expertise in the proper description and (MARC) coding for such materials.

When automating multimedia collections, another aspect of the automation process that requires consideration is the placement of barcode labels on nonbook materials. It is relatively easy to make a decision and provide instructions regarding barcoding of books; however, the variety of shapes and sizes of nonbook materials, as well as the use of removable covers and containers, presents a greater challenge. Libraries may want to standardize the types of containers (e.g., plastic bags for sound cassette kits, boxes for videocassettes) that are used as much as possible to simplify the method of barcoding and placement of barcodes. The placement of barcode labels and type of labels to be used involves a number of considerations, including, but not limited to: (1) the ease of the initial labeling of material; (2) the useful life of the label and how the placement affects it (e.g., wear-and-tear through use); (3) the ease of access to the label for circulation and inventory purposes; and (4) the number of items within a multi-item "kit" that should receive (duplicate) labels. Labels placed on the outside of an item (books, as well as media materials) are easier and faster to access than those placed on the inside. (A common fear of school librarians is that labels placed on the outside of an item are more likely to be picked off by school students than labels placed on the inside; however, this does not seem to be the case.) For purposes of having the barcode "read" for circulation or inventory purposes, it is necessary to have the barcode label on only one item of a kit, generally the container or the largest item. For identification purposes, it is useful to have duplicate eye-readable labels (i.e., just the numerics, not the barcode itself) to place on other major parts of a kit (such as when a kit is made up of three filmstrips and a sound cassette). Barcode labels with one, two, or three duplicate eye-readable labels can be ordered from barcode vendors; an alternative is to type the additional eye-readable labels or have them made through a computer program.

Pseudonyms

School library collections often include fiction materials written by authors under various pseudonyms. "Pseudonyms" are included in the discussion on collections in the section on public libraries, above.

Classification and Call Numbers

Non-unique Call Numbers

In general, school libraries use call numbers that are not unique to one given title or item. "Non-unique call numbers" are included in the discussion on classification and call numbers in the section on public libraries, above.

High Duplication Rates

Within a school district, there are usually multiple copies of a given item. "High duplication rates" are included in the discussion on classification and call numbers in the section on public libraries, above.

Biographies

School library collections often include numerous biographies. Call numbers for "biographies" are included in the discussion on classification and call numbers in the section on public libraries, above.

Patron Needs

Issues involved with "Bibliographic instruction" and "Sears subject headings" are included in the discussion on patron needs for public libraries, above. Both of these topics will also be of interest to those involved with school libraries.

The ALA publication *Cataloging correctly for kids* is highly recommended for school libraries, whether or not they are in the process of automation.[4] This joint publication of the American Association of School Librarians, Association for Library Services to Children, and the Resources and Technical Services Division provides information and instruction about the standards and practices that should be followed to provide quality access and description of materials for younger library users. When libraries automate, it is particularly important that they follow such standards, because library automation standards and systems are devised according to the standards. Libraries that do not follow the standards will find the automation harder to use, and it may require costly customization of software.

School libraries support the curriculum needs of their faculty and students, primarily by providing needed materials and information. Often, a specific item is needed at a particular time and location. In such cases, a "media booking" function, or other such function that supports the reserving of materials and equipment by individuals, is a highly useful feature of an automated system.

NOTES

1.   "Diacritics and special characters," *Cataloging service bulletin* 21: 60 (Summer 1983).

2.   "Library ceases distribution of CJK catalog cards," *Library of Congress information bulletin* 48 (45): 392 (November 6, 1989).

3.   The advantages of OCLC for cataloging for school libraries are also noted in: Lathrop, Ann, *Online and CD-ROM databases in school libraries: Readings* (Englewood, Colo.: Libraries Unlimited, 1989), 8.

4.   *Cataloging correctly for kids: An introduction to the tools* (Chicago: Cataloging of Children's Materials Committee, Resources and Technical Services Division, ALA, 1989).

RELATED READINGS

Byrne, Deborah. "School libraries and interlibrary loan." *Action for libraries* 16 [i.e., 15] (1-2) (January-February 1989).

Glossary

Access points: Those portions of a library catalog record under which a catalog user can search for an item in the catalog. In the more traditional card catalogs, access points are usually authors, titles, and subject headings. Within an automated system, virtually any portion of a library catalog record, such as the publisher name, notes, or illustration types, can conceivably be used as an access point, or search term.

American National Standards Institute: An organization that facilitates and oversees the development of standards in the United States. More commonly called "ANSI," this organization does not actually develop standards, but provides the structure and protocols for standards development by other organizations. ANSI is part of the larger International Organization for Standards (called "ISO").

ANSI: see American National Standards Institute.

Authority control: A type of quality control within library catalogs that basically consists of establishing one standard form of a name or word under which library patrons should search within a catalog. In addition, authority control also involves the creation of cross-reference names or terms from which catalog users can be directed to the established form.

Authority record: An authority record includes the established form of a name or word that is used as an access point in a library catalog, as well as cross-references from other names or terms.

Bibliographic record: A bibliographic record includes the description of an item to be used in a library catalog, as well as author, title, and subject added entries, call number, and other relevant information.

Content designation: Within a MARC record, content designation involves the use of specific codes (i.e., MARC tags, indicators, and subfield codes) to identify a particular piece of information within any given part of the record.

Delimiter: Within the MARC formats, delimiters are used to identify and differentiate between separate elements within a field. The delimiter sign ($\neq$) is used with a MARC subfield code (e.g., $\neq b$) in front of each data element to identify subfields within MARC fields.

Field: A MARC field is one or more elements of data that are identified by a MARC tag. Typically, data elements are grouped together within fields according to groupings used within traditional catalog records. For example, the place of publication, the publisher name, and the date of publication (in addition to some other relevant data elements) are all included as part of the MARC field tagged "260."

Fixed field: Within the MARC formats, there are several fields which are a fixed number of characters in length (such as the Leader, the 005, 007, and 008 fields). Within these fields, each character is defined by its relative position in the field; subfield codes are not used to define each element of data. Within some environments, any one or a combination of these fields are informally known as "MARC fixed fields."

Holdings data: Information in regard to the numbers of copies or volumes of a bibliographic item that a library holds, as well as other information in regard to the location and condition of the item.

Indicator: Within the MARC format, an indicator is a one-character code (generally a number, although an alphabetic character may be used) that is used to provide instructions to the computer or to give further information about the contents of a field within a MARC record. MARC variable data fields may contain one or two indicators, or both indicator positions may be defined as "blank."

International Organization for Standards: An umbrella organization for the facilitation of standards development within and among nations. This group is commonly referred to as "ISO" (for "International Standards Organization"). The American sub-organization is the American National Standards Institute (commonly referred to as "ANSI").

ISO: see International Organization for Standards.

Subfield code: Within the MARC format, subfield codes are one-character codes (generally, these are lowercase alphabetic characters, although numbers may be used) that identify individual elements of information within a MARC field. MARC subfield codes are immediately preceded by a delimiter sign ($\neq$) and they are placed in front of the specific information that they identify.

Tag: Within the MARC format, tags are three-character numeric codes (from 001 to 999) that identify a field of information within a MARC record.

Index

Abstract note, 106-7
Academic libraries, 238-45
Added entries, 114-20. *See also* Field 7XX
ALA character set, 193
ALA filing rules, 173-75
Alphabetic identifiers, 39
American National Standard for Bibliographic Information Interchange on Magnetic Tape, 13
American National Standard for Information Sciences Bibliographic Information Interchange, 31
American Library Association, 12. *See also* names of ALA committees
American National Standards Institute. *See* NSI
Analytical entries, 242
Anglo-American Cataloging Rules, 28
Annotation note, 106-7
ANSI standard Z39.2, 11, 13, 18, 31, 34
Archival and Manuscripts control formats, 32
Archival materials, 242-43
ASCII, 125-26
Audience code, 67-68
Audiovisual collections, 247, 251-52
Authorities: A MARC Format, 32
Authority control, 209-11
    processing, 158-66
Authority format, 216-31
Authority records, use of, 227-30
Authority work, 209-11
Avram, Henriette D., 9

Bibliographic titles. *See* Tag X40
Bibliographies, 180-82
Bibliography note, 105
Biography code, 73

Bit, 124-25
Book catalogs, 179
Book formats, 32
Books, codes for, 52-121. *See also individual field numbers,* e.g., Field 008
    leader codes, 53-61
Brief records. *See* Minimal-level catalog records
Byte, 124-25

Call numbers, 84-88, 244-45, 248-49, 252-53
Catalog maintenance, 196-97
CD-ROM catalogs, 178-79
Circulation module software, 194
Coded data, 39
Collection analysis, 182-84
COM catalogs, 175-78
Communications formats, 32-33
Computer disks, 123-25
Computer Files formats, 32
Computer filing. *See* Filing rules
Computer hardware
    routines, 189-90
    speed, 190-91
    storage capability, 188-89
Computer software
    input and output capabilities, 192-93
Computer tapes, 123-25
Conference publication code, 70-71
CONSER, 15-16
Content designation, 11, 18
Contents code, 68-69
Contents note, 106
Control information. *See* Field 0XX
Control number code, 74-76
Cooperative Online Serials Program. *See* CONSER

Copy code, 76-77
Corporate name, 90-91. *See also* Tag X10
    as added entry, 115-16
    as subject added entry, 109-10
    establishing name authority, 212
Cross-referencing, 228

Database (of MARC records)
    characteristics, 172
    maintenance, 196-97
    preprocessing, 172
    production schedules, 172
Date of publication, 62-65
Date of transaction code, 77-78
Deduping, 144-49, 194, 196
Deletes, 30
Dewey Decimal call number, 87-88
Direct access to data, 123-25
Display constants, 28
Documentation, 197
*Documentation Format for Bibliographic
    Information Interchange on Magnetic
    Tape*, 31
Duplication of records. *See* Deduping

EBCDIC, 125-26
Edition or copy code, 76-77
Edition statement, 96-97

Festschrift code, 71
Fiction code, 72
Field 005, 23
Field 007, 23
Field 008, 23, 62-74
Field 0XX, 22, 36, 45-46, 74-88
Field 1XX, 22, 36, 45-47
Field 2XX, 22, 36, 45, 47
Field 3XX, 22, 36, 45, 47
Field 4XX, 22, 36, 45, 47
Field 5XX, 22, 30, 36, 45, 47
Field 6XX, 22, 36, 45, 48
Field 7XX, 22, 36, 45, 48
Field 8XX, 22, 36, 45, 48
Field 9XX, 22, 36, 45, 48-49
Filing indicator, 26
    correction, 152-54
Filing rules, 173-75
Films formats, 32

Floppy disks
    care and storage, 140-41
    characteristics, 139
    data arrangement, 139
Foreign language materials, 243
Form of item code, 68
*Format Integration and Its Effect on the
    USMARC Bibliographic Format*, 14
Formatted contents note, 106
Full-level catalog records, 28
    A—Mandatory if applicable, 29
    M—Mandatory, 29
    O—Optional, 29
    U—Unused, 29

General note, 104-5
Geographic names. *See also* Tag X51
    as subject added entry, 113-14
    establishing name authority, 214
Global changes, 229-30
Government documents, 241-42
Government publications code, 69-70

Holdings codes, 233-37
Holdings consolidation, 149-52

Illustration code, 66-67
Index code, 71-72
Indicators, 25, 37-38, 50
Integration of MARC format, 120-21
ISBN, 82-83
ISO 2709, 31

Jurisdiction as name authority, 212

Knapp, John F., 9

Language code, 73, 83-84
LC filing rules, 173-75
Library of Congress
    and LSP, 231
    call number, 86
    experiments with MARC, 9-11
Library of Congress Control Number, 80-81
Library of Congress Subject Headings, 210
Linked Systems Project, 230-31
Local call numbers, 88
LSP, 230-31

Machine-Readable Bibliographic Information committee. *See* MARBI
Machine-Readable Data Files formats, 32
Machine-readable records, 1
Main entry, 89-94. *See also* Field 1XX
Manuscripts formats, 32
Manuscripts, 242-43
Maps formats, 32
MARBI, 12-14, 31
MARC
    authority format, 209-31
    format integration, 120-21
    future of, 120-21
    history of, 2-11
MARC Formats for Bibliographic Data, 32
MARC I pilot project, 8-10
MARC II
    communications format — origin of, 8-11
    origin of, 8-16
MARC record
    content designation, 19, 30-31, 34
    data content, 31
    directory, 20-21
    fixed field codes, 23-24, 41-44
    fixed-length record, 2-8
    format integration, 29-30
    full authority records, 192-93
    leader, 20-21
    loading into online system, 195-96
    organization of, 35
    record content, 19
    structure of, 1-2, 19-28, 31
    variable fields, 20-22, 36, 45-51
MARC tapes, 26-38
    backups, 134
    care and storage, 130-33
    characteristics, 127-30
    data arrangement (transmission format), 135-38
    origin of, 9
    processing service pricing, 166-69
    processing, 142-69
    screen display arrangement, 135-38
    shipment, 135
    storage, 134
Meeting name, 91-92. *See also* Tag X11
    as added entry, 116-17
    as subject added entry, 110
    establishing name authority, 212
Microforms, 240-41
    Minimal-level catalog records, 28, 30
Misfiled entries, 196
Modules, 191-92

Multimedia collections, 247, 251-52
Music formats, 32

NACO, 15, 231
Name authority, 212-14
    cross reference example, 211
    record example, 211
Name changes, 30
Name/title, establishaing n/t authority, 212
Names. *See types of names*, e.g., Personal names, Geographic names, etc.
National Coordinated Cataloging Operations. *See* NACO
National Coordinated Cataloging Program. *See* NCCP
NCCP, 15
Notes, 104-7. *See also* Field 5XX
Numeric codes, 25
Numeric identifiers, 39
Numeric tag, 20

OCLC, 15-16, 231
OCLC-MARC, 13
Offset character
    5, 53-54
    6, 55-57
    17, 58-60
    18, 60-61
Online authority file, 227-28
Online systems, 187-207
    comparison to manual systems, 187-88
    evaluation, 197
    loading records, 195-96
    maintenance of database, 196-97
    trouble shooting, 197-207

Paperback materials, 246-47, 251
Patron needs, 244-45, 249, 253
Personal names, 89-90. *See also* Tag X00
    as added entry, 114-15
    as subject added entry, 108-9
    establishing name authority, 212
    with subject subdivision, 215
Physical description, 98-99. *See also* Field 3XX
Physical description code, 78-79
Place of publication, 65-66
Printed catalogs, 179
Pseudonyms, 247
Public access catalog module software, 194

Public libraries, 245-50
Publication, distribution, etc., 97-98

Rather, Lucia J., 9
Repeatability
    field and subfield, 27-28, 50
    of tag patterns, 49-50
Reporting system, 197
Research Libraries Group. *See* RLG
Reserved field. *See* Field 9XX
Responsible Parties Rule, 33
RLG, 15-16, 231

School libraries, 250-53
Scope note, 106-7
Sears subject headings, 249-50
See also references, 226
See references, 225-26
Sequential access to data, 123-25
Serial publications, 239-40
Serials formats, 32
Serials union listing, 240
Series added entries. 101-2. *See also*
    Field 8XX
    uniform title, 119
Series statements, 99-101, 103-4. *See also*
    Field 4XX
Smart barcode processing, 154-58
Special collections, 243
Special select, 150-52
Specifications, local, 148-49, 150-52, 154,
    156-58, 164-66
    flexibility, 193
    for database software, 185-86
    for system, 191-94
Standardization, 1-2
Statistical reporting, 191
    module software, 194
Subfield codes, 26, 37-39, 50-51
Subjects - Subjects, 107-14, 214-15. *See also*
    Field 6XX
Summary note, 106-7

Tag 9, 49
Tag X00, 22, 37
Tag X10, 22, 37
Tag X11, 22, 37
Tag X30, 22, 37
Tag X40, 22, 37
Tag X50, 22, 37
Tag X51, 22, 37
Technical reports, 241
Title, 94-96. *See also* Field 2XX
Topical terms. *See also* Tag X50
    as subject added entry, 112
    establishing name authority, 214
Troubleshooting
    database, 200-207
    hardware, 198-99
    software, 199-200

Uniform title, 92-94. *See also* Tag X30
    as added entry, 117-18
    as subject added entry, 111
    establishing name authority, 213
USMARC, 12-14. *See also* MARC II
    content of data elements, 18
    underlying principles, 31-39
USMARC advisory group, 13-14
USMARC format for bibliographic data, 18-19
USMARC Format for Holdings Data, 32

Variable control fields, 20-24, 38
Variable data fields, 38-39. *See also* "Field"
    followed by the number
    indicator positions, 20, 22
    subfield code, 20, 22
Variable data fields, 20, 24-27, 38-39
Variant title as added entry, 118-19
Vendors
    evaluation of, 186
    responsibilities, 145-48, 149-50, 153-54,
        156, 162-64
    selection of, 184-86
Visual Materials formats, 32

Workstations, 195